ph²

To Clara and Fanette

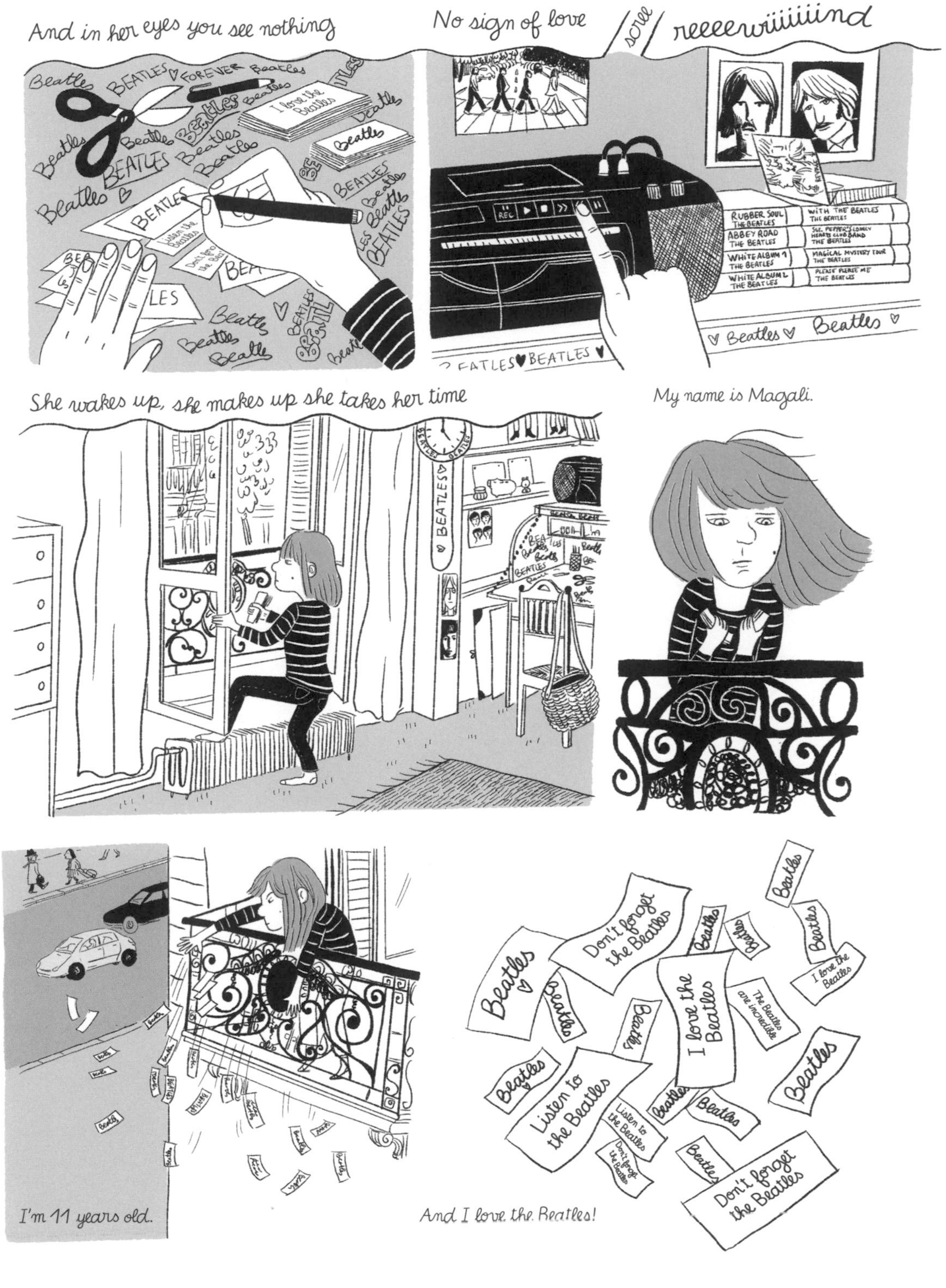
And in her eyes you see nothing
BEATLES FOREVER
I love the Beatles
No sign of love
scree
reeeewiiiiiind
REC
RUBBER SOUL THE BEATLES
WITH THE BEATLES THE BEATLES
ABBEY ROAD THE BEATLES
SGT. PEPPER'S LONELY HEARTS CLUB BAND THE BEATLES
WHITE ALBUM 1 THE BEATLES
MAGICAL MYSTERY TOUR THE BEATLES
WHITE ALBUM 2 THE BEATLES
PLEASE PLEASE ME THE BEATLES
She wakes up, she makes up she takes her time
My name is Magali.
I'm 11 years old.
Don't forget the Beatles
I love the Beatles
The Beatles are incredible
Listen to the Beatles
And I love the Beatles!

Nowhere Girl

Magali le Huche

NOBROW

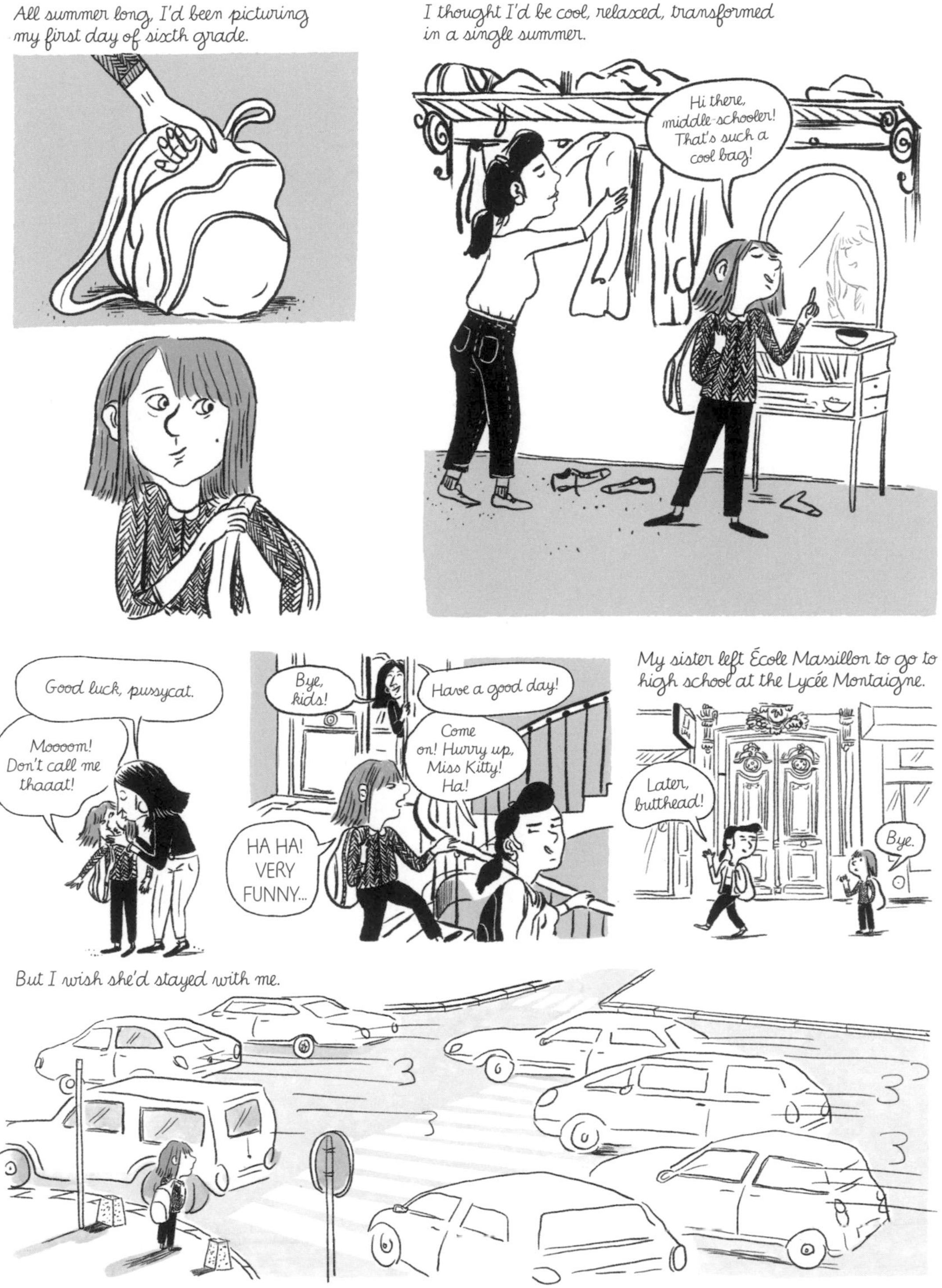
All summer long, I'd been picturing my first day of sixth grade.
I thought I'd be cool, relaxed, transformed in a single summer.
Hi there, middle-schooler! That's such a cool bag!
Good luck, pussycat.
Moooom! Don't call me thaaat!
Bye, kids!
Have a good day!
Come on! Hurry up, Miss Kitty! Ha!
HA HA! VERY FUNNY...
My sister left École Massillon to go to high school at the Lycée Montaigne.
Later, butthead!
Bye.
But I wish she'd stayed with me.

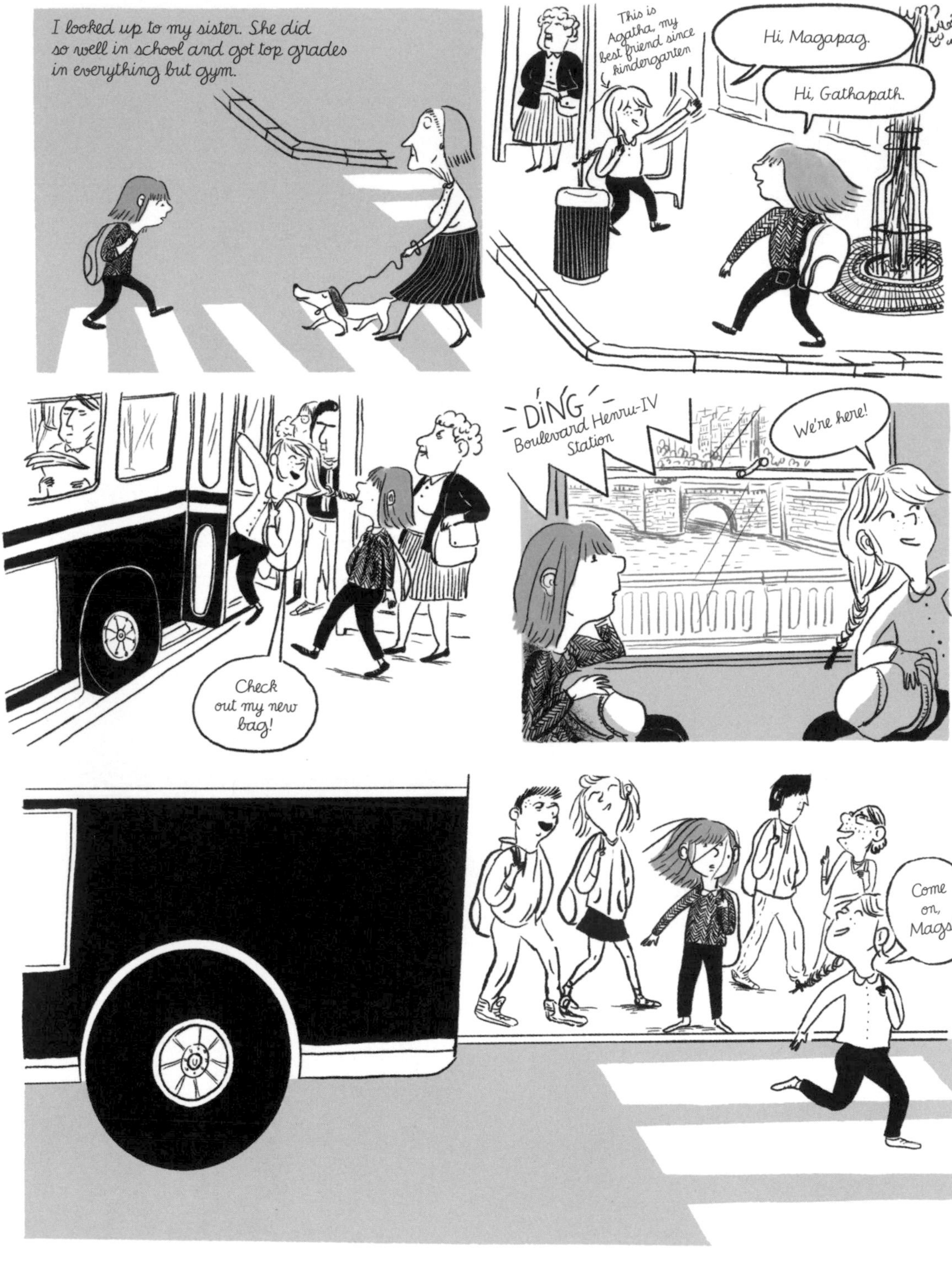
I looked up to my sister. She did so well in school and got top grades in everything but gym.
This is Agatha, my best friend since kindergarten
Hi, Magapag.
Hi, Gathapath.
Check out my new bag!
DING
Boulevard Henru-IV Station
We're here!
Come on, Mags!

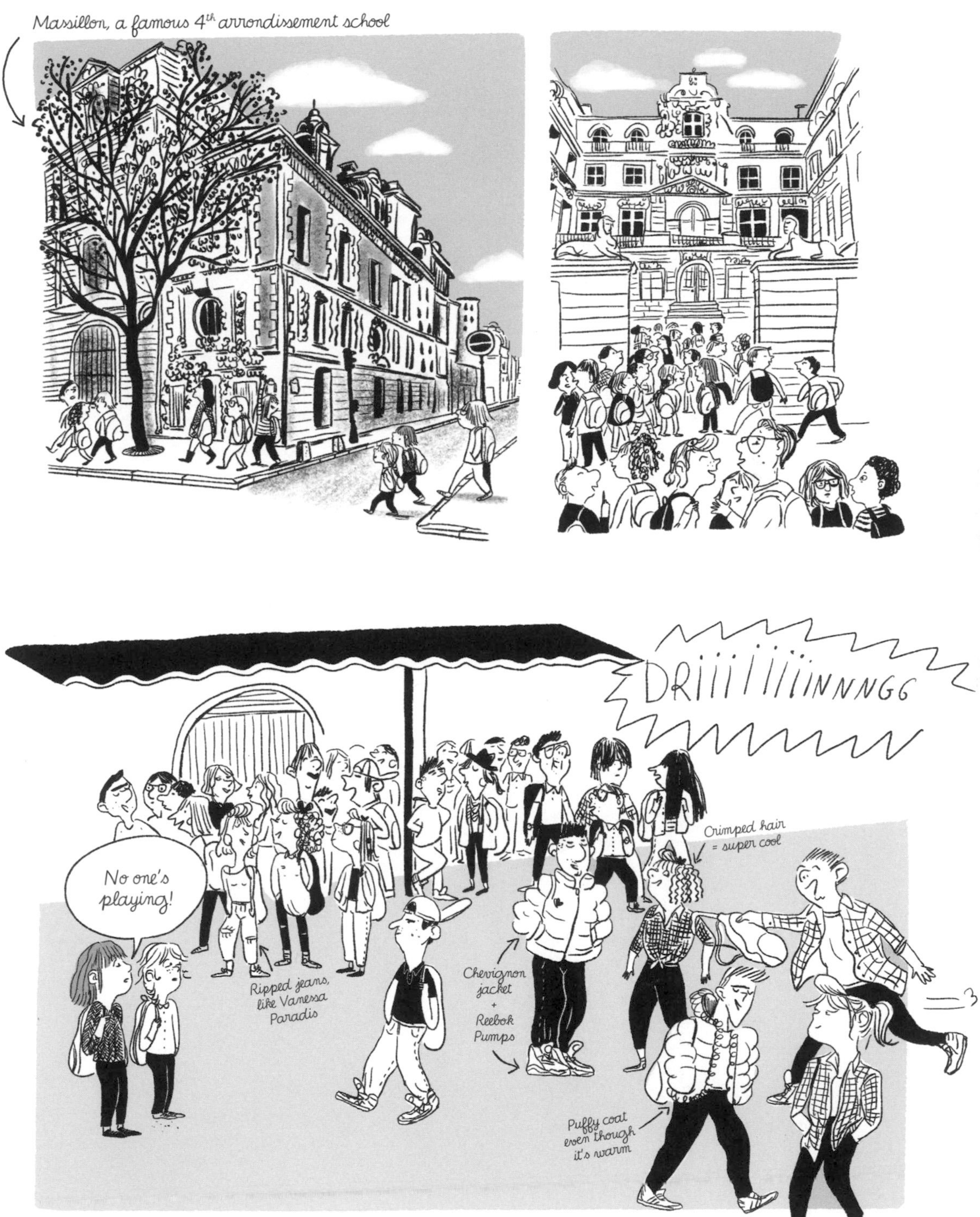
Massillon, a famous 4th arrondissement school
DRIIIIIIIIINNNGG
No one's playing!
Ripped jeans, like Vanessa Paradis
Chevignon jacket + Reebok Pumps
Crimped hair = super cool
Puffy coat even though it's warm

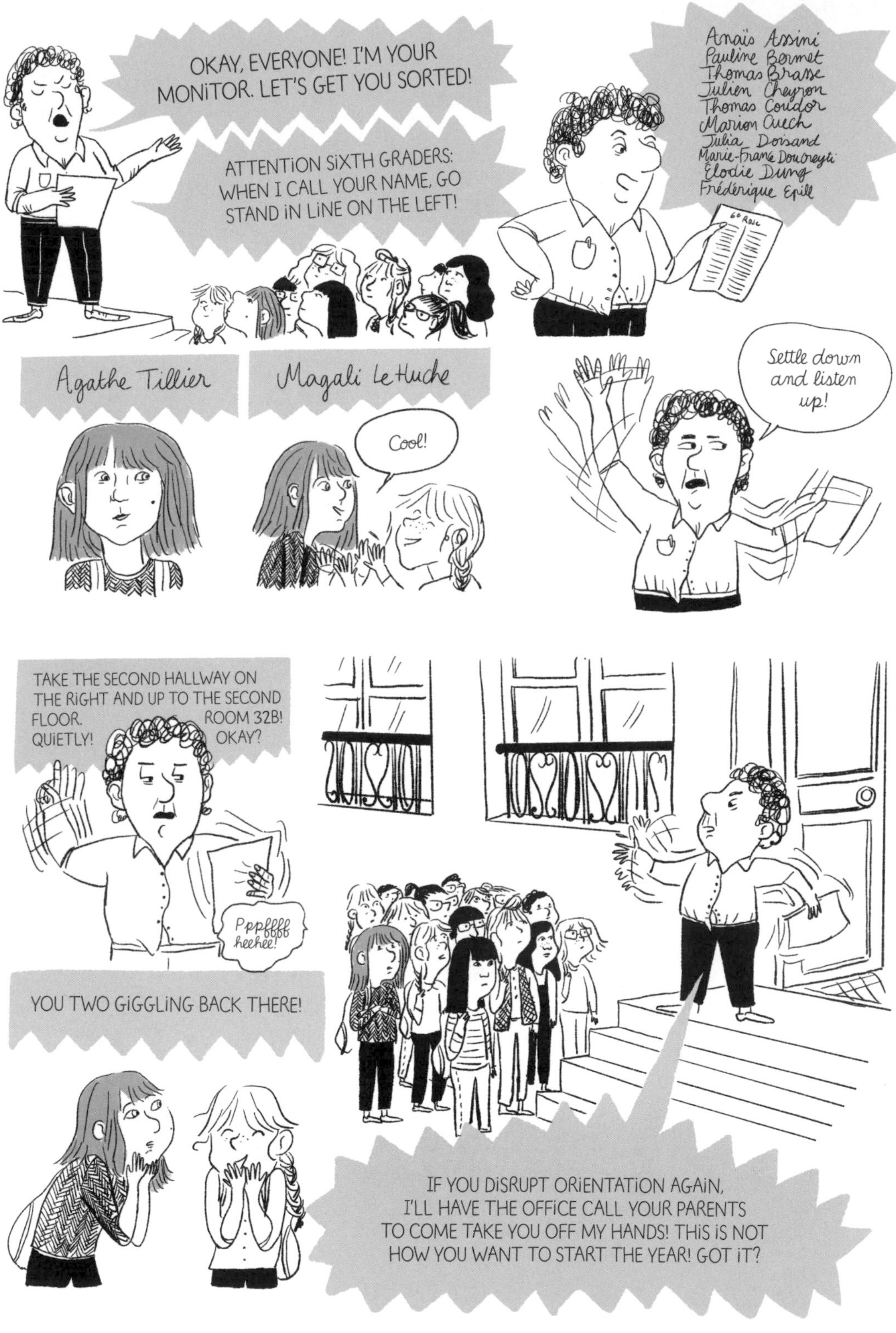

OKAY, EVERYONE! I'M YOUR MONITOR. LET'S GET YOU SORTED!
ATTENTION SIXTH GRADERS: WHEN I CALL YOUR NAME, GO STAND IN LINE ON THE LEFT!
Anaïs Assini
Pauline Bermet
Thomas Brasse
Julien Cheyron
Thomas Coudor
Marion Cuech
Julia Doisand
Marie-France Doumeyti
Élodie Dung
Frédérique Epill
Agathe Tillier
Magali Le Huche
Cool!
Settle down and listen up!
TAKE THE SECOND HALLWAY ON THE RIGHT AND UP TO THE SECOND FLOOR.
ROOM 32B!
QUIETLY!
OKAY?
Pppffff heehee!
YOU TWO GIGGLING BACK THERE!
IF YOU DISRUPT ORIENTATION AGAIN, I'LL HAVE THE OFFICE CALL YOUR PARENTS TO COME TAKE YOU OFF MY HANDS! THIS IS NOT HOW YOU WANT TO START THE YEAR! GOT IT?

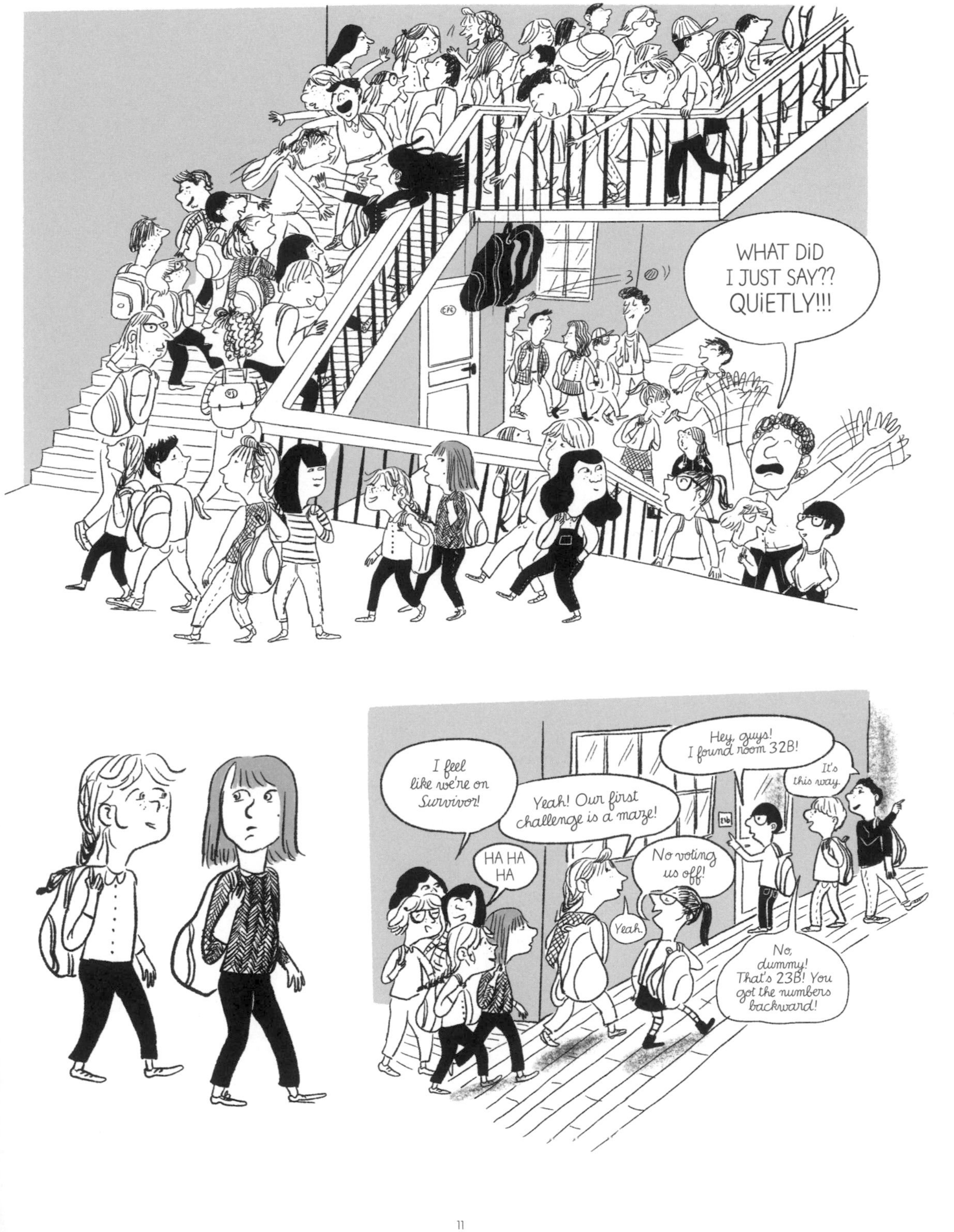
WHAT DiD I JUST SAY?? QUiETLY!!!
I feel like we're on Survivor!
Yeah! Our first challenge is a maze!
HA HA HA
Hey, guys! I found room 32B!
It's this way.
No voting us off!
Yeah.
No, dummy! That's 23B! You got the numbers backward!

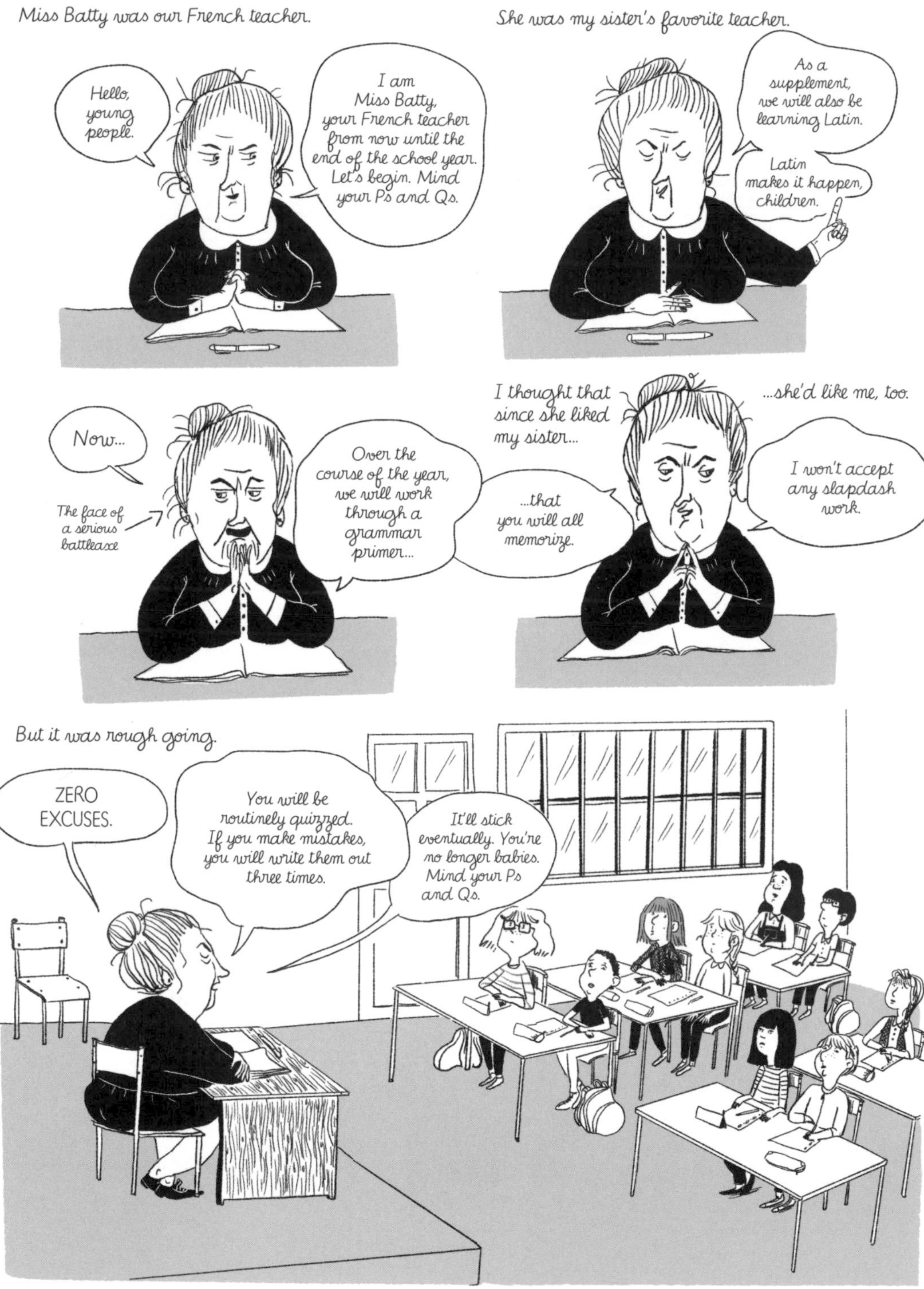

Miss Batty was our French teacher.
Hello, young people.
I am Miss Batty, your French teacher from now until the end of the school year. Let's begin. Mind your Ps and Qs.
She was my sister's favorite teacher.
As a supplement, we will also be learning Latin.
Latin makes it happen, children.
Now...
The face of a serious battleaxe
Over the course of the year, we will work through a grammar primer...
I thought that since she liked my sister...
...she'd like me, too.
...that you will all memorize.
I won't accept any slapdash work.
But it was rough going.
ZERO EXCUSES.
You will be routinely quizzed. If you make mistakes, you will write them out three times.
It'll stick eventually. You're no longer babies. Mind your Ps and Qs.

I thought my teachers had to love me. This belief inevitably led to me acting like a big suck-up.

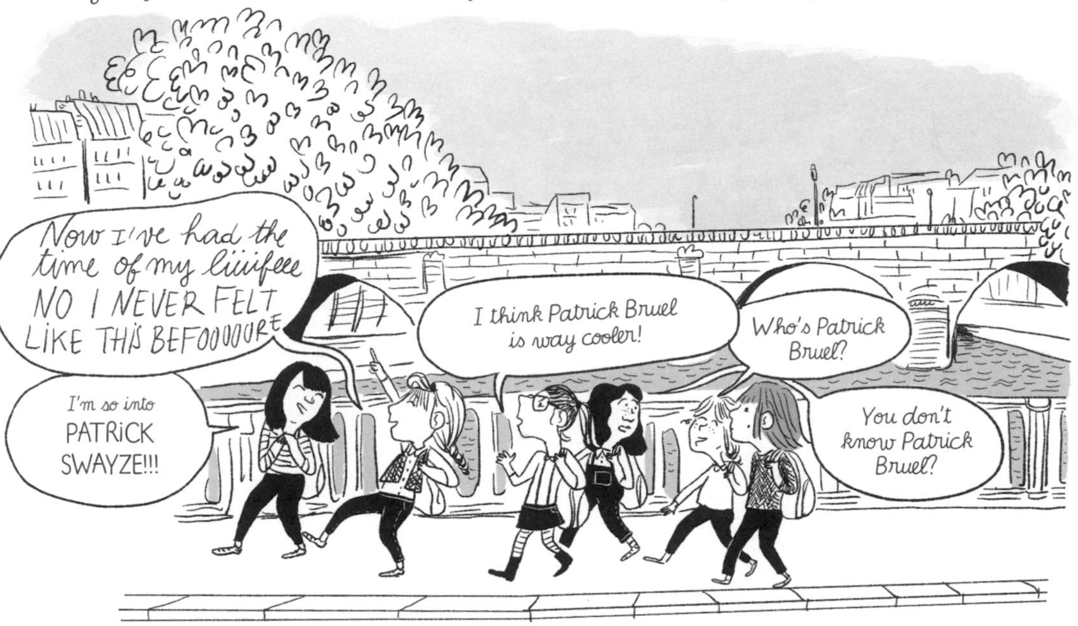
Now I've had the time of my liiifeee NO I NEVER FELT LIKE THIS BEFOOOOURE
I'm so into PATRICK SWAYZE!!!
I think Patrick Bruel is way cooler!
Who's Patrick Bruel?
You don't know Patrick Bruel?

In elementary school, everyone competed to be the teacher's pet.

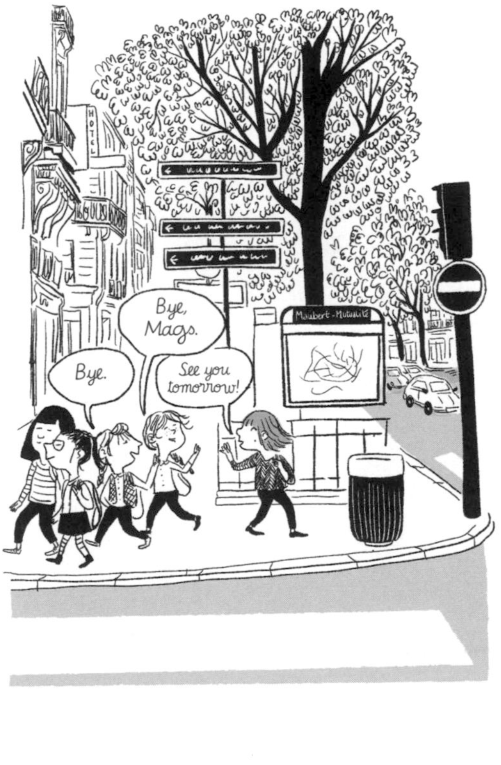
Bye, Mags.
Bye.
See you tomorrow!

But in spite of all my efforts, I never managed to climb the ranks and be a model student.

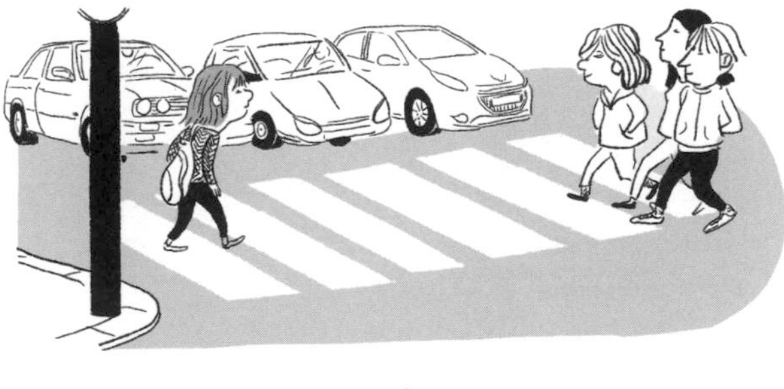

My workbooks were always a bit messy, and my grades were only average.

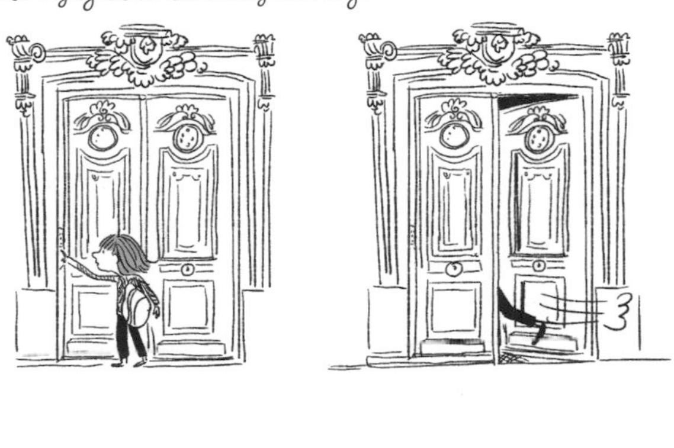

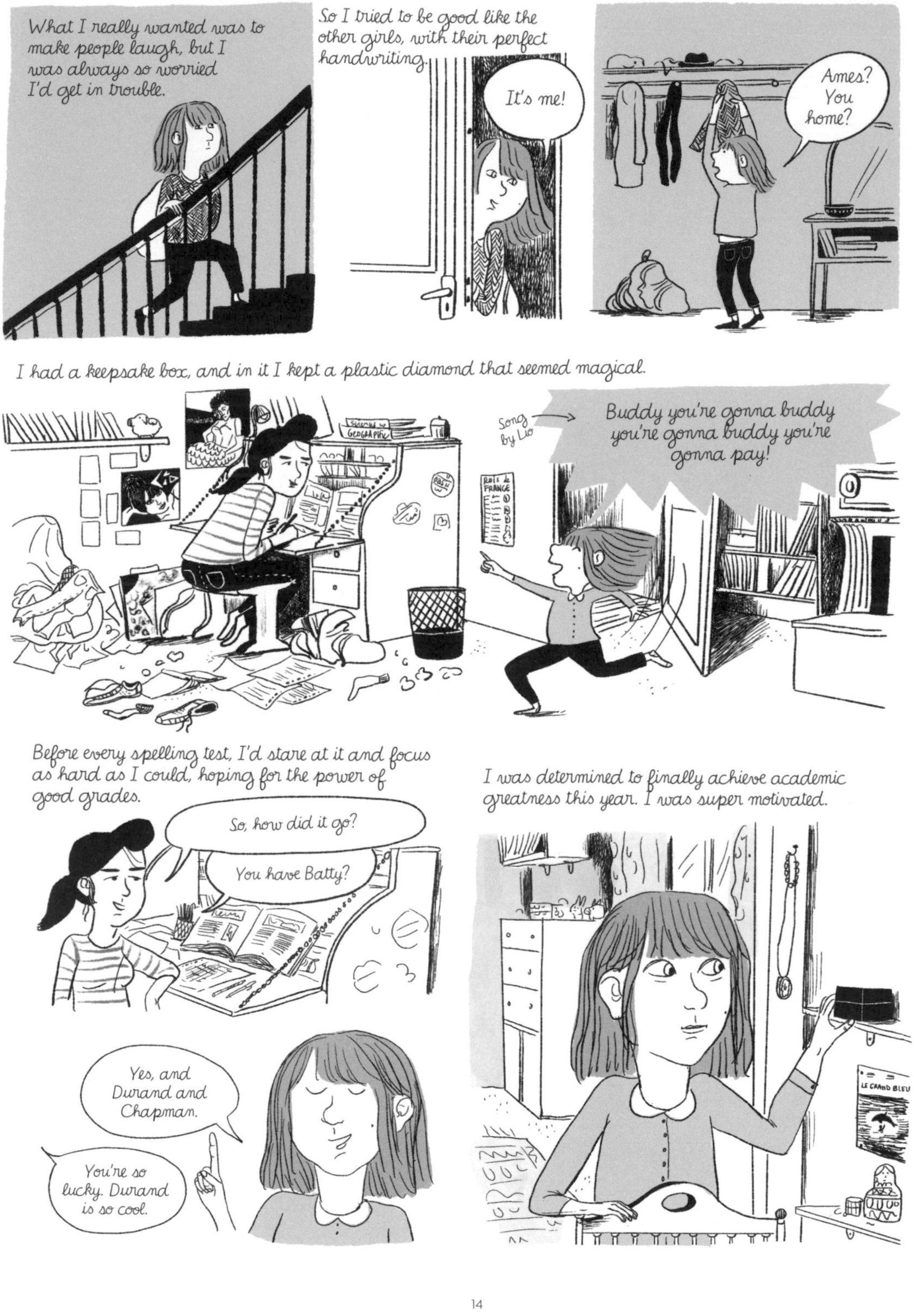
What I really wanted was to make people laugh, but I was always so worried I'd get in trouble.
So I tried to be good like the other girls, with their perfect handwriting.
It's me!
Ames? You home?
I had a keepsake box, and in it I kept a plastic diamond that seemed magical.
GEOGRAPHIE
Song by Lio
Buddy you're gonna buddy you're gonna buddy you're gonna pay!
Rois de FRANCE
Before every spelling test, I'd stare at it and focus as hard as I could, hoping for the power of good grades.
So, how did it go?
You have Batty?
Yes, and Durand and Chapman.
You're so lucky. Durand is so cool.
I was determined to finally achieve academic greatness this year. I was super motivated.
LE GRAND BLEU

I'd be an overachiever, and all my teachers would love me.

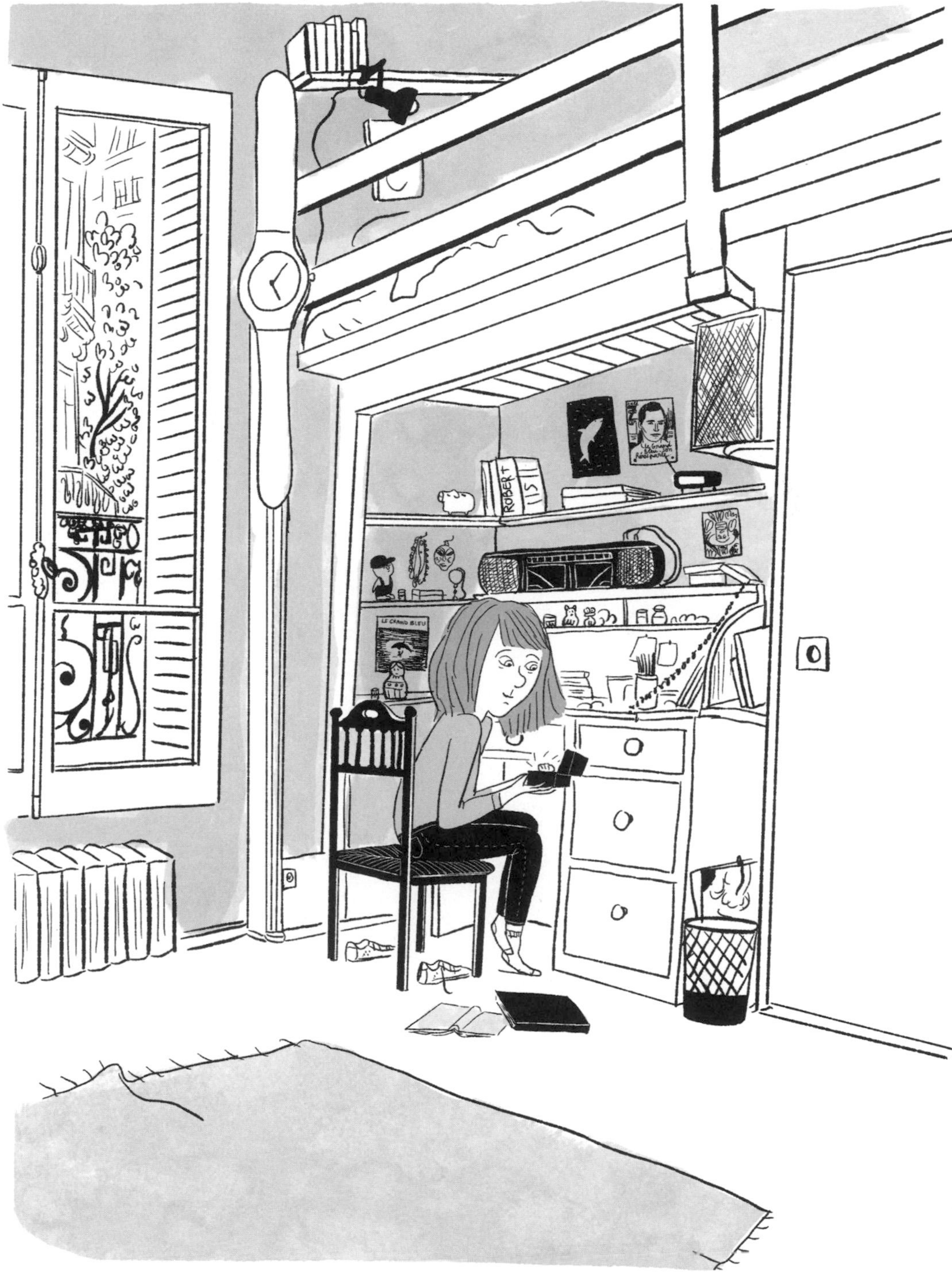
ROBERT
Le Grand Bleu · son Rénovasprale
LE GRAND BLEU

My sister and I knew the TV line-up by heart. First there was MacGyver at 6:30, followed by Who's the Boss? at 8.

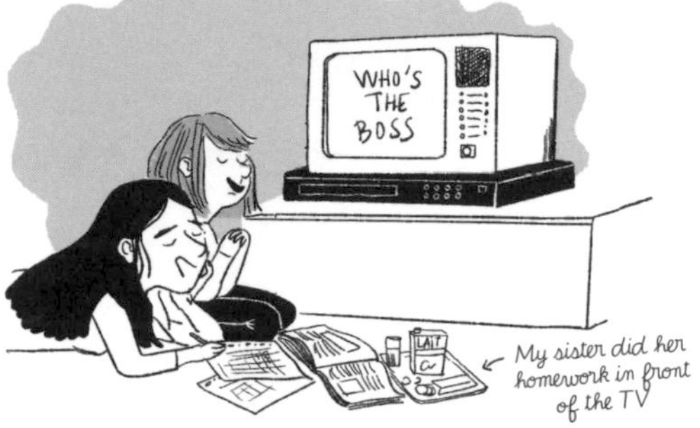
WHO'S THE BOSS
LAIT
My sister did her homework in front of the TV

We loved that show. If we had to miss an episode, we'd record it.

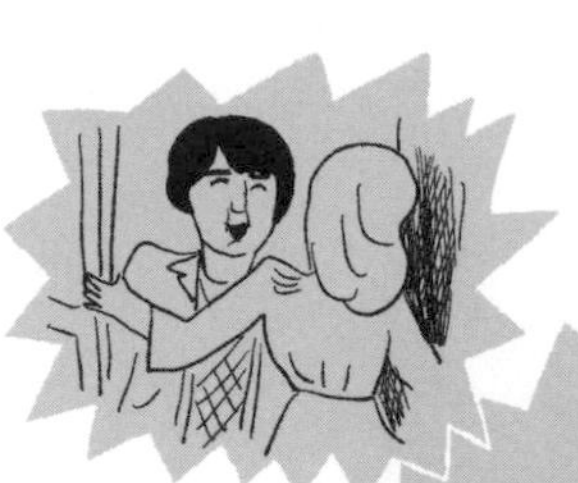

We were fans of Tony Micelli.

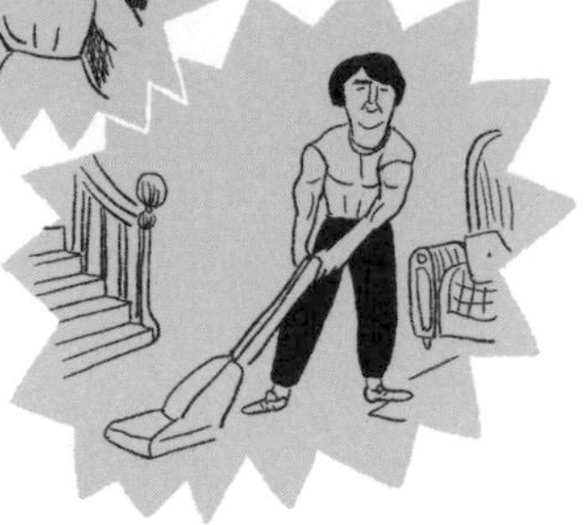

Our parents generally got home late.

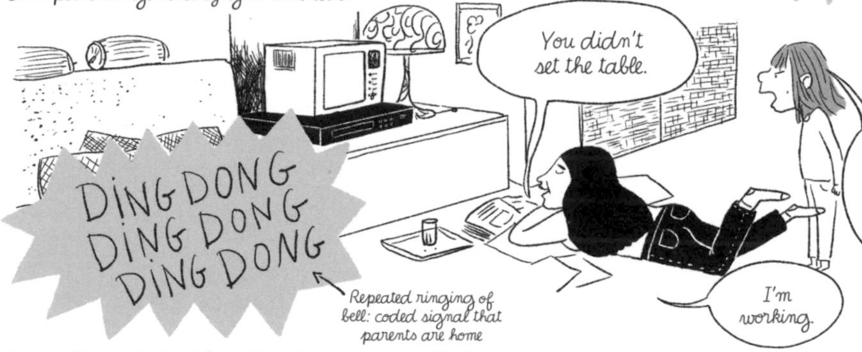
You didn't set the table.
YOU COULD DO iT FOR ONCE!!
DiNG DONG DiNG DONG DiNG DONG
Repeated ringing of bell: coded signal that parents are home
I'm working.

My mother, who had been listening to people all day, was usually seized with an irrepressible urge to talk.

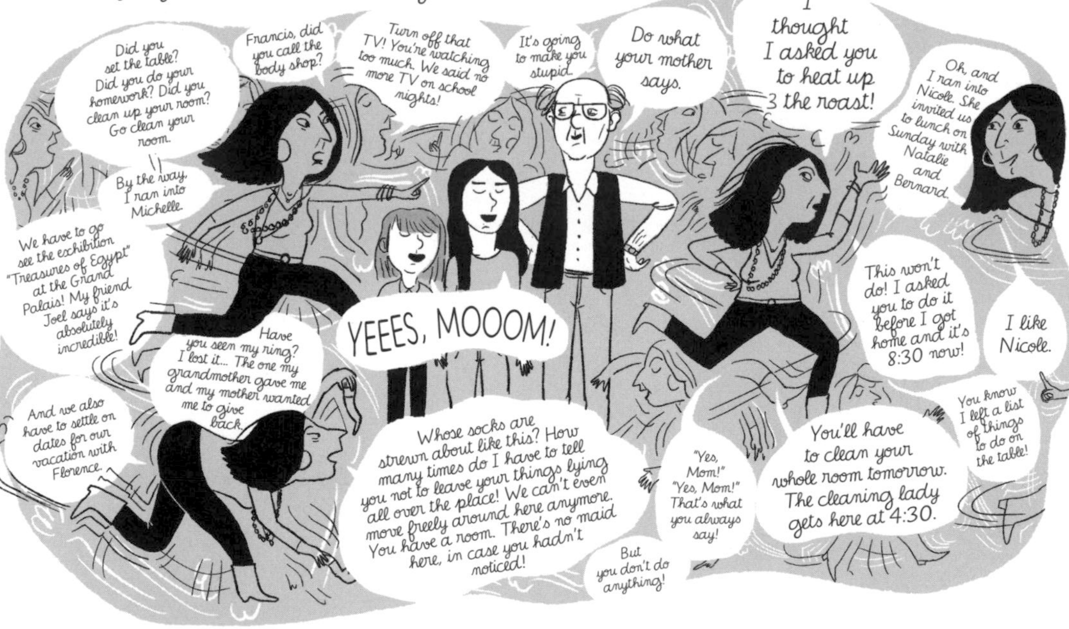
Did you set the table? Did you do your homework? Did you clean up your room? Go clean your room.
Francis, did you call the body shop?
Turn off that TV! You're watching too much. We said no more TV on school nights!
It's going to make you stupid.
Do what your mother says.
I thought I asked you to heat up the roast!
Oh, and I ran into Nicole. She invited us to lunch on Sunday with Natalie and Bernard.
By the way, I ran into Michelle.
We have to go see the exhibition "Treasures of Egypt" at the Grand Palais! My friend Joel says it's absolutely incredible!
YEEES, MOOOM!
This won't do! I asked you to do it before I got home and it's 8:30 now!
I like Nicole.
Have you seen my ring? I lost it... The one my grandmother gave me and my mother wanted me to give back.
And we also have to settle on dates for our vacation with Florence.
Whose socks are strewn about like this? How many times do I have to tell you not to leave your things lying all over the place! We can't even move freely around here anymore. You have a room. There's no maid here, in case you hadn't noticed!
"Yes, Mom!" "Yes, Mom!" That's what you always say!
But you don't do anything!
You'll have to clean your whole room tomorrow. The cleaning lady gets here at 4:30.
You know I left a list of things to do on the table!

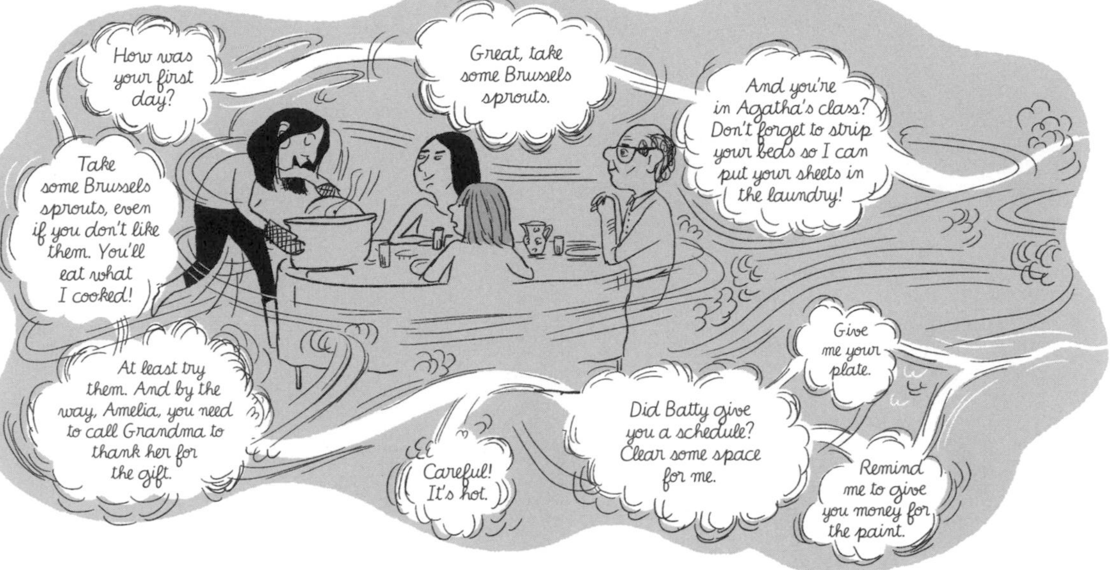
How was your first day?
Take some Brussels sprouts, even if you don't like them. You'll eat what I cooked!
Great, take some Brussels sprouts.
And you're in Agatha's class? Don't forget to strip your beds so I can put your sheets in the laundry!
At least try them. And by the way, Amelia, you need to call Grandma to thank her for the gift.
Careful! It's hot.
Did Batty give you a schedule? Clear some space for me.
Give me your plate.
Remind me to give you money for the paint.

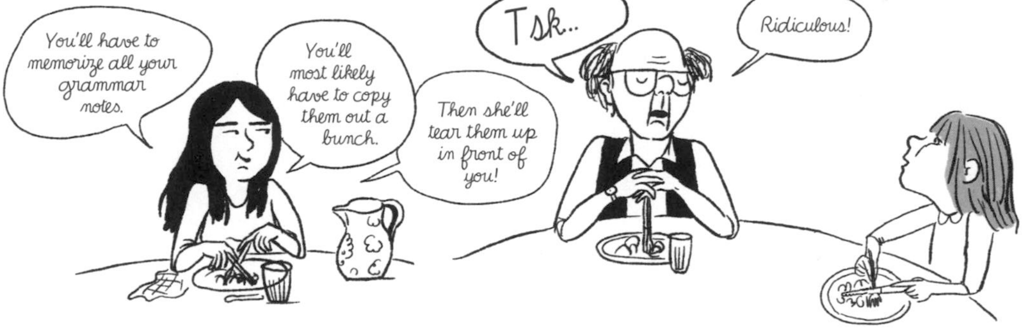
You'll have to memorize all your grammar notes.
You'll most likely have to copy them out a bunch.
Then she'll tear them up in front of you!
Tsk...
Ridiculous!

My parents were sort of super-therapists. They created safe spaces for people to talk--people struggling with learning disabilities, people with mental illnesses, people who were grieving or depressed, and more. Anyone who needed someone to listen.

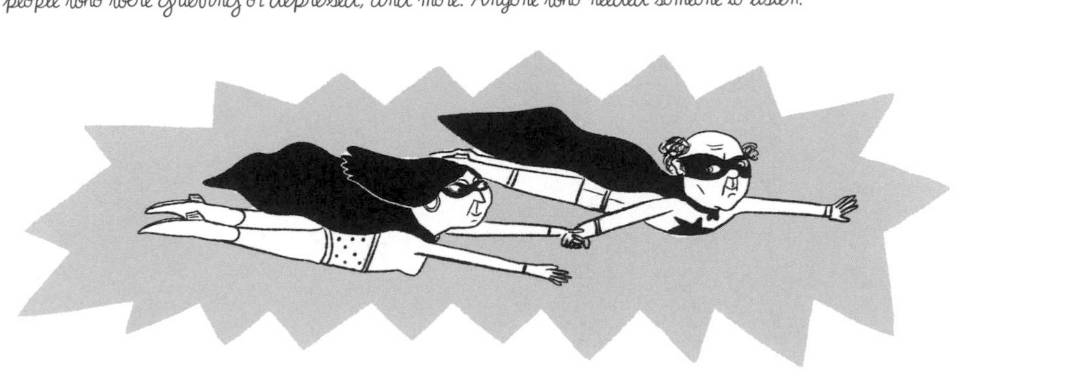

They were in great demand.

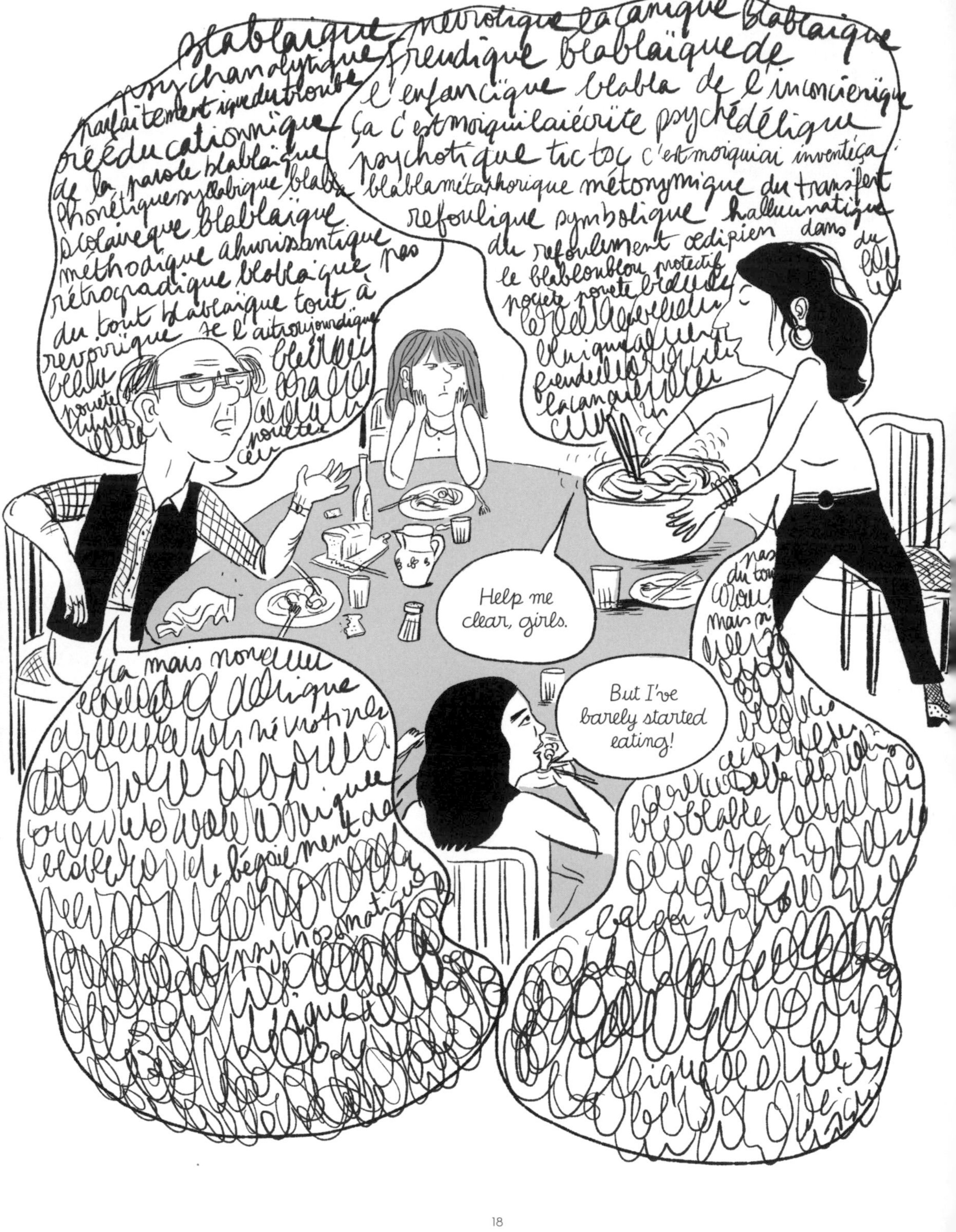
blablaïque
psychanalytique
rééducationnique
de la parole blablaïque
scolaireque blablaïque
méthodique ahurissantique
rétrogradique blablaïque pas
du tout blablaïque tout à
névrotique lacanique blablaïque
freudique blablaïque de
l'enfancique blabla de l'inconscienique
ça c'est moiquilaiécrite psychédélique
psychotique tic toc c'est moiquiai inventéça
blablamétaphorique métonymique du transfert
refoulique symbolique hallucinatique
du refoulement oedipien dans
Help me clear, girls.
But I've barely started eating!

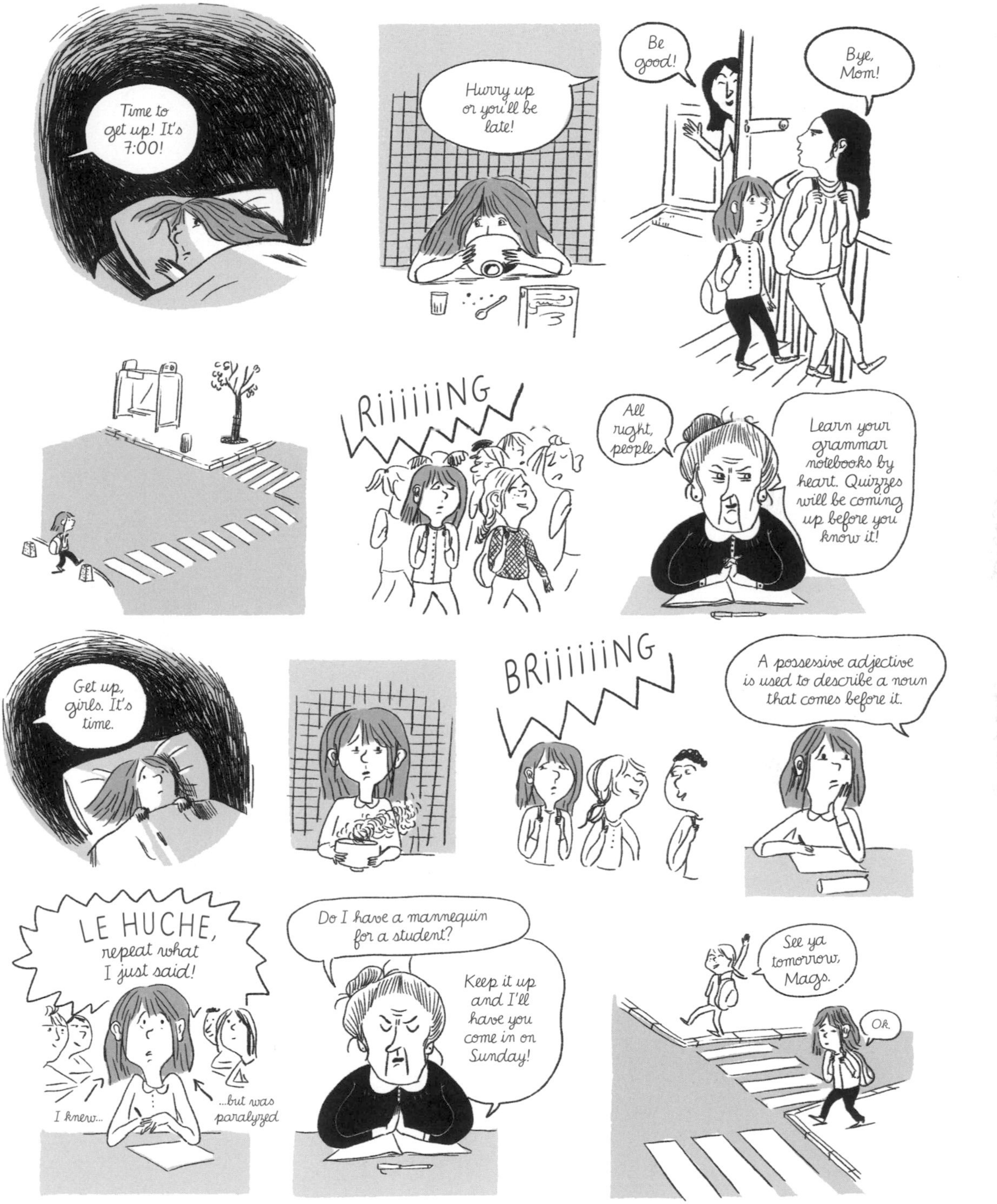

Time to get up! It's 7:00!
Hurry up or you'll be late!
Be good!
Bye, Mom!
RiiiiiiNG
All right, people.
Learn your grammar notebooks by heart. Quizzes will be coming up before you know it!
Get up, girls. It's time.
BRiiiiiiNG
A possessive adjective is used to describe a noun that comes before it.
LE HUCHE, repeat what I just said!
I knew...
...but was paralyzed
Do I have a mannequin for a student?
Keep it up and I'll have you come in on Sunday!
See ya tomorrow, Mags.
Ok.

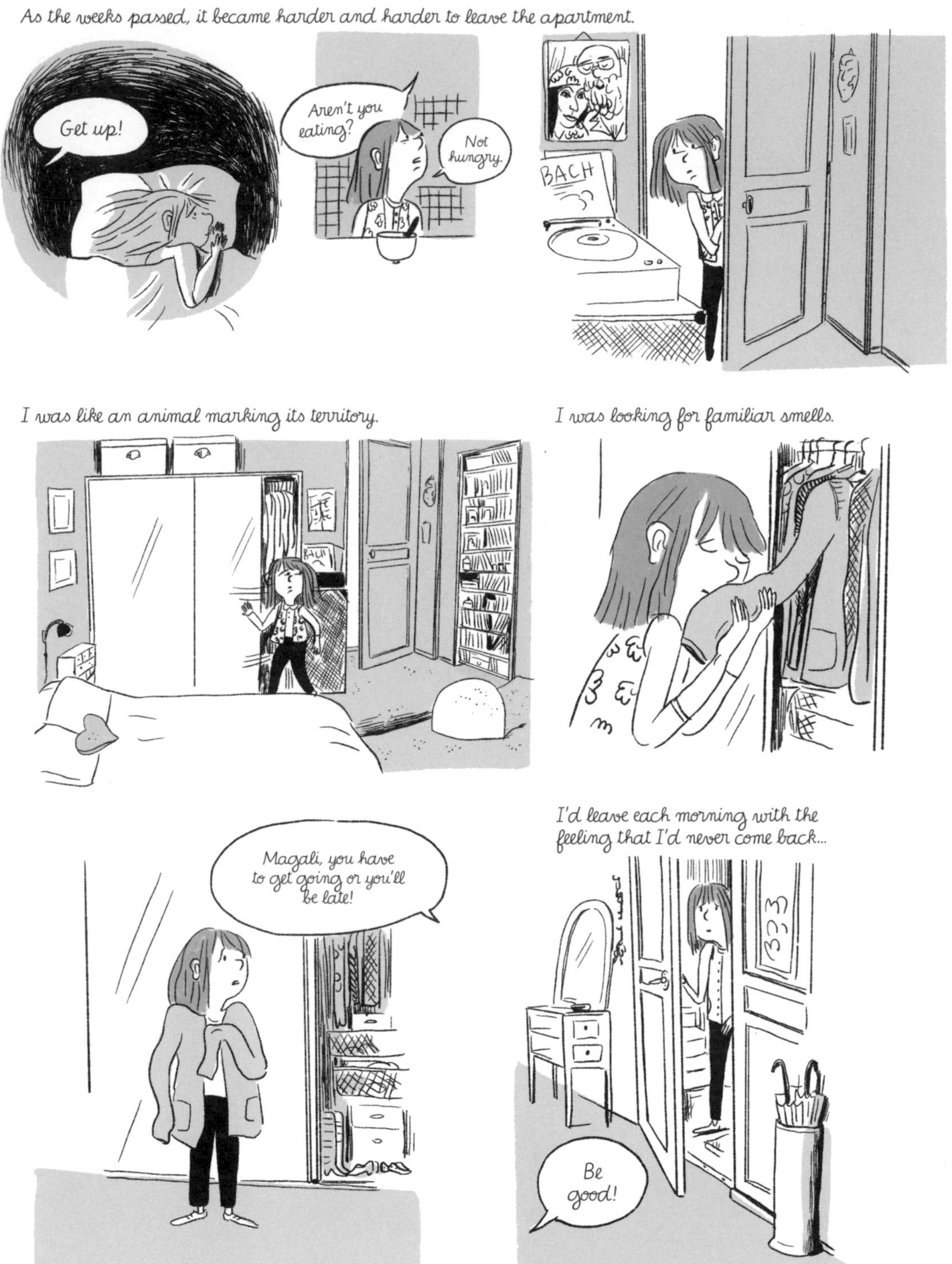
As the weeks passed, it became harder and harder to leave the apartment.
Get up!
Aren't you eating?
Not hungry.
BACH
I was like an animal marking its territory.
I was looking for familiar smells.
Magali, you have to get going or you'll be late!
I'd leave each morning with the feeling that I'd never come back...
Be good!

...and that each morning I left a bit of my childhood at home.

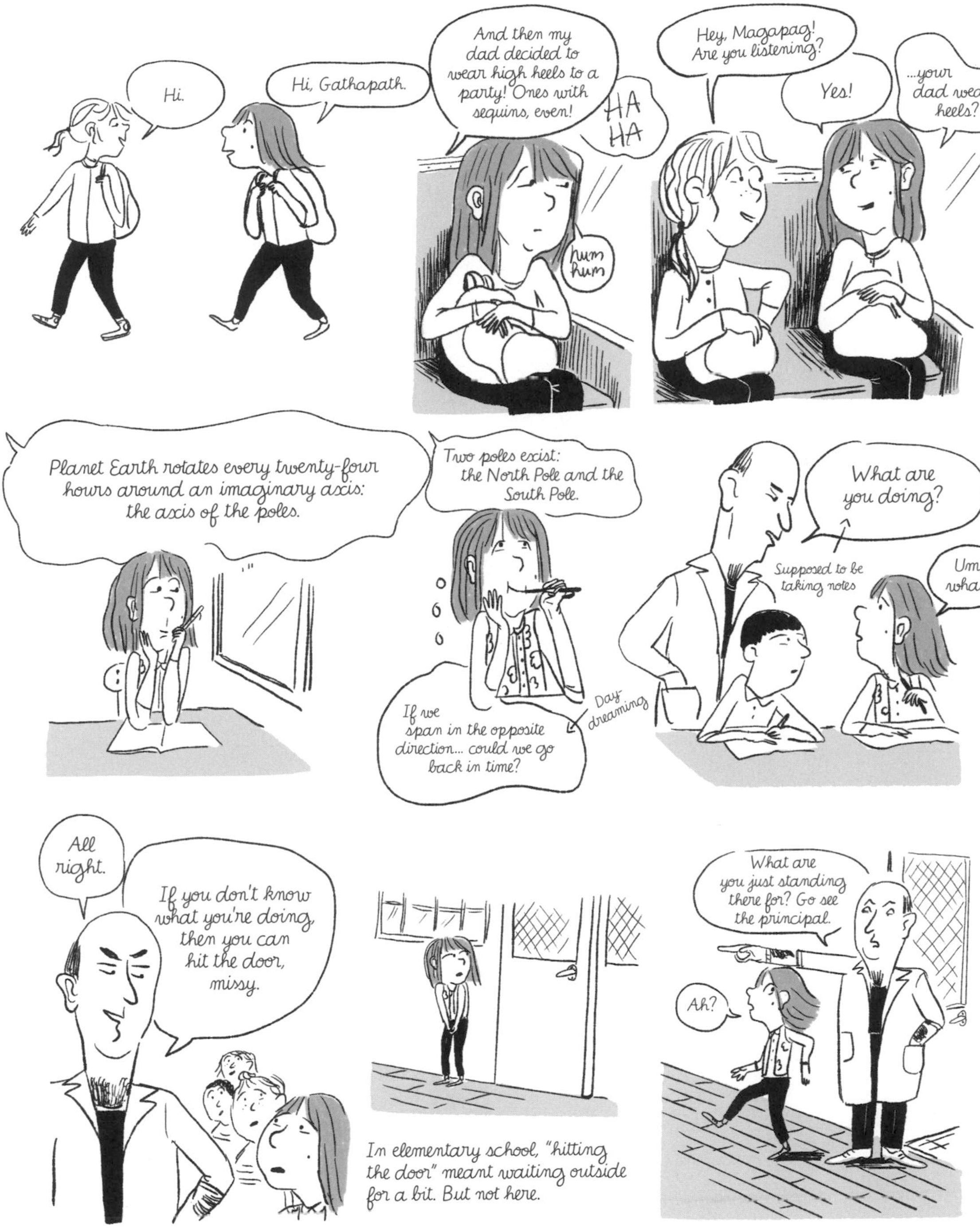

Hi.
Hi, Gathapath.
And then my dad decided to wear high heels to a party! Ones with sequins, even!
HA HA
hum hum
Hey, Magapag! Are you listening?
Yes!
...your dad wears heels?
Planet Earth rotates every twenty-four hours around an imaginary axis: the axis of the poles.
Two poles exist: the North Pole and the South Pole.
If we span in the opposite direction... could we go back in time?
Day-dreaming
What are you doing?
Supposed to be taking notes
Um, what?
All right.
If you don't know what you're doing, then you can hit the door, missy.
In elementary school, "hitting the door" meant waiting outside for a bit. But not here.
What are you just standing there for? Go see the principal.
Ah?

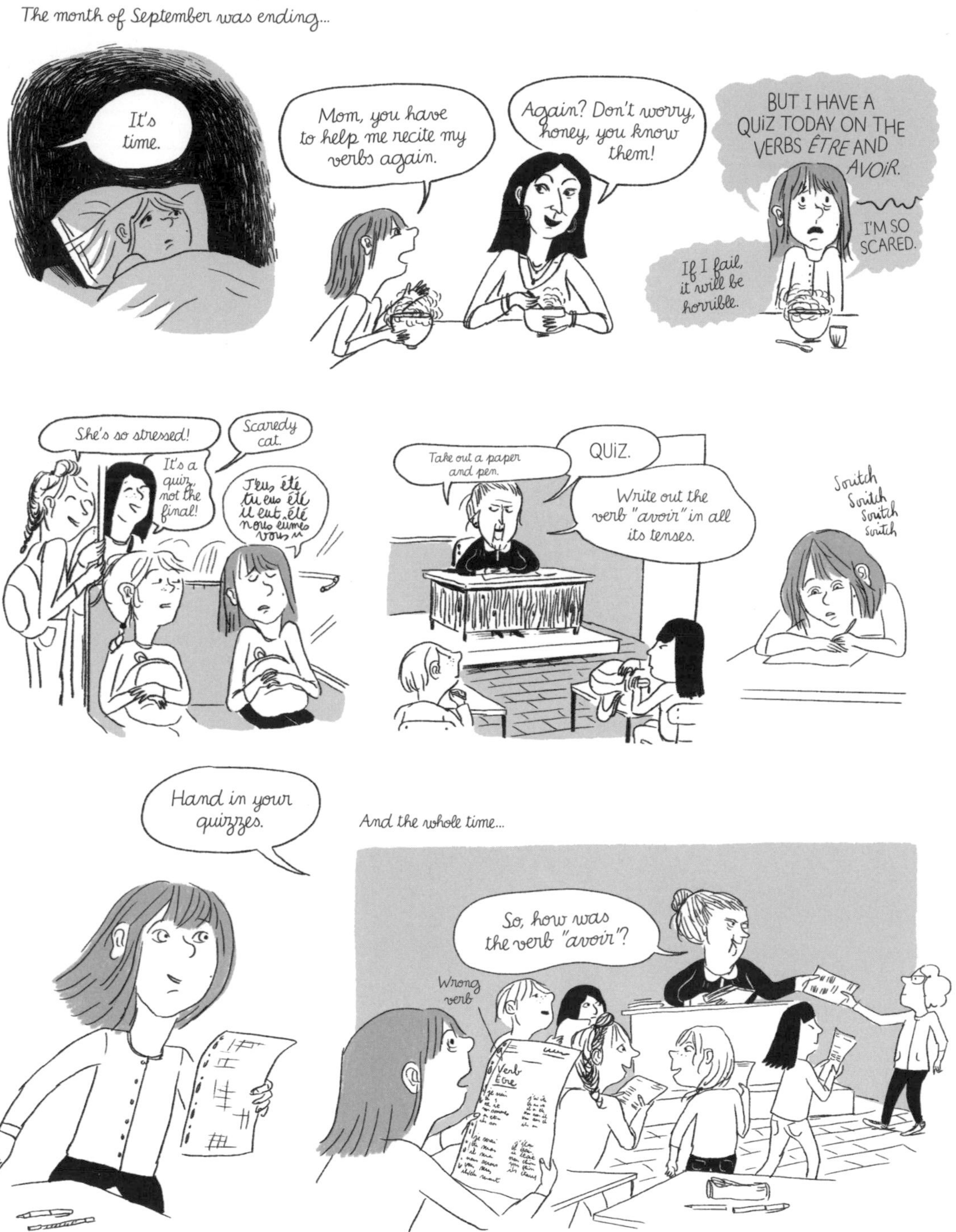
The month of September was ending...
It's time.
Mom, you have to help me recite my verbs again.
Again? Don't worry, honey, you know them!
BUT I HAVE A QUIZ TODAY ON THE VERBS ÊTRE AND AVOIR.
If I fail, it will be horrible.
I'M SO SCARED.
She's so stressed!
It's a quiz, not the final!
Scaredy cat.
J'eus été
tu eus été
il eut été
nous eûmes
vous "
Take out a paper and pen.
QUIZ.
Write out the verb "avoir" in all its tenses.
Switch
Swilch
Switch
switch
Hand in your quizzes.
And the whole time...
So, how was the verb "avoir"?
Wrong verb
Verb Être

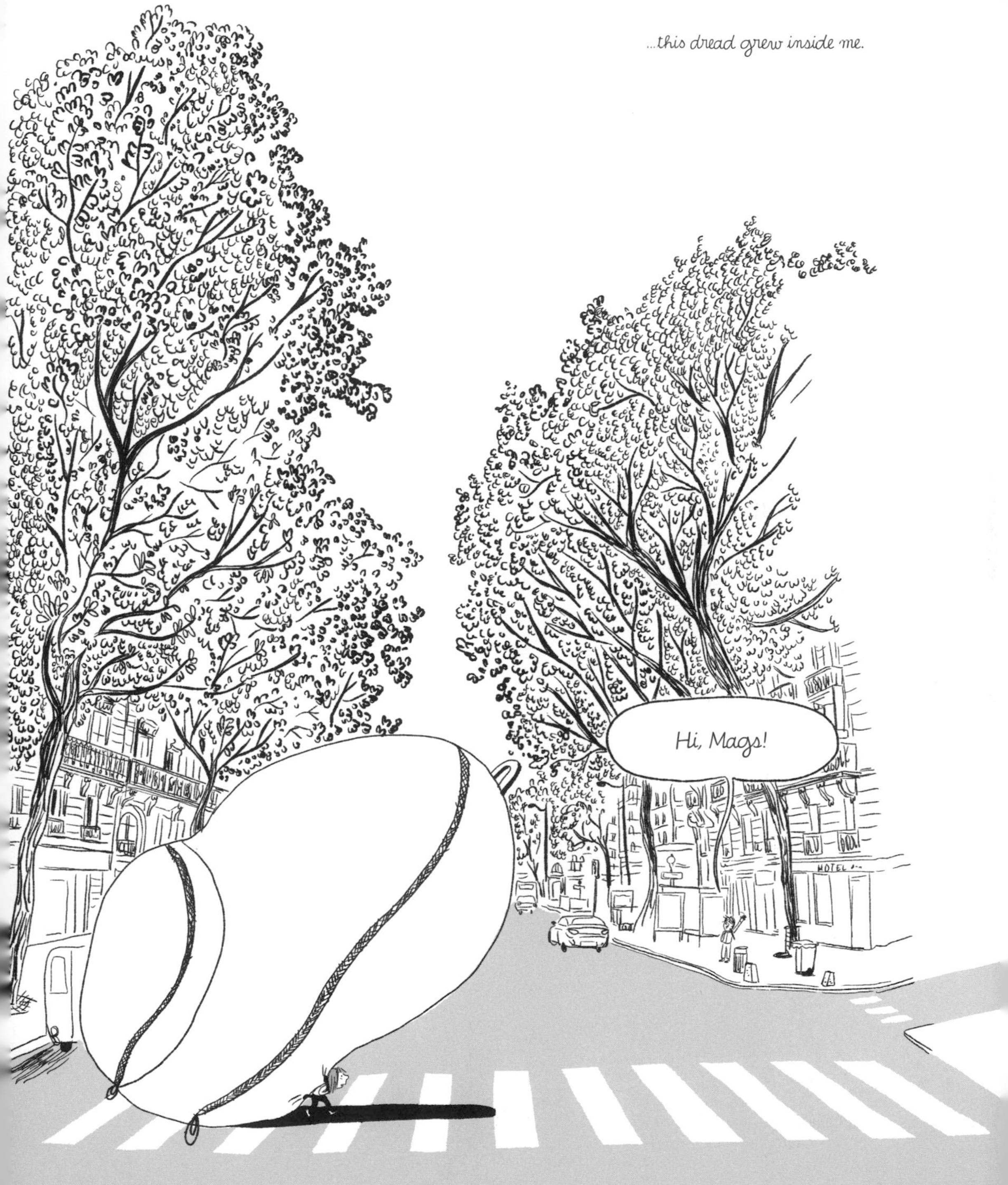
...this dread grew inside me.
Hi, Mags!
HOTEL

I was always a groupie at heart.

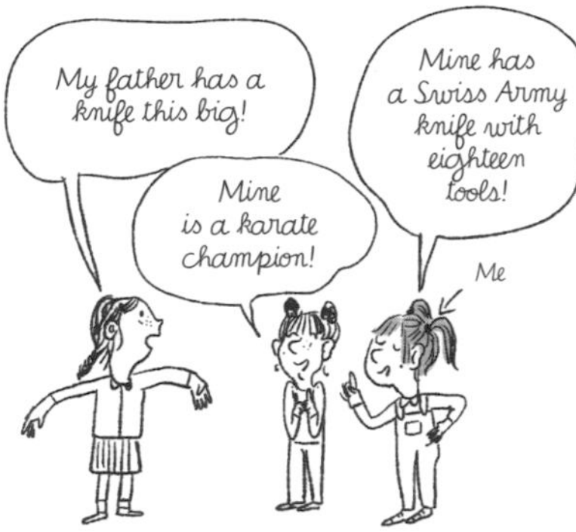
My father has a knife this big!
Mine is a karate champion!
Mine has a Swiss Army knife with eighteen tools!
Me

In kindergarten, we were all in love with our fathers.

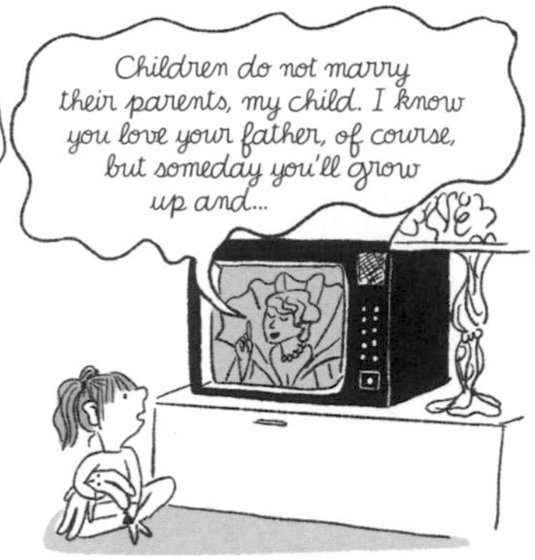
Children do not marry their parents, my child. I know you love your father, of course, but someday you'll grow up and...

I learned that I was supposed to pick some other person and marry them. But who?

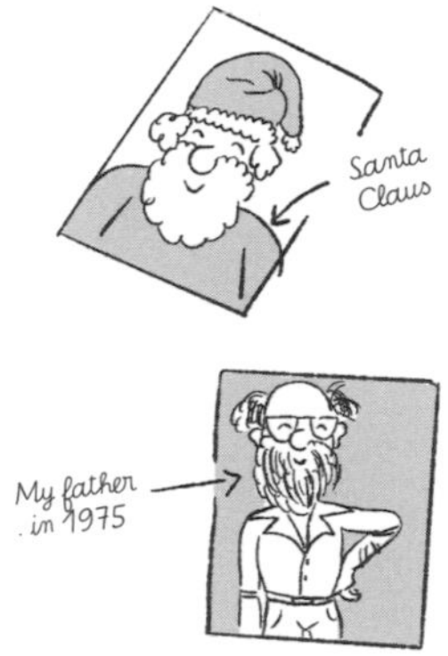
Santa Claus
My father in 1975

I decided on Santa Claus. Bald, bearded, and kind, he had a lot in common with my father.

And then one day:

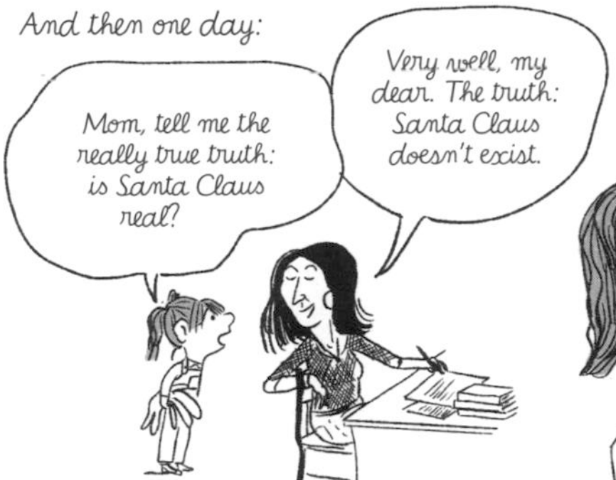
Mom, tell me the really true truth: is Santa Claus real?
Very well, my dear. The truth: Santa Claus doesn't exist.

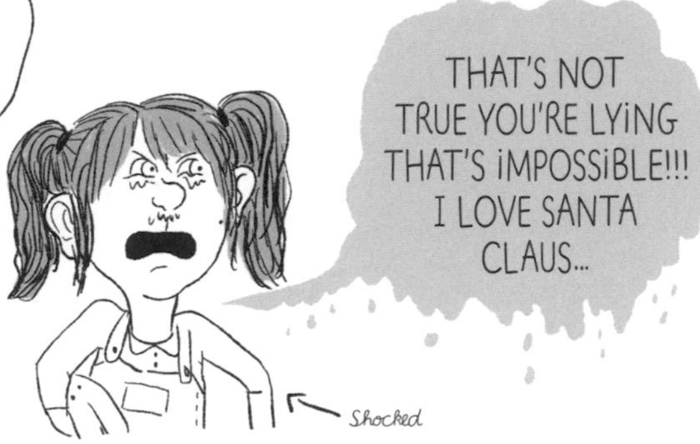
THAT'S NOT TRUE YOU'RE LYiNG THAT'S iMPOSSiBLE!!! I LOVE SANTA CLAUS...
Shocked

It was terrible.

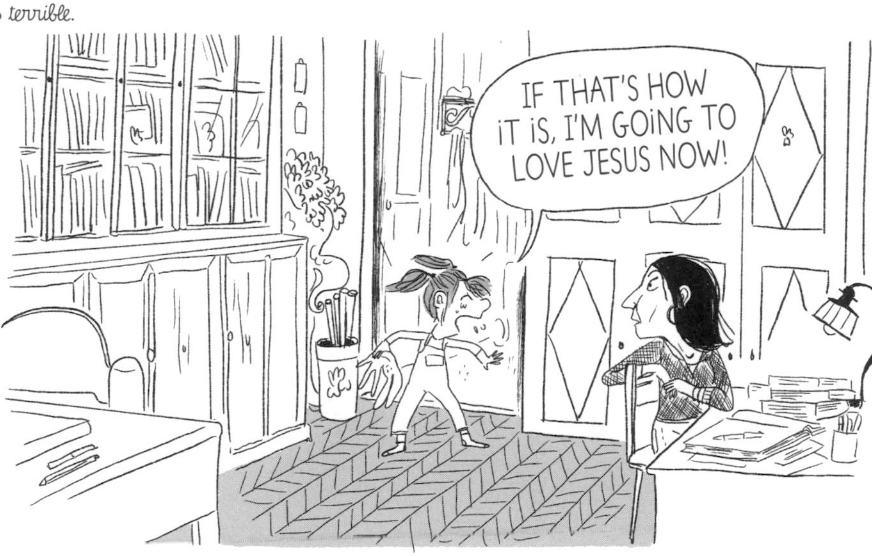
IF THAT'S HOW iT iS, I'M GOiNG TO LOVE JESUS NOW!

Jesus... My first crush...

Buff even when half-dead
Nails + blood = totally rock 'n' roll
Ribs visible
Manly body hair
Teensy sheet = only piece of clothing
Little folds in sheet arousing all my curiosity

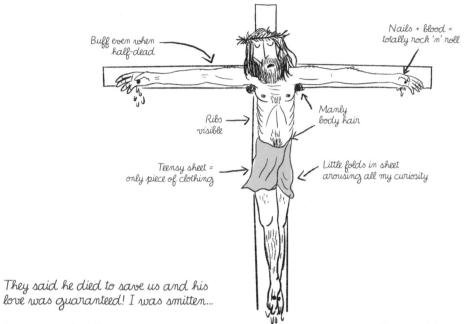

They said he died to save us and his love was guaranteed! I was smitten...

I was crazy about Jesus.

I love you, too.

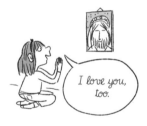

I played pretend church services.

This is my body.

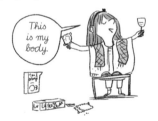

Jesus and I lasted four years...

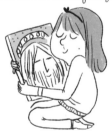

Then there was Christophe Lambert.

The body that made me forget Jesus

Next, MacGyver.

The same intense eyes

And Jean-Marc Barr.

That dreamy stare toward some distant horizon
First cliché female fantasy

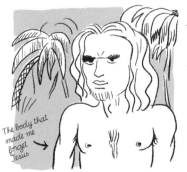

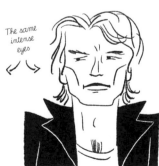

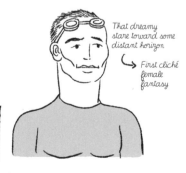

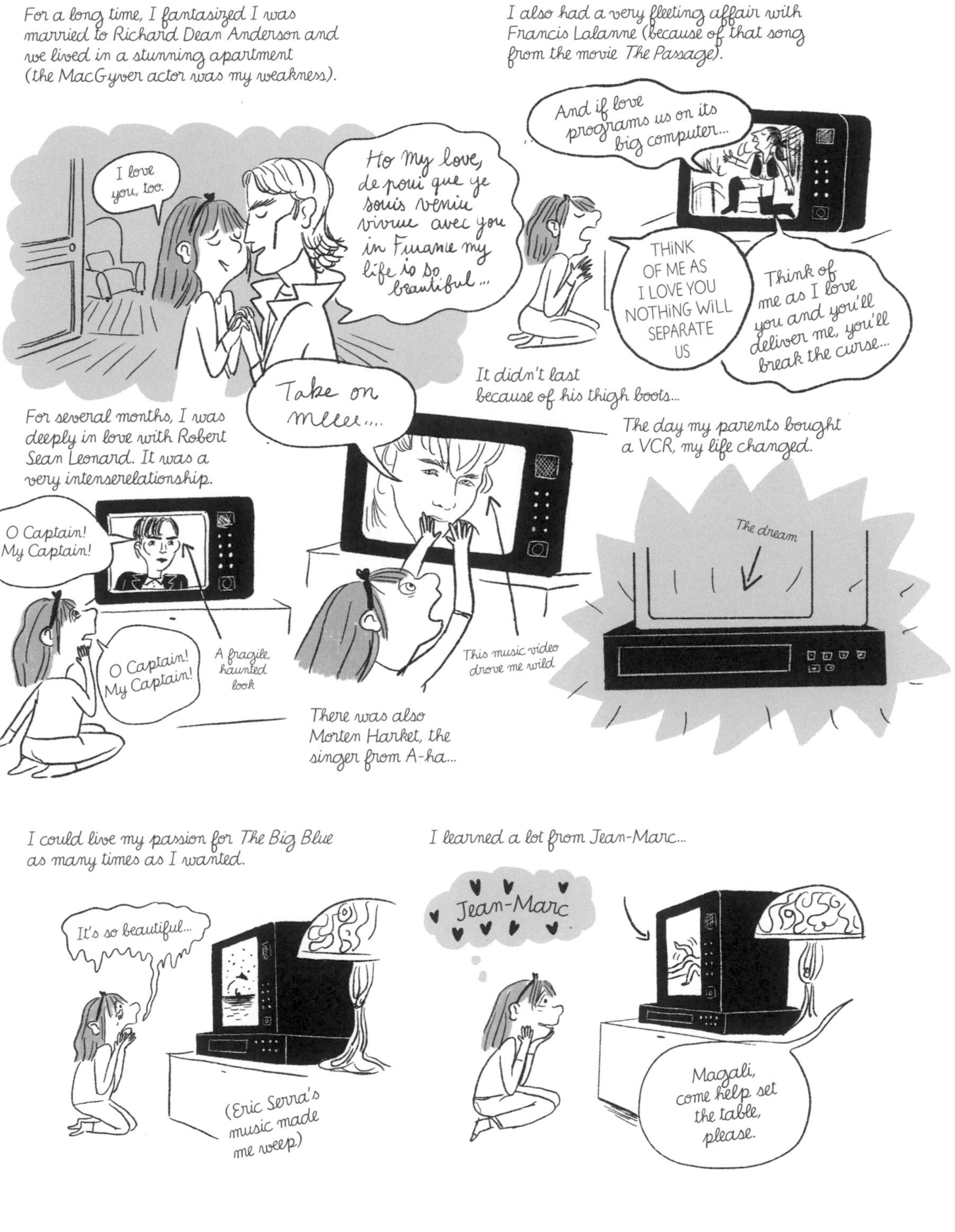
For a long time, I fantasized I was married to Richard Dean Anderson and we lived in a stunning apartment (the MacGyver actor was my weakness).
I love you, too.
Ho my love, de poui que ye souis veniu vivrue avec you in Fuance my life is so beautiful...
I also had a very fleeting affair with Francis Lalanne (because of that song from the movie The Passage).
And if love programs us on its big computer...
THINK OF ME AS I LOVE YOU NOTHING WILL SEPARATE US
Think of me as I love you and you'll deliver me, you'll break the curse...
It didn't last because of his thigh boots...
For several months, I was deeply in love with Robert Sean Leonard. It was a very intenserelationship.
O Captain! My Captain!
O Captain! My Captain!
A fragile, haunted look
Take on meee....
This music video drove me wild
There was also Morten Harket, the singer from A-ha...
The day my parents bought a VCR, my life changed.
The dream
I could live my passion for The Big Blue as many times as I wanted.
It's so beautiful...
(Eric Serra's music made me weep)
I learned a lot from Jean-Marc...
Jean-Marc
Magali, come help set the table, please.

I could go back and rewind or fast forward to skip ahead whenever I wanted, as often as I wanted.

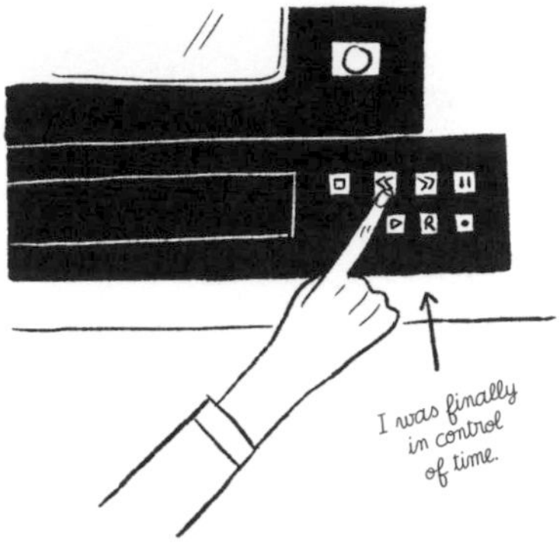
I was finally in control of time.

My parents couldn't work the VCR at all. So my sister did everything. At first, she recorded all the *Cinéma de minuit* movies.

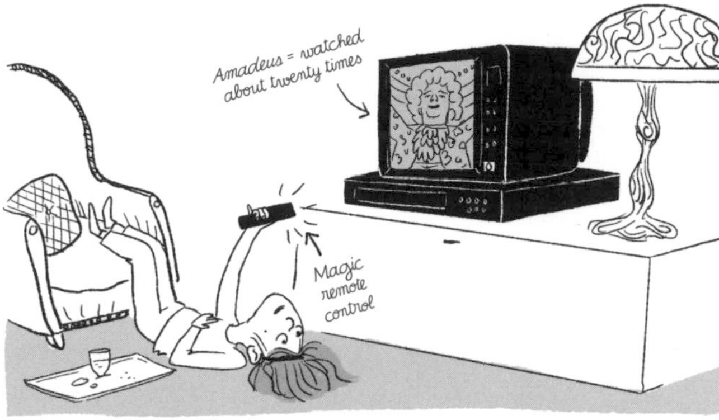
Amadeus = watched about twenty times
Magic remote control

That's how I stumbled across *Bonnie and Clyde*, which I watched a dozen times, much of it on rewind.

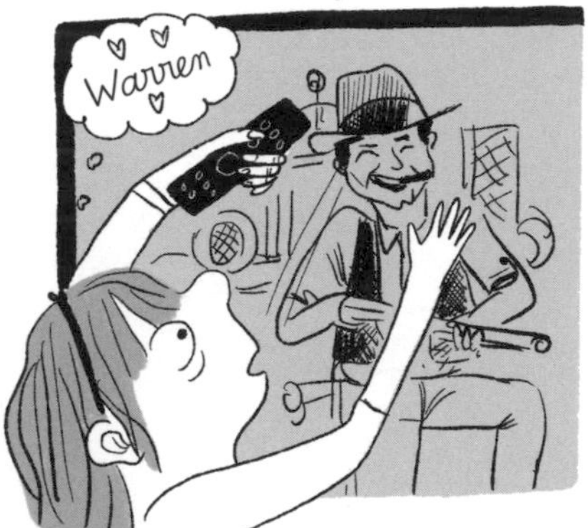
Warren

I watched Little Big Man around ten times, at least two of those in slow-mo (over multiple days).

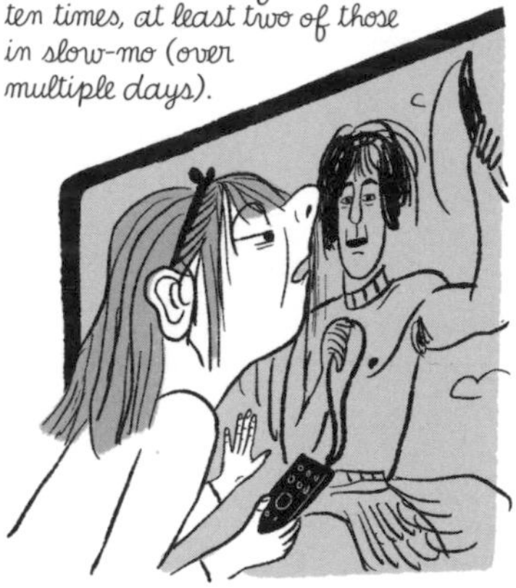

I spent a lot of time in front of the TV...

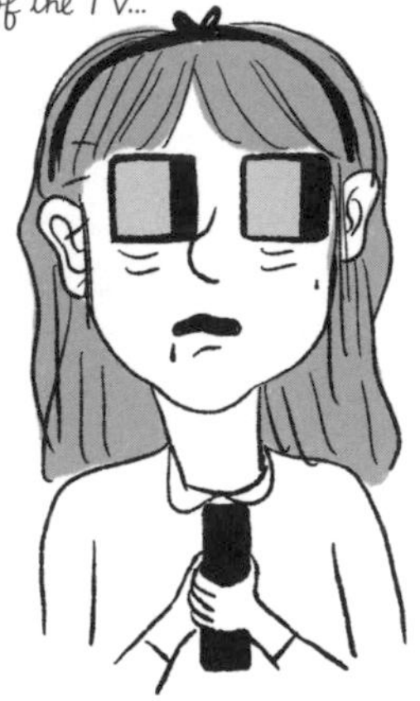

When my parents came home and I had to turn it off, it was a bit like coming down from a drug.

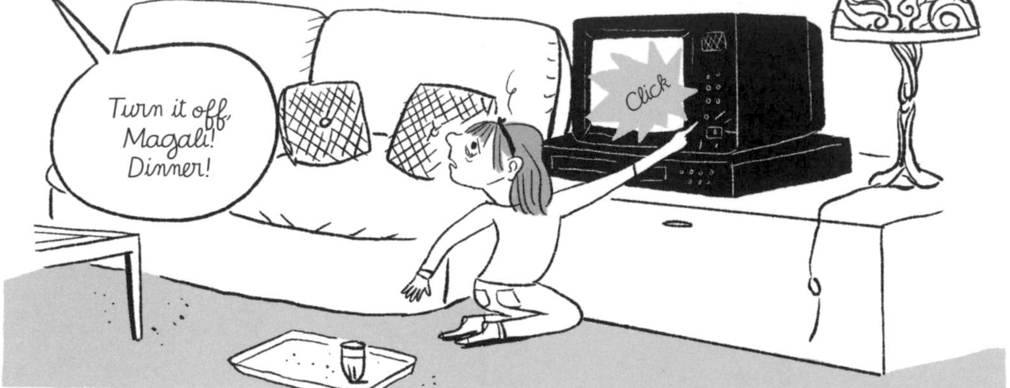
Turn it off, Magali! Dinner!
Click

I loved everything my sister listened to: Madonna! Michael Jackson! The music filled me with longing, but it was kind of her property.

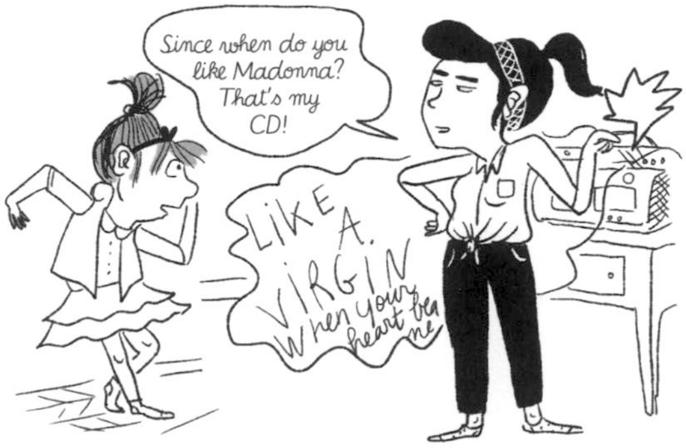
Since when do you like Madonna? That's my CD!
LIKE A VIRGIN When your heart bea... me

I had four tapes I listened to on a loop...

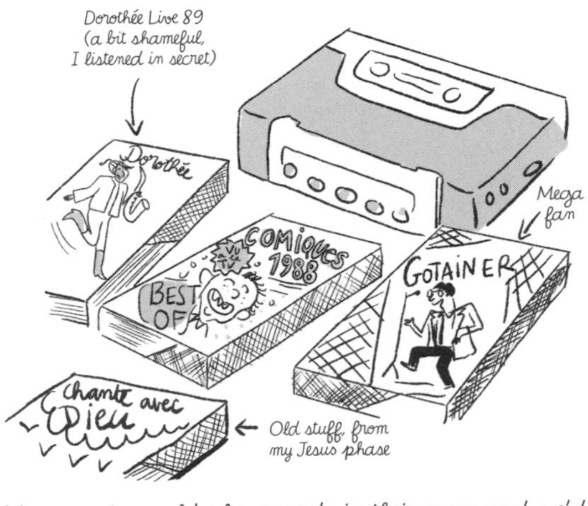
Dorothée Live 89 (a bit shameful, I listened in secret)
Dorothée
COMIQUES 1988
BEST OF
GOTAINER
Mega fan
Chante avec Dieu
Old stuff, from my Jesus phase

I loved dancing while listening to music.

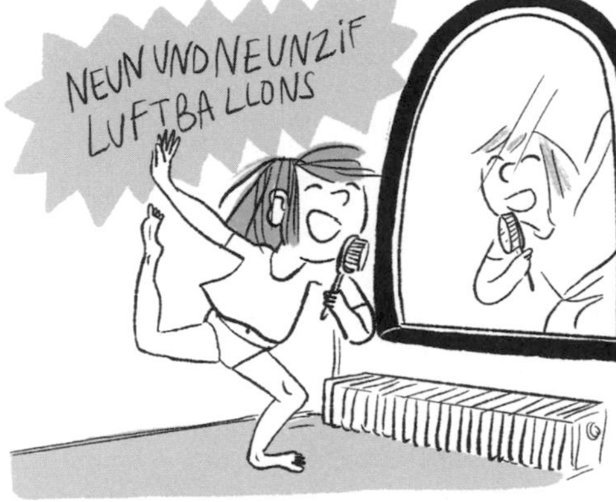
NEUN UND NEUNZIF LUFTBALLONS

(My parents had eclectic taste)

My parents would play records in their room and we'd hear the music in the living room at the end of the hall.

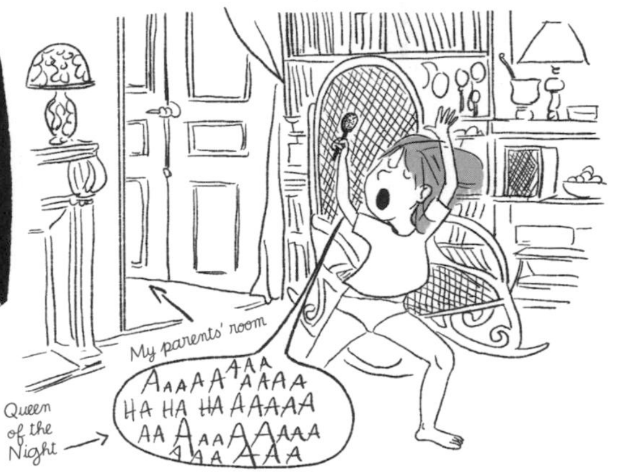
My parents' room
AAAAAAAAAAAA HA HA HA AAAAA AA AAAAAAAA AAAAAA
Queen of the Night

When I wasn't watching TV, I spent my time dressing up. I could be all different types of people! Anything was possible. I was totally into it.

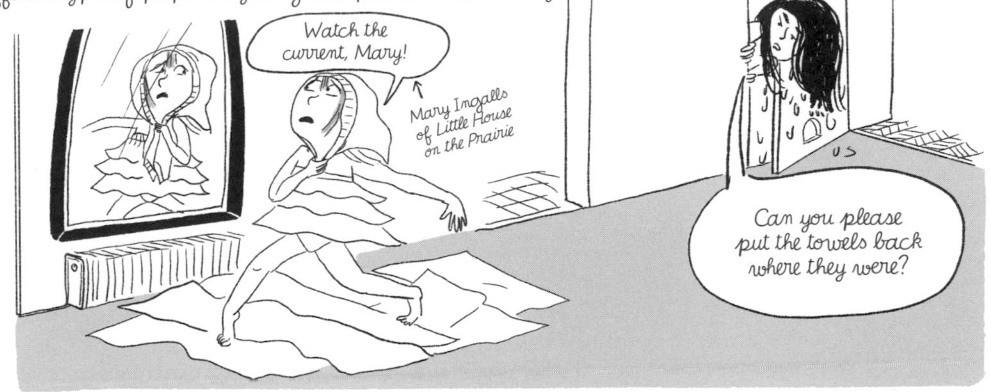
Watch the current, Mary!
Mary Ingalls of Little House on the Prairie
Can you please put the towels back where they were?

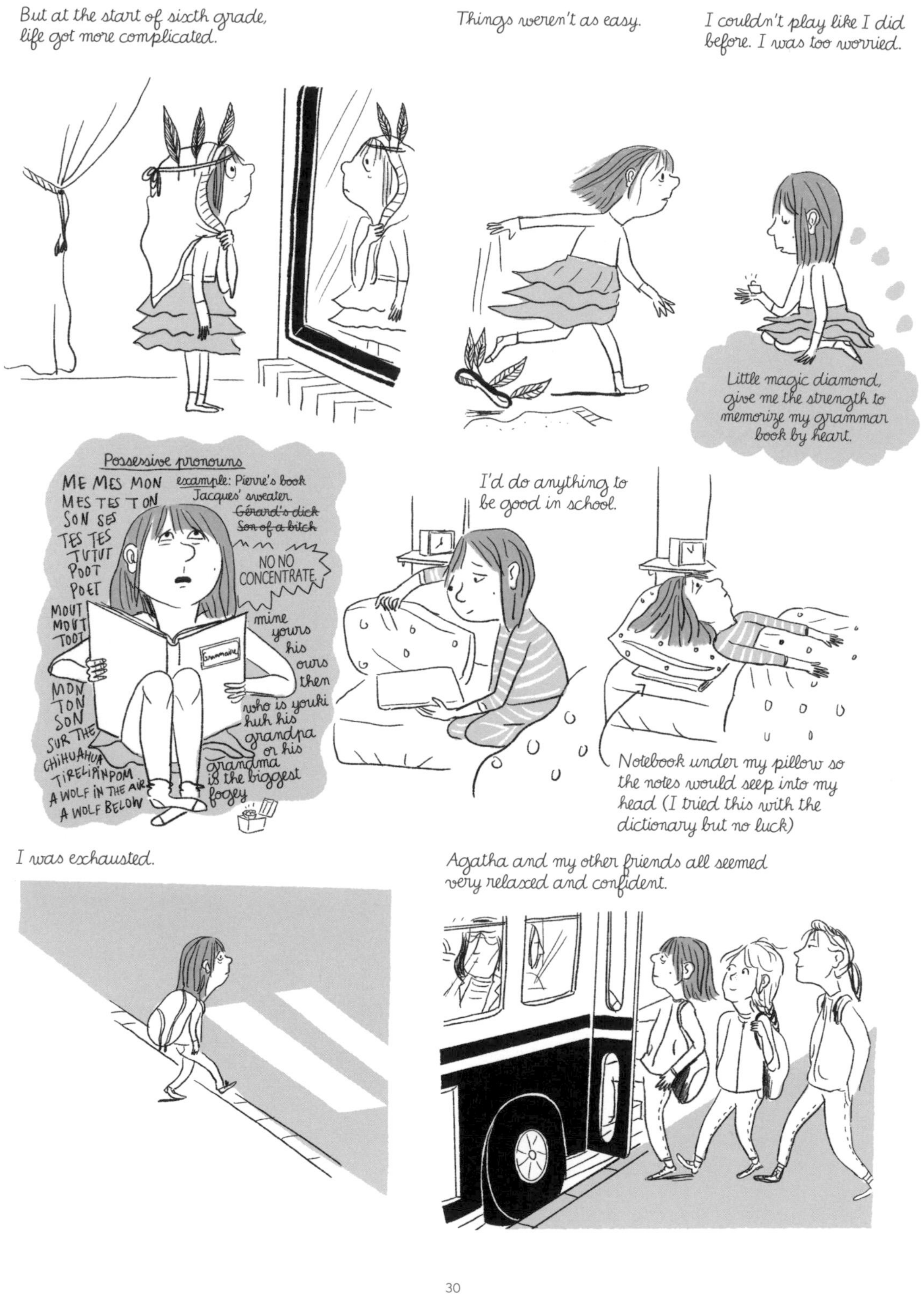
But at the start of sixth grade, life got more complicated.
Things weren't as easy.
I couldn't play like I did before. I was too worried.
Little magic diamond, give me the strength to memorize my grammar book by heart.
Possessive pronouns
ME MES MON
MES TES T ON
SON SES
TES TES
TUTUT
POOT
POET
MOUT
MOUT
TOOT
MON
TON
SON
SUR THE
CHIHUAHUA
TIRELIPINPOM
A WOLF IN THE AIR
A WOLF BELOW
example: Pierre's book
Jacques' sweater.
~~Gérard's dick~~
~~Son of a bitch~~
NO NO CONCENTRATE.
mine
yours
his
ours
then
who is youki
huh his
grandpa
or his
grandma
is the biggest
fogey
Grammaire
I'd do anything to be good in school.
Notebook under my pillow so the notes would seep into my head (I tried this with the dictionary but no luck)
I was exhausted.
Agatha and my other friends all seemed very relaxed and confident.

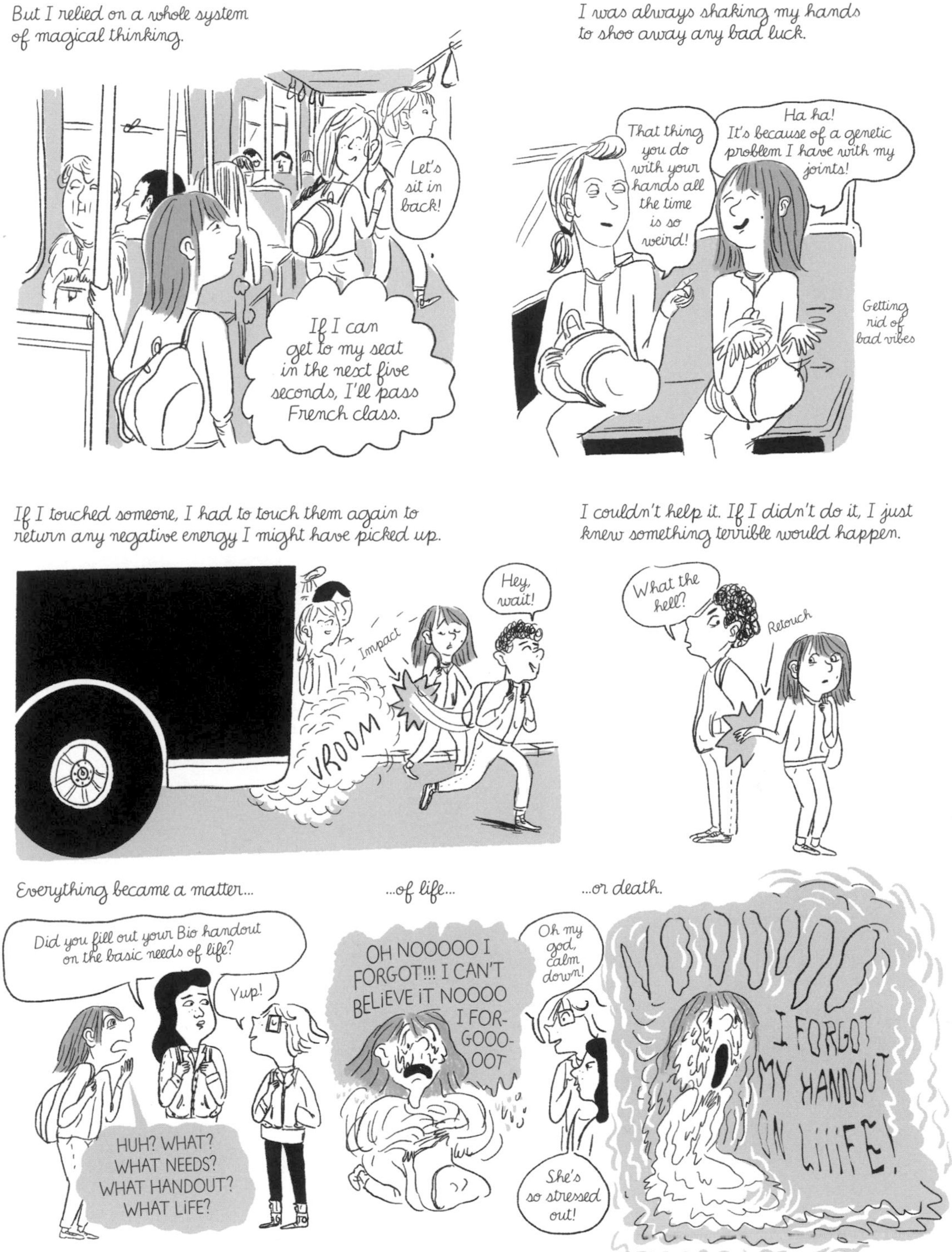
But I relied on a whole system of magical thinking.
Let's sit in back!
If I can get to my seat in the next five seconds, I'll pass French class.
I was always shaking my hands to shoo away any bad luck.
That thing you do with your hands all the time is so weird!
Ha ha! It's because of a genetic problem I have with my joints!
Getting rid of bad vibes
If I touched someone, I had to touch them again to return any negative energy I might have picked up.
Impact
VROOM
Hey, wait!
I couldn't help it. If I didn't do it, I just knew something terrible would happen.
What the hell?
Retouch
Everything became a matter...
Did you fill out your Bio handout on the basic needs of life?
Yup!
HUH? WHAT? WHAT NEEDS? WHAT HANDOUT? WHAT LIFE?
...of life...
OH NOOOOO I FORGOT!!! I CAN'T BELIEVE IT NOOOO I FORGOOOOOT
Oh my god, calm down!
She's so stressed out!
...or death.
NOOOOOO
I FORGOT MY HANDOUT ON LIIIFE!

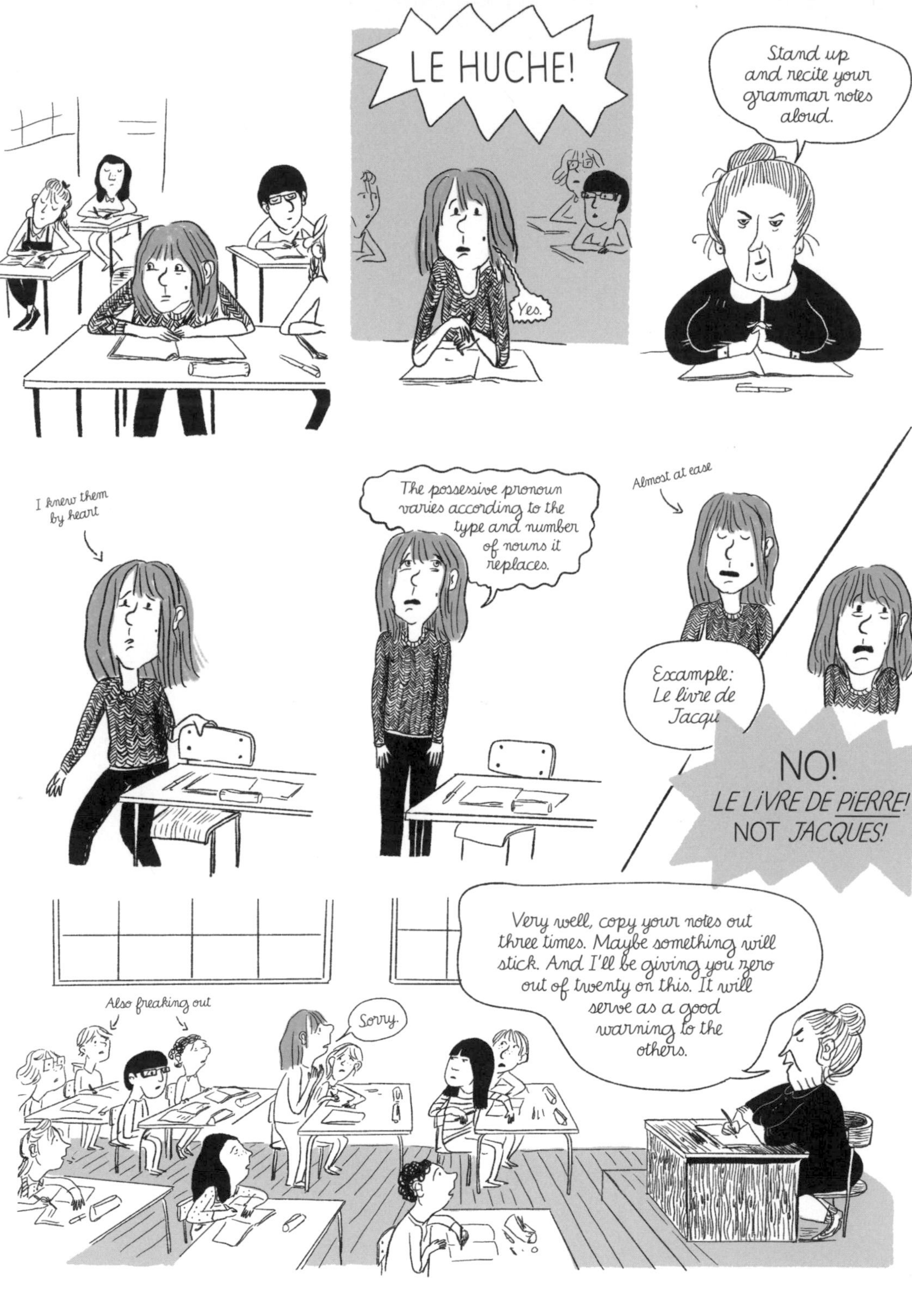

LE HUCHE!
Yes.
Stand up and recite your grammar notes aloud.
I knew them by heart
The possessive pronoun varies according to the type and number of nouns it replaces.
Almost at ease
Example: Le livre de Jacqu
NO! LE LIVRE DE PIERRE! NOT JACQUES!
Very well, copy your notes out three times. Maybe something will stick. And I'll be giving you zero out of twenty on this. It will serve as a good warning to the others.
Also freaking out
Sorry.

One Sunday afternoon, when I was trying to play to pass the time, my sister decided to listen to a new record.

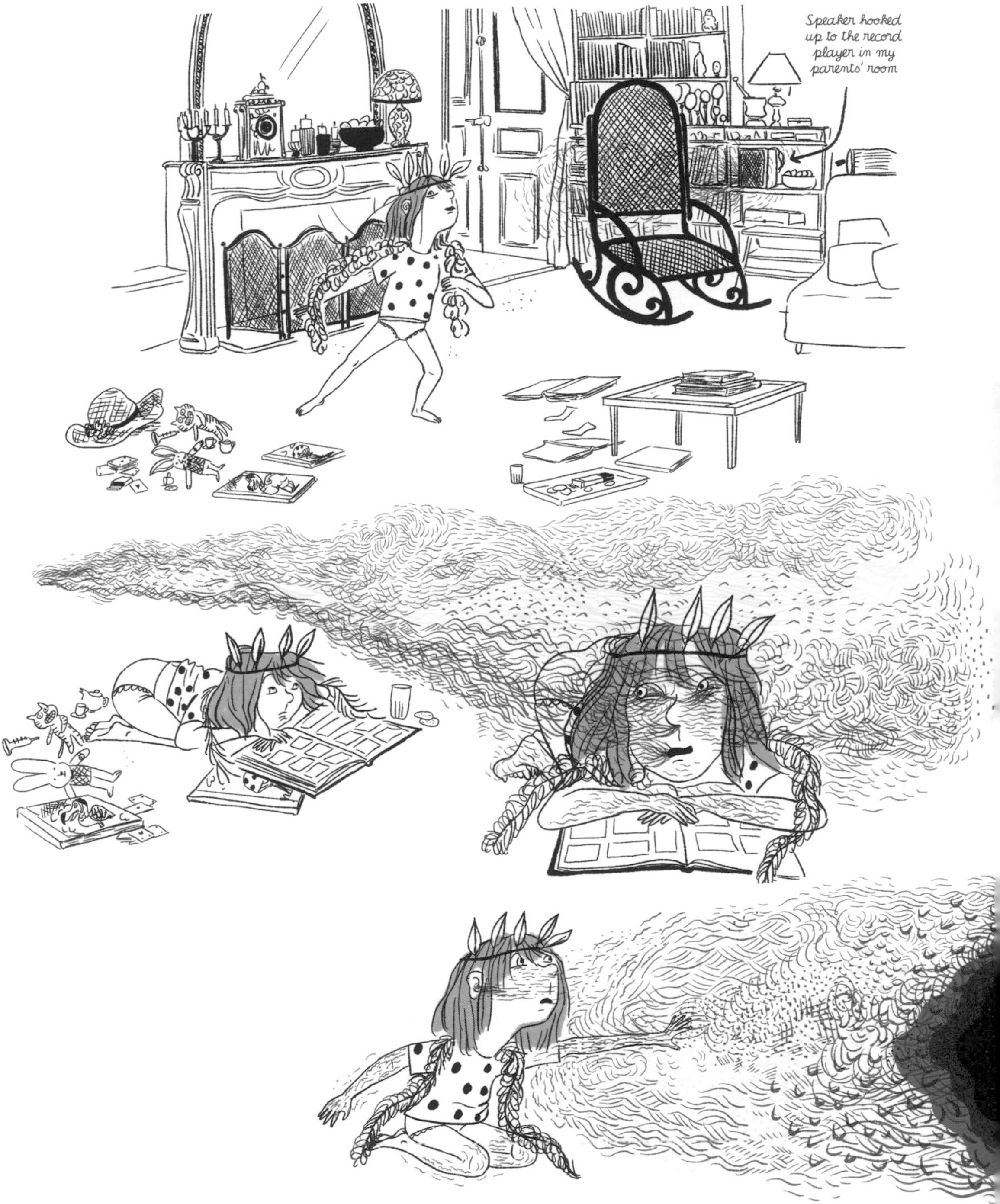
Speaker hooked up to the record player in my parents' room

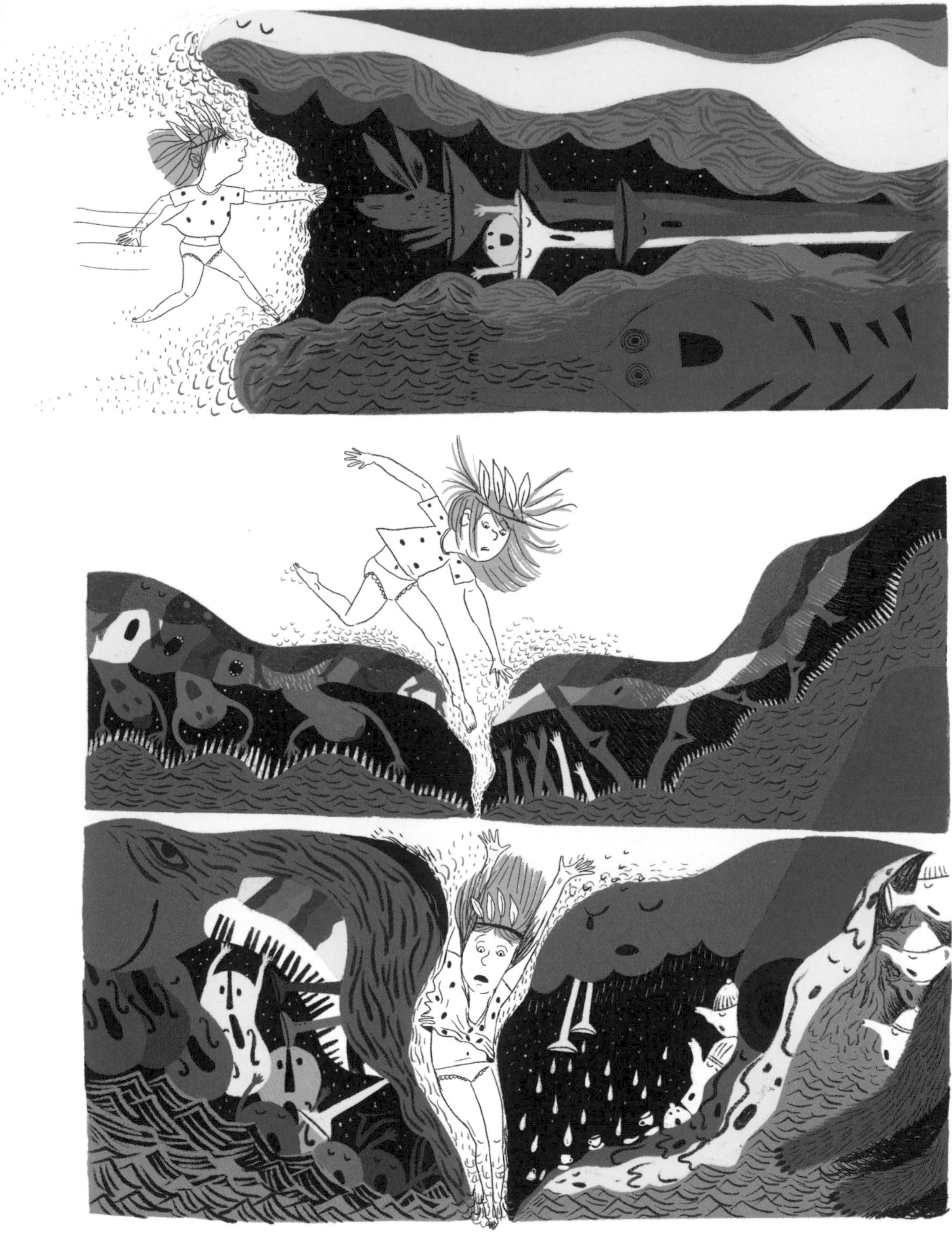

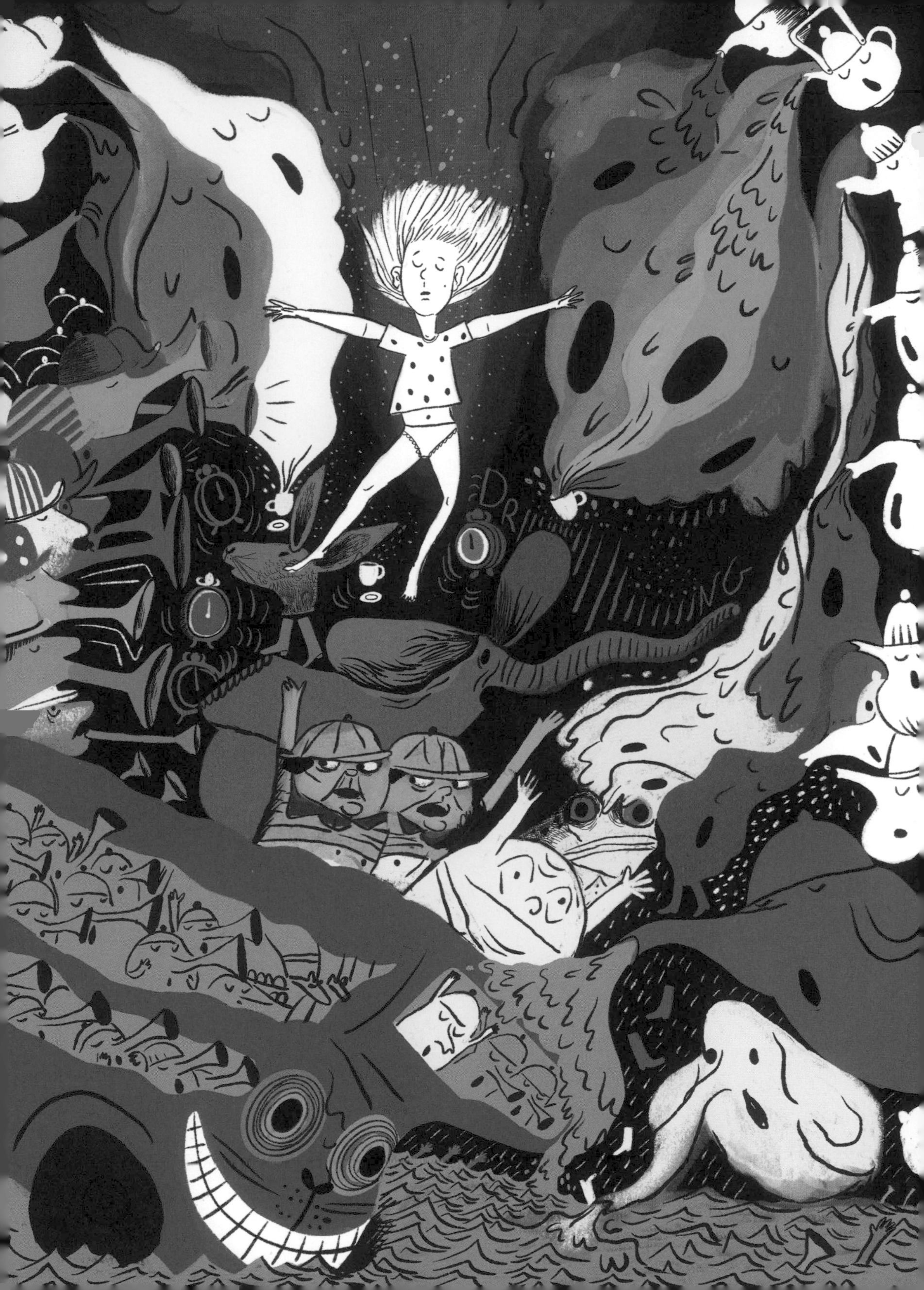

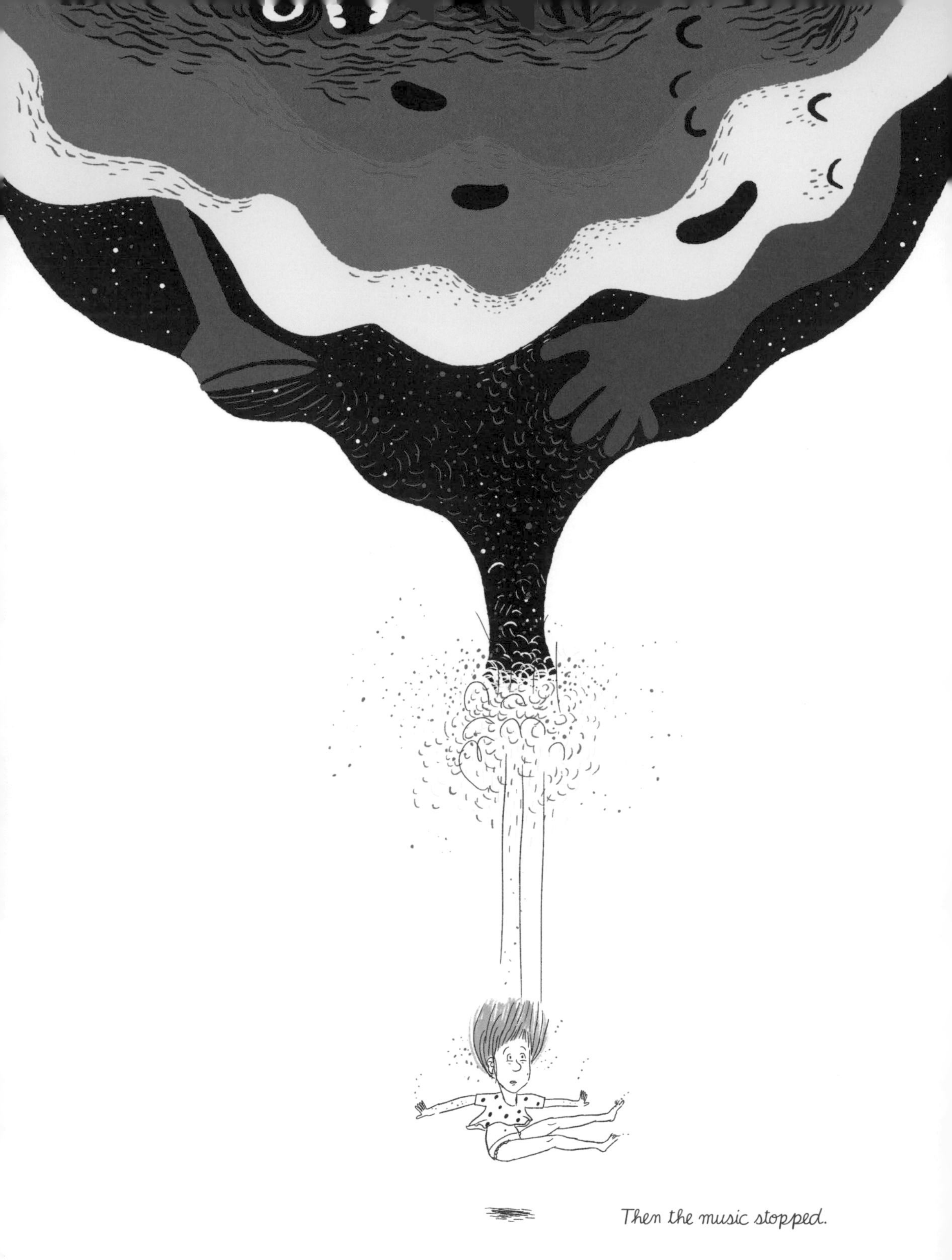

Then the music stopped.

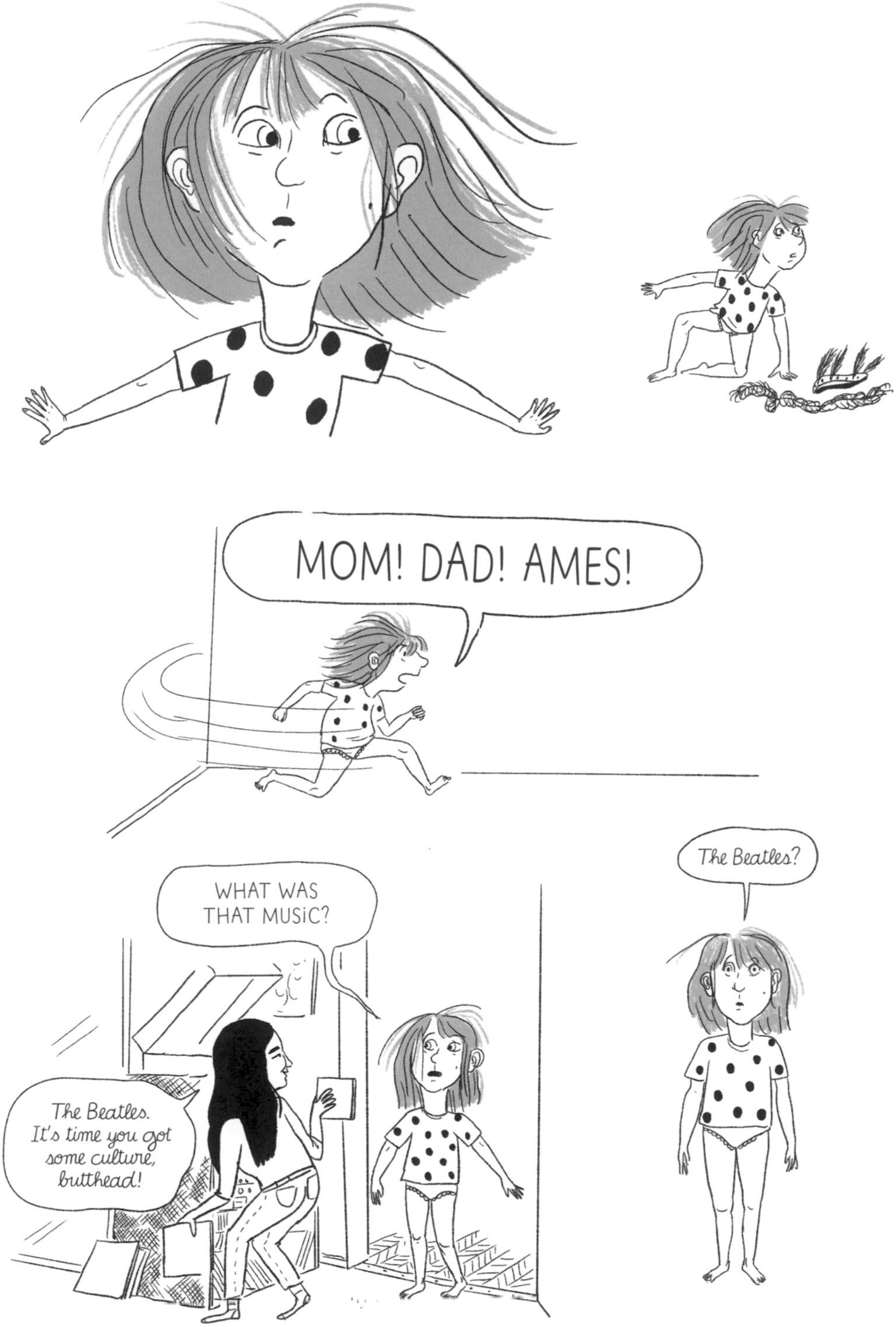
MOM! DAD! AMES!
WHAT WAS THAT MUSiC?
The Beatles. It's time you got some culture, butthead!
The Beatles?

I spent the fall break listening to With the Beatles and Sgt. Pepper's Lonely Hearts Club Band, the only two Beatles CDs my parents owned.

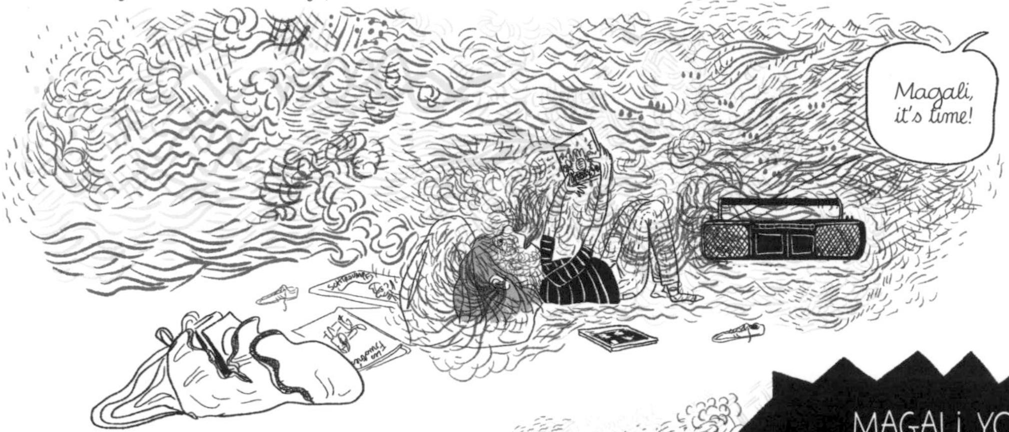
Magali, it's time!

1963 and 1967 seemed so much better than 1990...

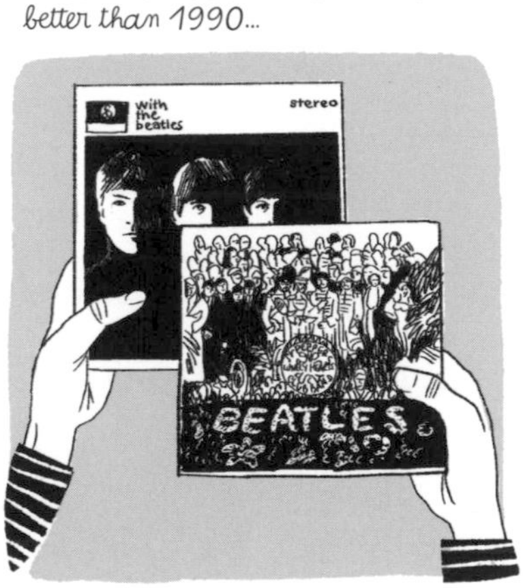
with the beatles
stereo
BEATLES

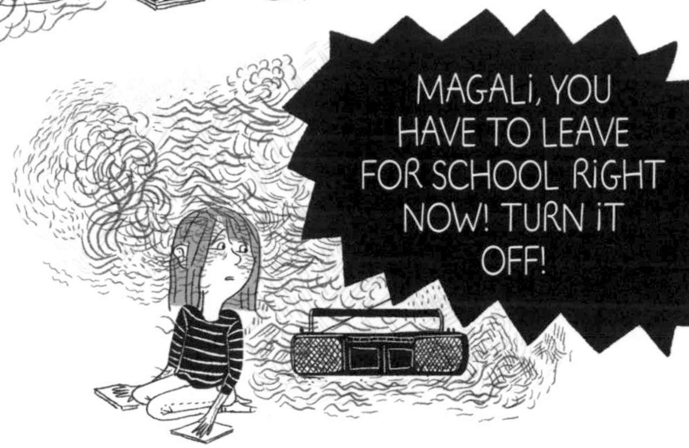
MAGALI, YOU HAVE TO LEAVE FOR SCHOOL RIGHT NOW! TURN IT OFF!

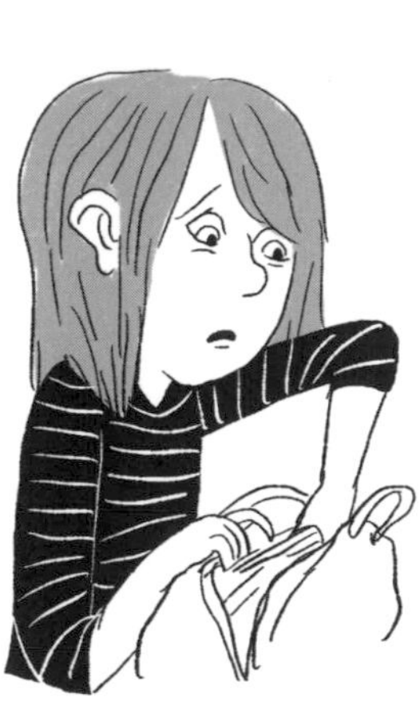

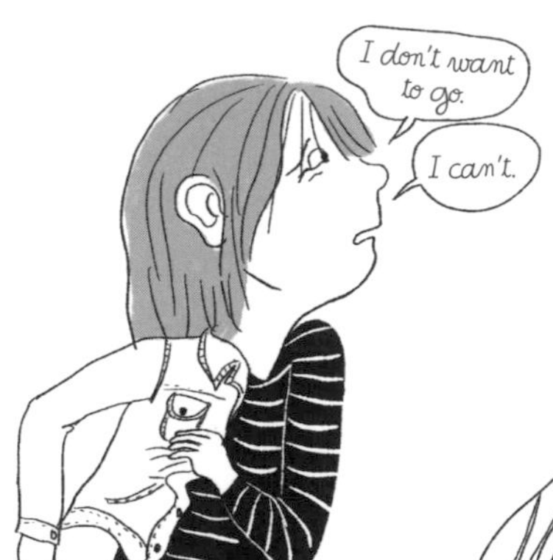
I don't want to go.
I can't.

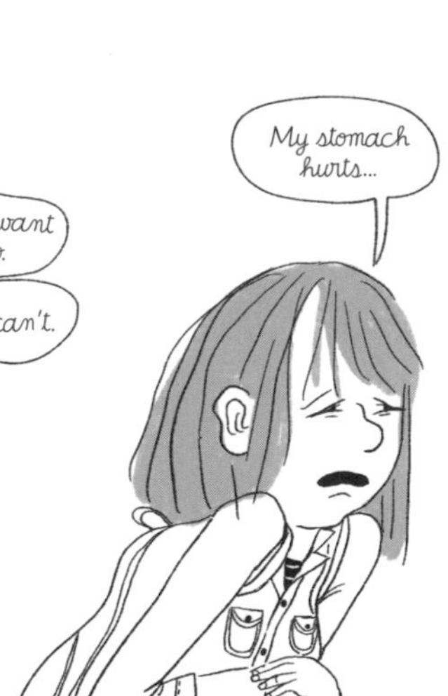
My stomach hurts...

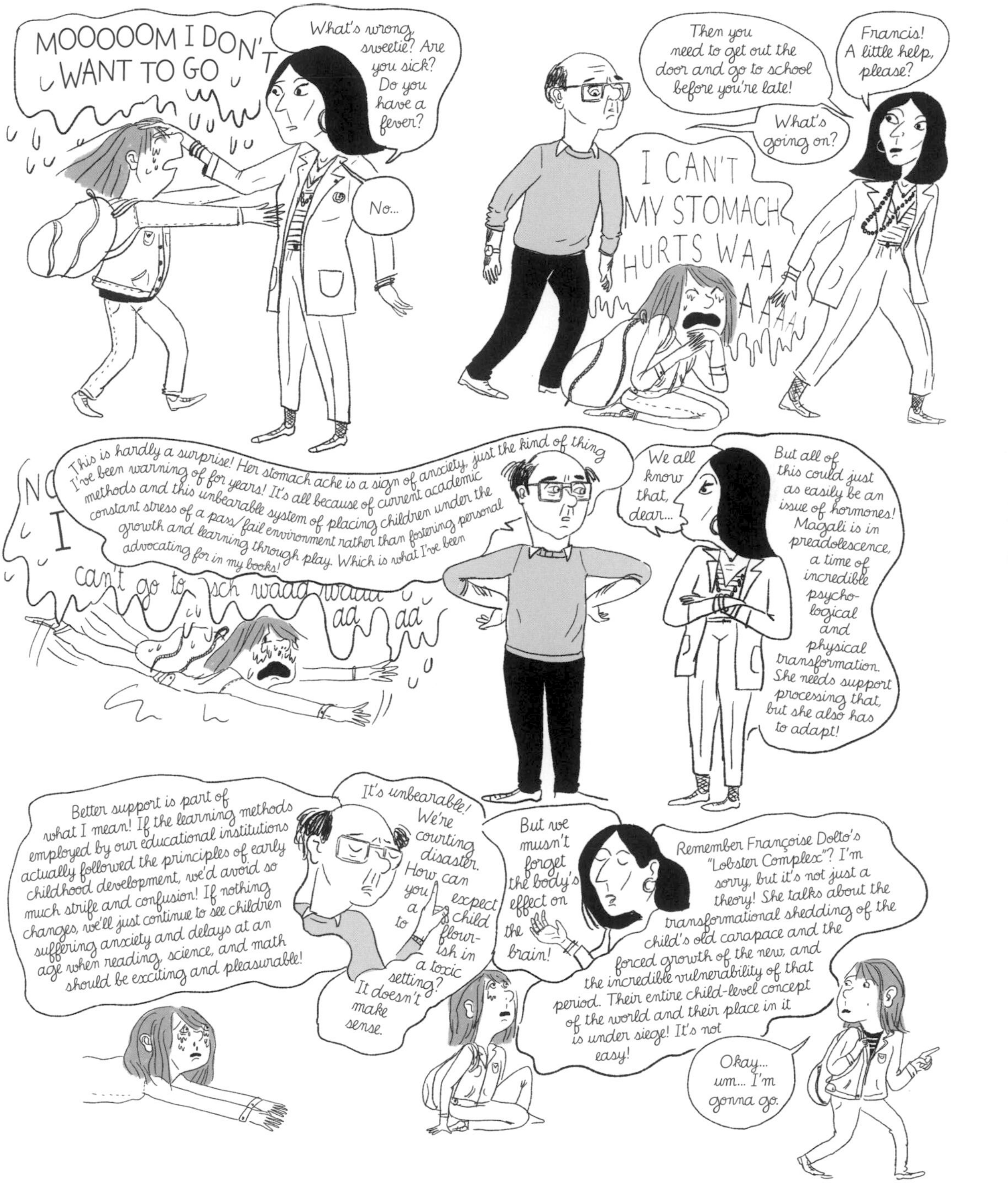
MOOOOOM I DON'T WANT TO GO
What's wrong, sweetie? Are you sick? Do you have a fever?
No...
Then you need to get out the door and go to school before you're late!
Francis! A little help, please?
What's going on?
I CAN'T MY STOMACH HURTS WAA AAAA
NO I
can't go to sch waaa waaa aa aa
This is hardly a surprise! Her stomach ache is a sign of anxiety, just the kind of thing I've been warning of for years! It's all because of current academic methods and this unbearable system of placing children under the constant stress of a pas/fail environment rather than fostering personal growth and learning through play. Which is what I've been advocating for in my books!
We all know that, dear...
But all of this could just as easily be an issue of hormones! Magali is in preadolescence, a time of incredible psychological and physical transformation. She needs support processing that, but she also has to adapt!
Better support is part of what I mean! If the learning methods employed by our educational institutions actually followed the principles of early childhood development, we'd avoid so much strife and confusion! If nothing changes, we'll just continue to see children suffering anxiety and delays at an age when reading, science, and math should be exciting and pleasurable!
It's unbearable! We're courting disaster. How can you expect a child to flourish in a toxic setting? It doesn't make sense.
But we mustn't forget the body's effect on the brain!
Remember Françoise Dolto's "Lobster Complex"? I'm sorry, but it's not just a theory! She talks about the transformational shedding of the child's old carapace and the forced growth of the new, and the incredible vulnerability of that period. Their entire child-level concept of the world and their place in it is under siege! It's not easy!
Okay... um... I'm gonna go.

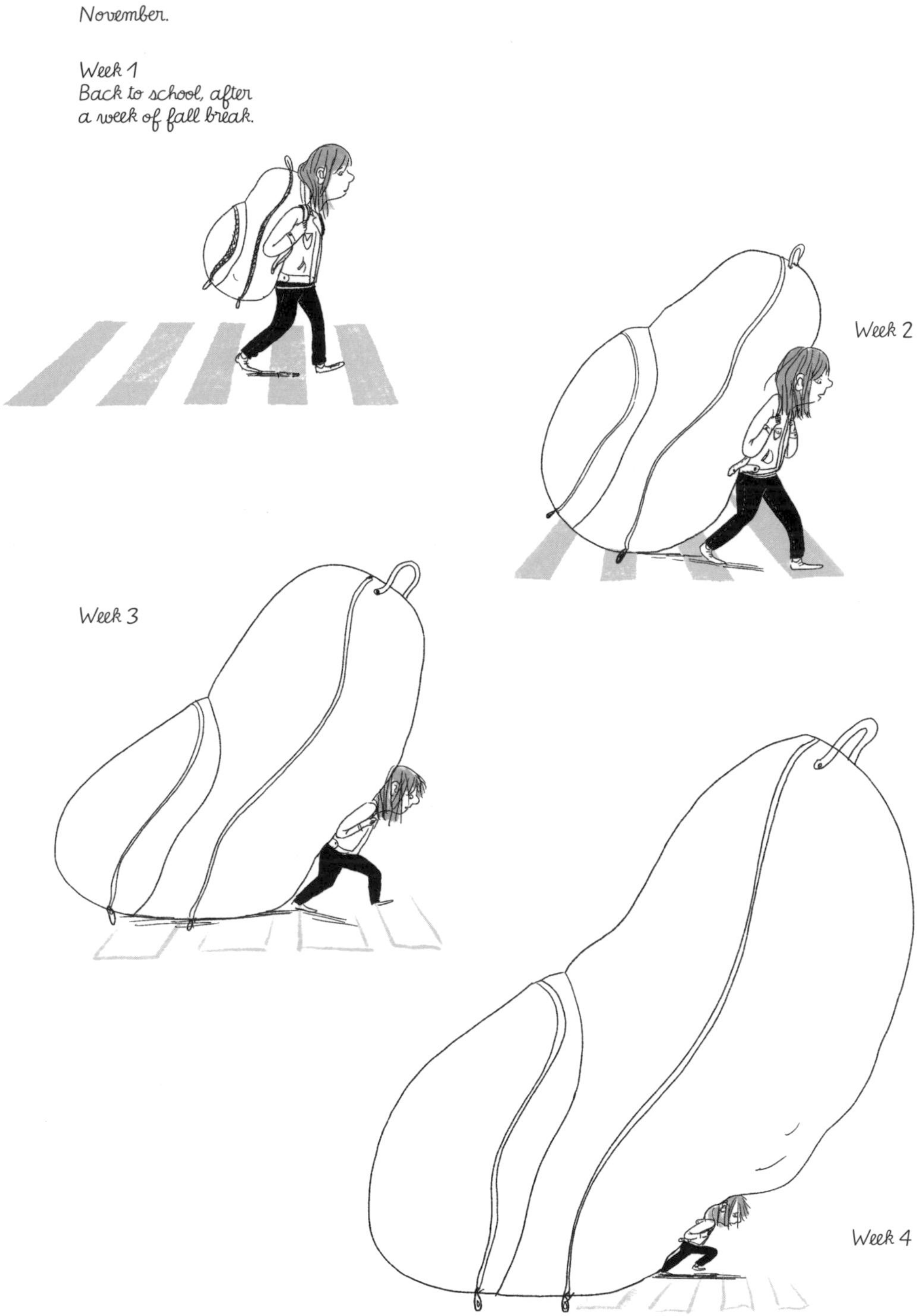
November.
Week 1
Back to school, after
a week of fall break.
Week 2
Week 3
Week 4

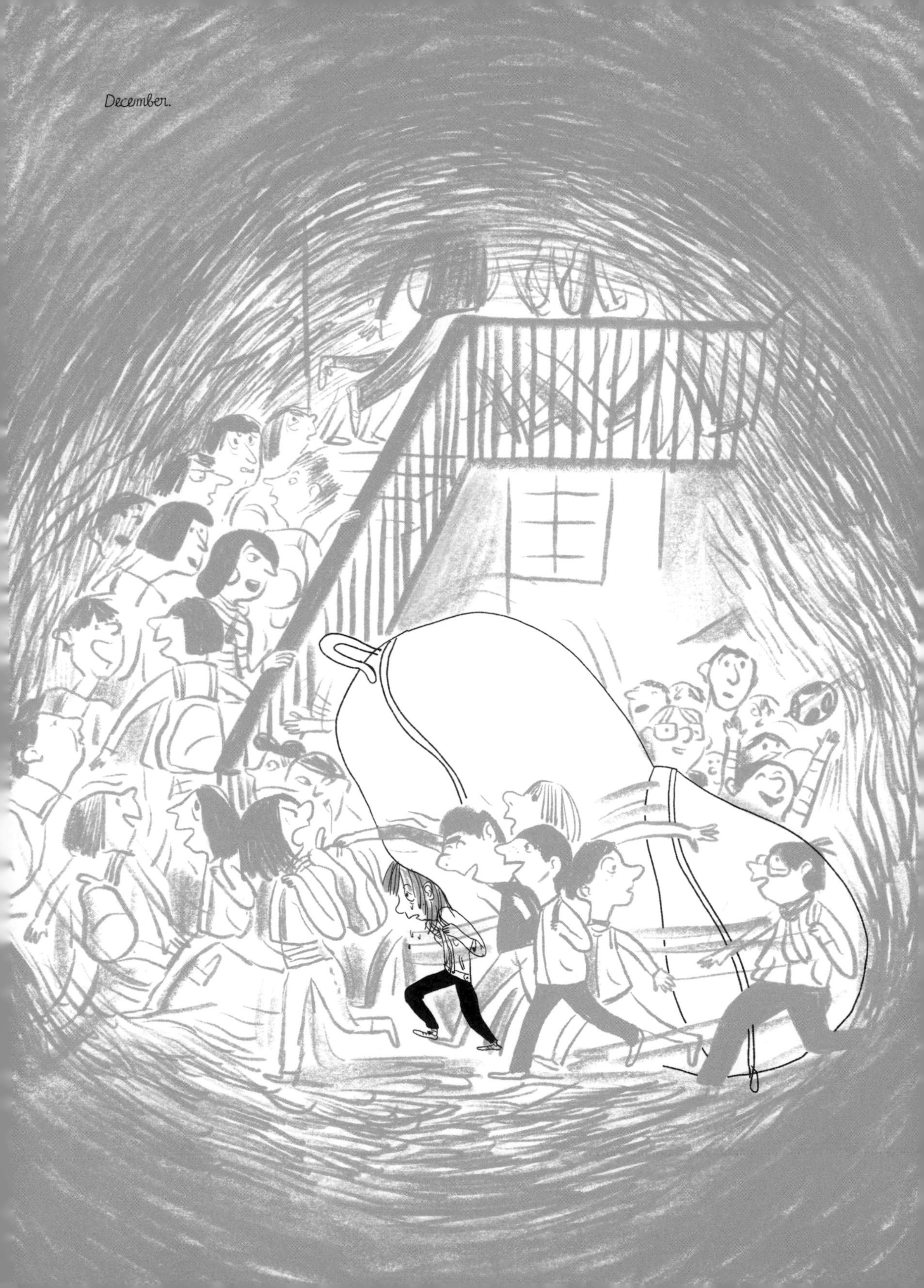
December.

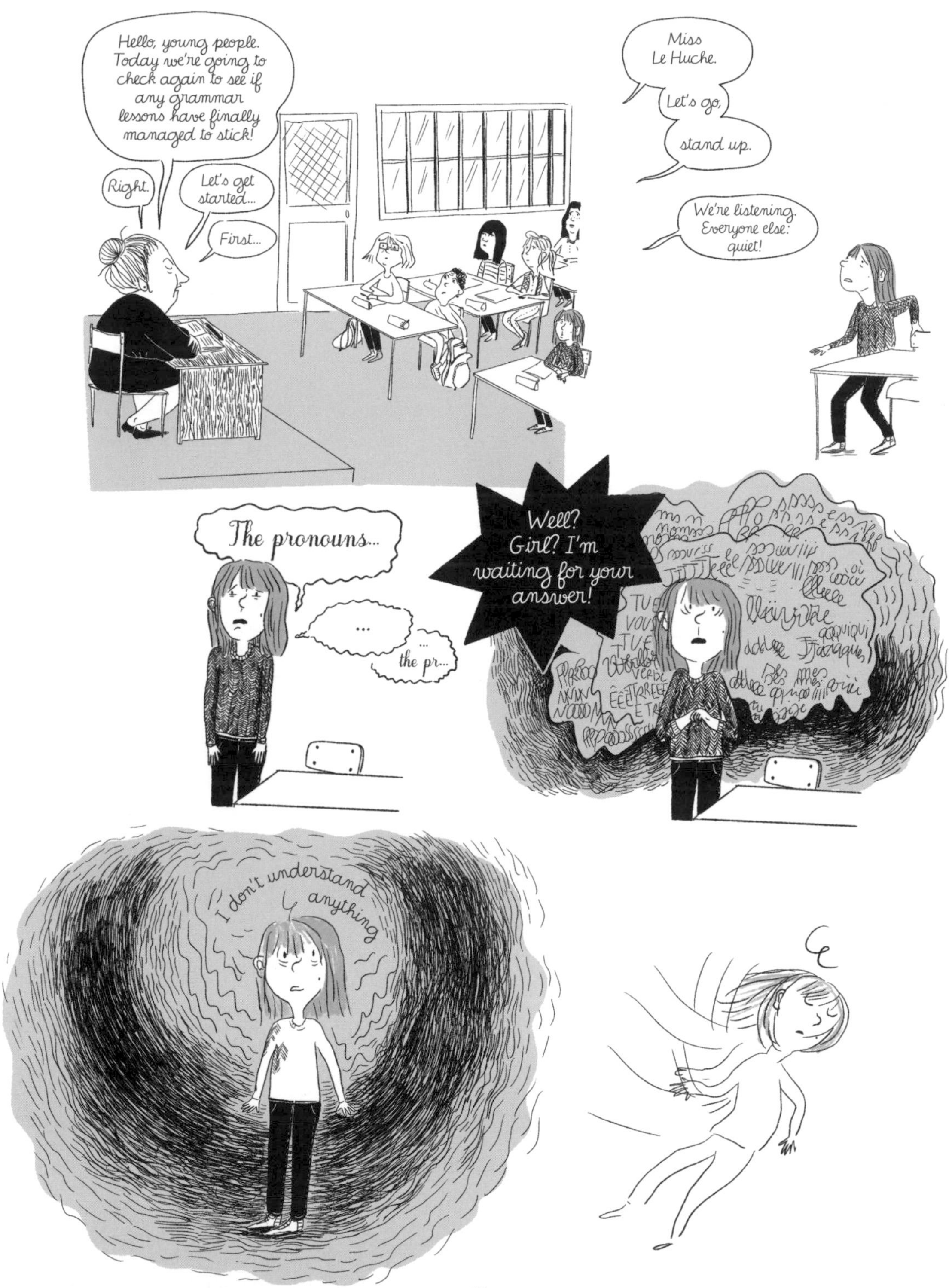

Hello, young people. Today we're going to check again to see if any grammar lessons have finally managed to stick!
Right.
Let's get started...
First...
Miss Le Huche.
Let's go,
stand up.
We're listening. Everyone else: quiet!
The pronouns...
...
... the pr...
Well? Girl? I'm waiting for your answer!
I don't understand anything

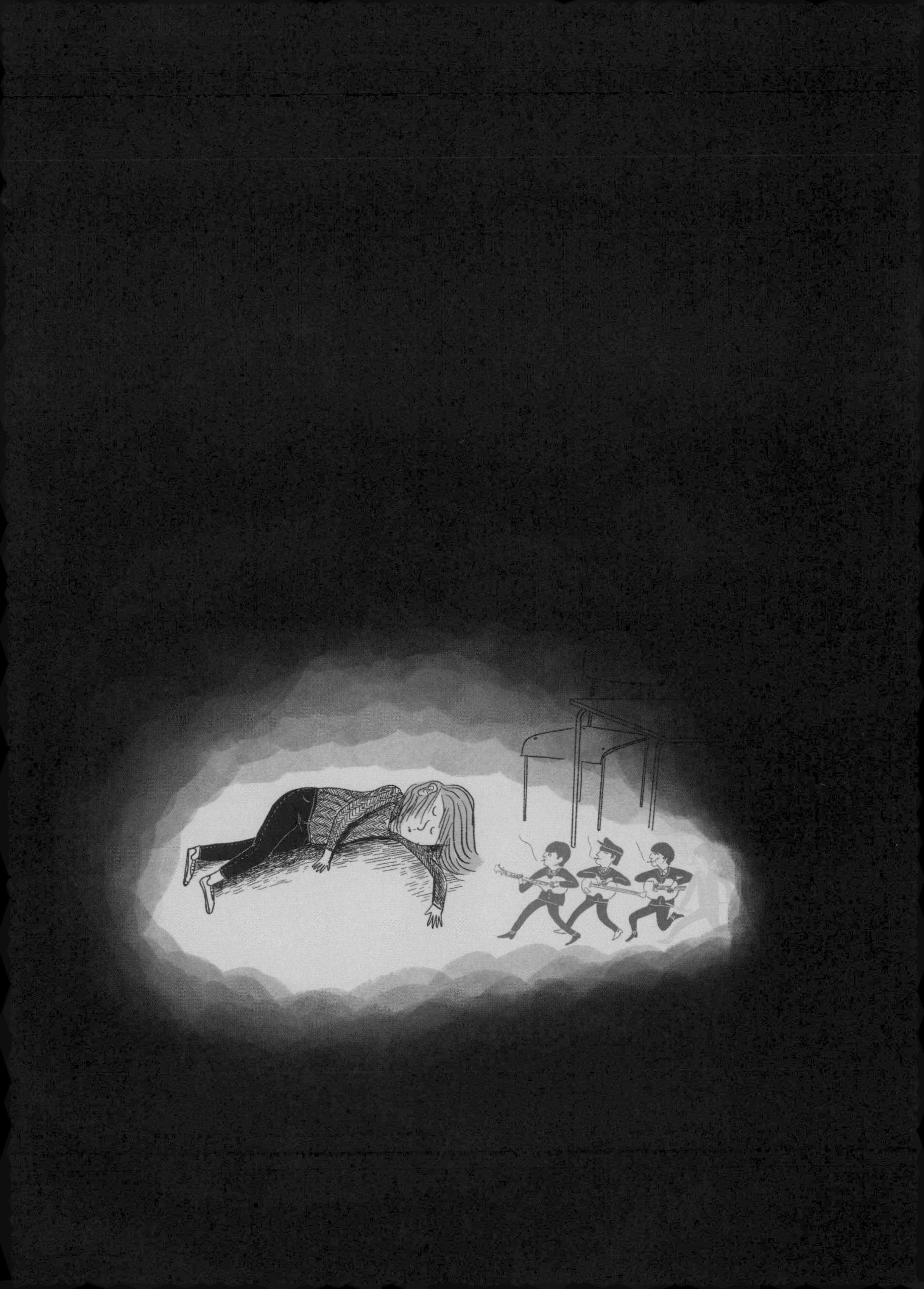

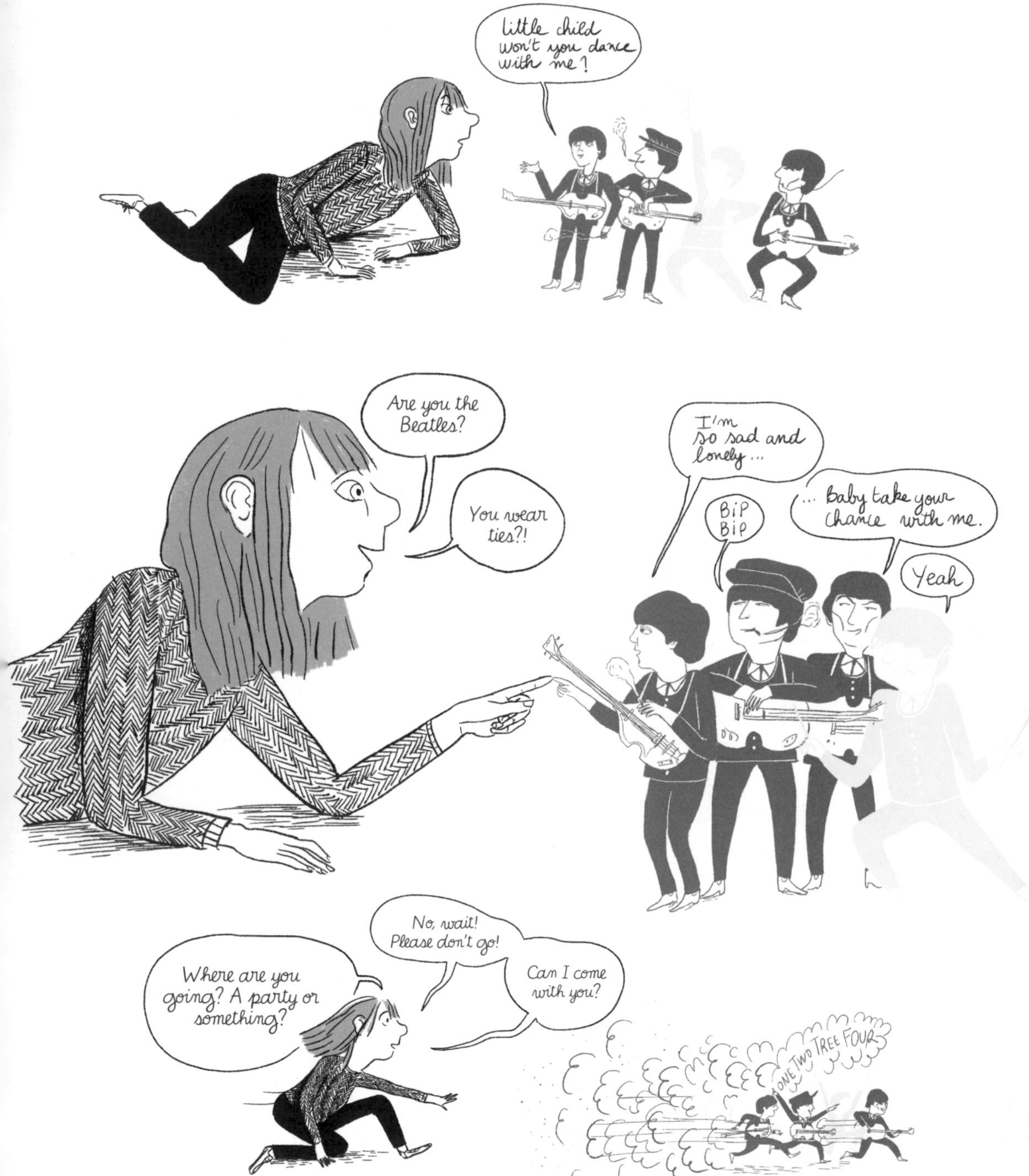
little child won't you dance with me?
Are you the Beatles?
You wear ties?!
I'm so sad and lonely...
BiP BiP
... Baby take your chance with me.
Yeah
Where are you going? A party or something?
No, wait! Please don't go!
Can I come with you?
ONE TWO TREE FOUR

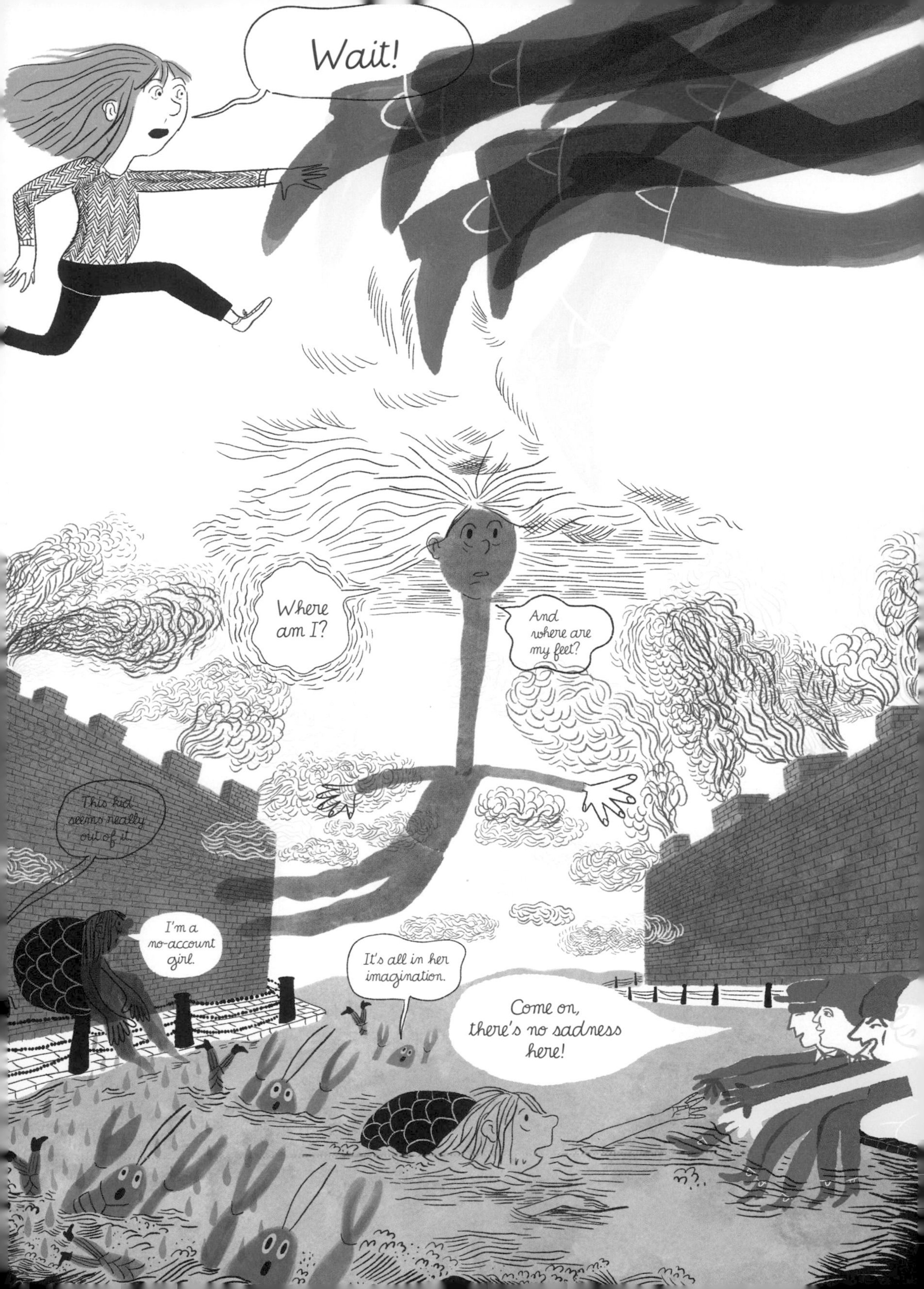
Wait!
Where am I?
And where are my feet?
This kid seems really out of it.
I'm a no-account girl.
It's all in her imagination.
Come on, there's no sadness here!

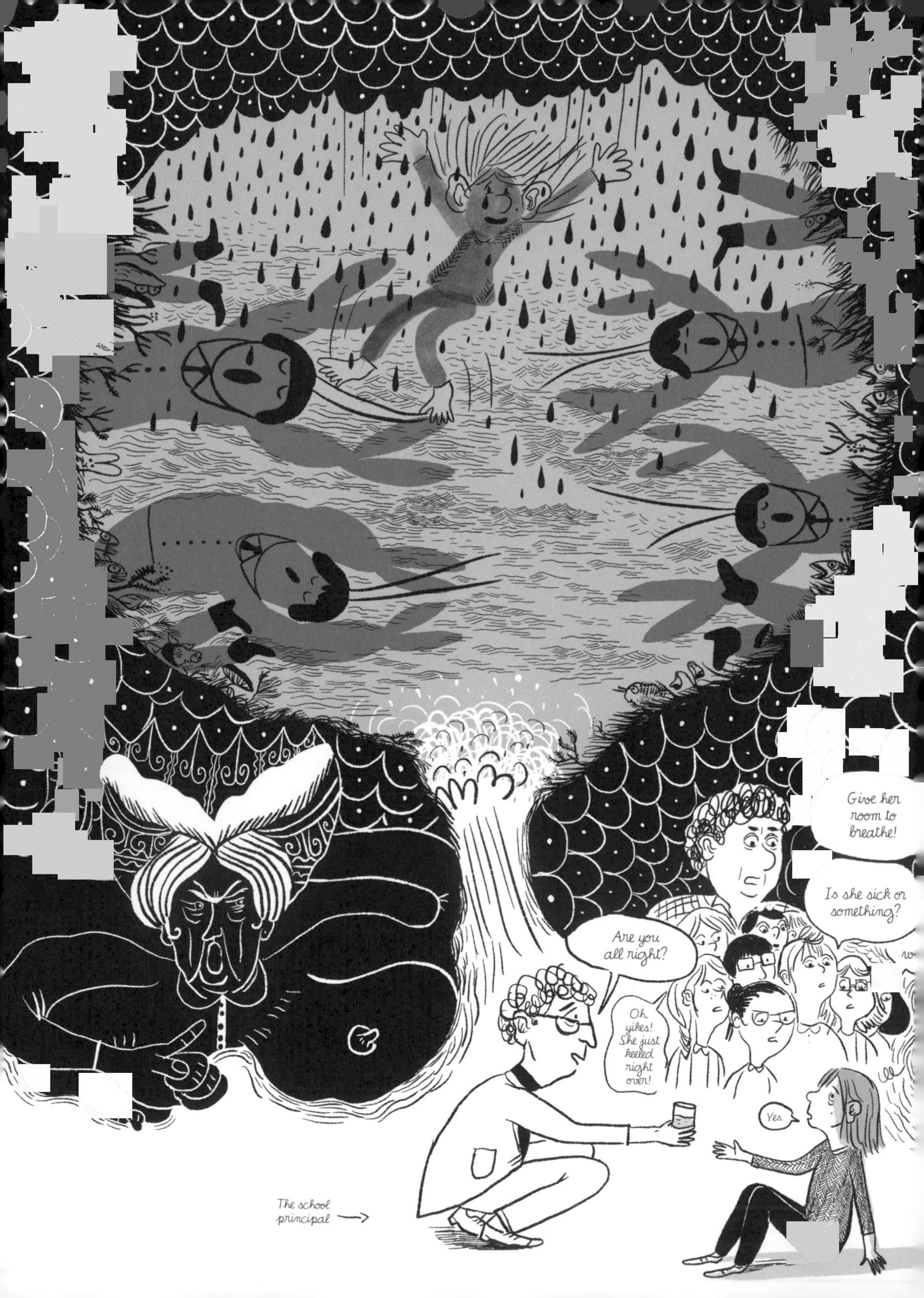
Give her room to breathe!
Is she sick or something?
Are you all right?
Oh, yikes! She just keeled right over!
Yes.
The school principal

This time I had proof that I wasn't okay.

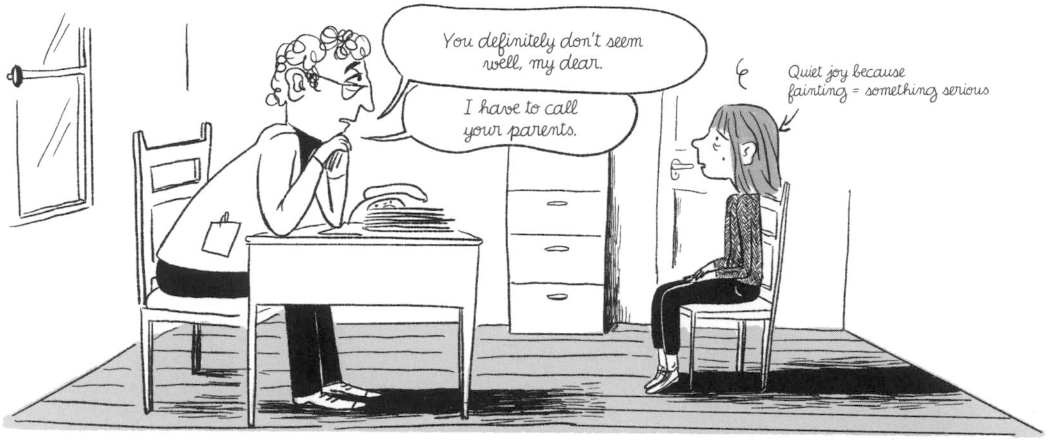
You definitely don't seem well, my dear.
I have to call your parents.
Quiet joy because fainting = something serious

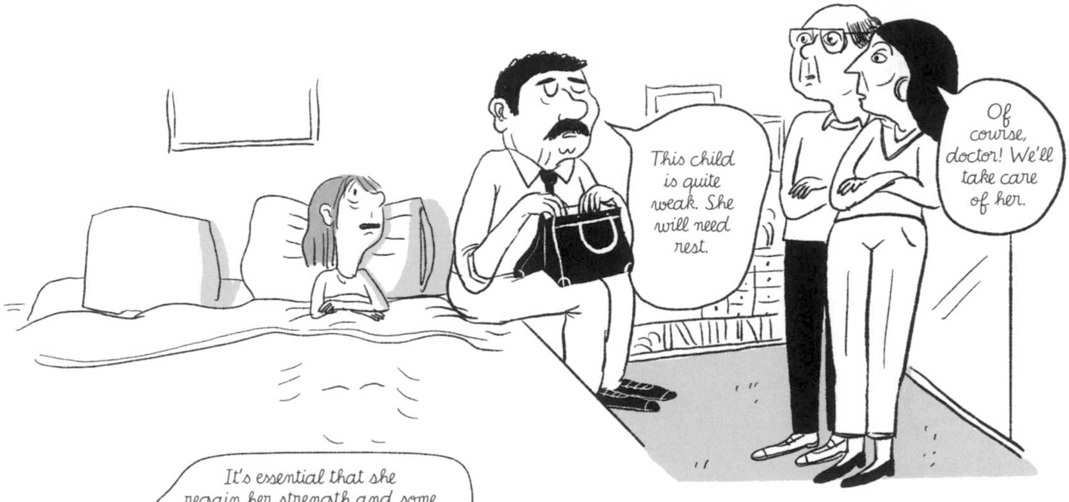
This child is quite weak. She will need rest.
Of course, doctor! We'll take care of her.

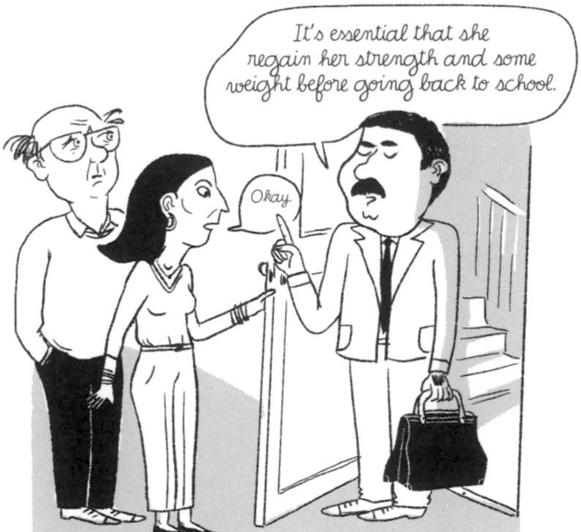
It's essential that she regain her strength and some weight before going back to school.
Okay.

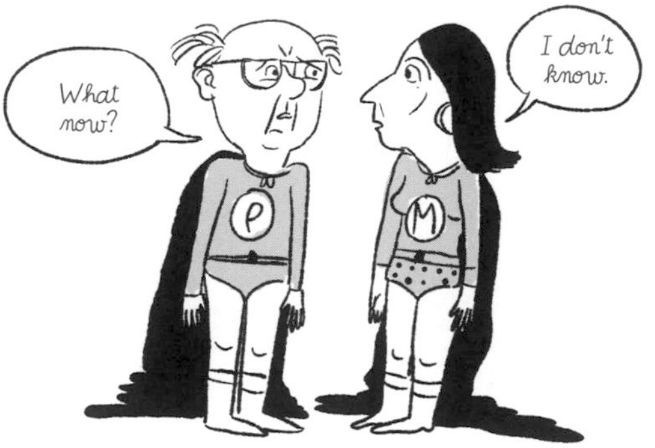
What now?
I don't know.

Phase 1 accomplished: worry my parents.

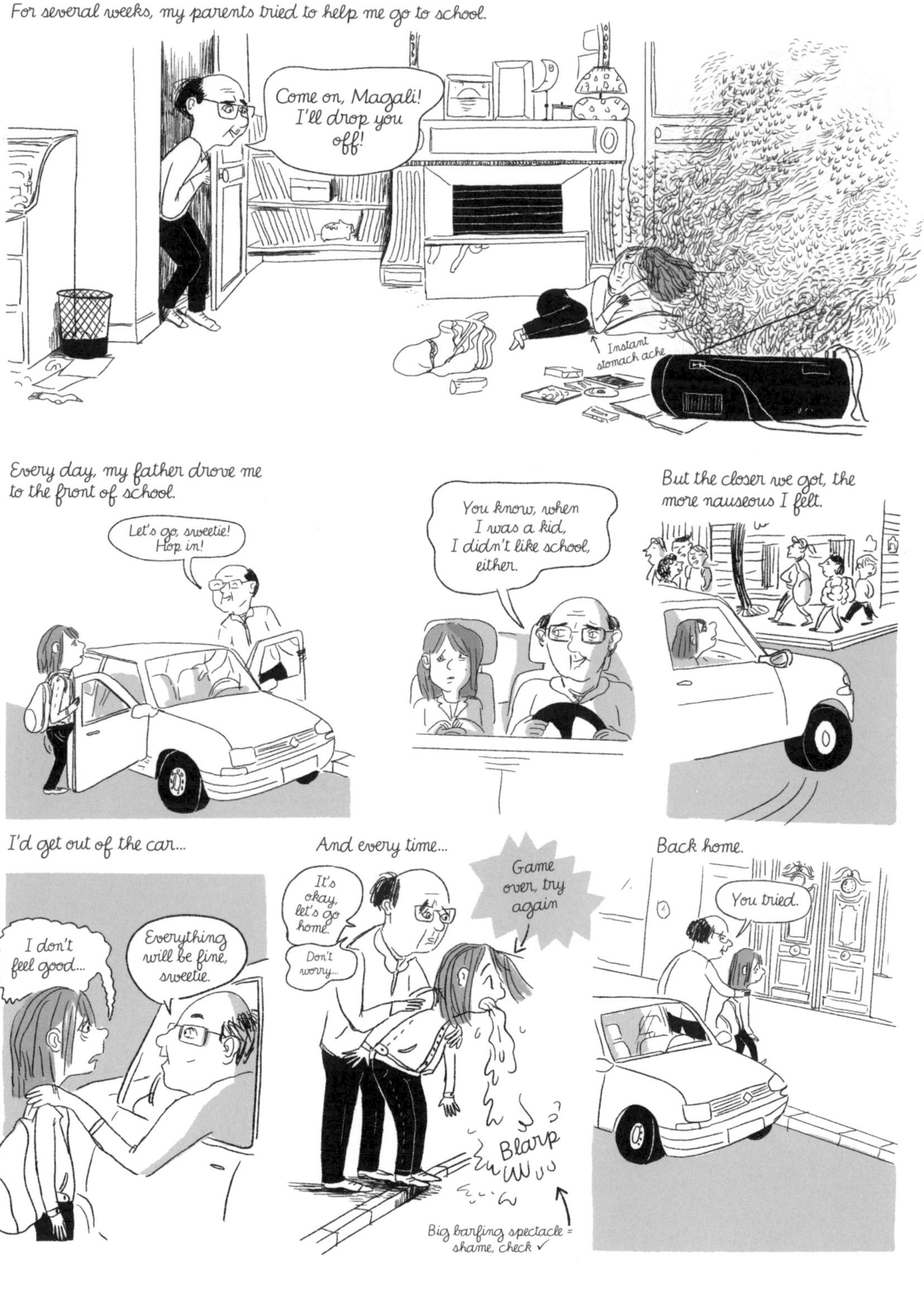
For several weeks, my parents tried to help me go to school.
Come on, Magali! I'll drop you off!
Instant stomach ache
Every day, my father drove me to the front of school.
Let's go, sweetie! Hop in!
You know, when I was a kid, I didn't like school, either.
But the closer we got, the more nauseous I felt.
I'd get out of the car...
I don't feel good...
Everything will be fine, sweetie.
And every time...
It's okay, let's go home.
Don't worry...
Game over, try again
Blarp
Big barfing spectacle = shame, check ✓
Back home.
You tried.

We kept trying up to Christmas vacation.

Okay, let's go!

Game over, try again

It's time!

But once we got to school, it was always the same thing.

Okay, let's go...

Game over

It's okay! Don't stress! We'll figure this out!

My dad, always an optimist

One day, right before vacation, I made it inside.

I'm so happy you're here today, Mags!

I miss you when you're not here!

Agatha, #1 comforter

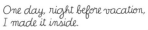

Leave her alone!

HA HA HA HA

Oh look, it's the big baby who can't go to school because she's too scaaaared!

HAHA

Are you going to pass out today?

Do I smell vomit?!

Freaking out

HA HA HA HA HA

You gonna throw up at lunch?

HA HA gross !!!!

HA HA HA HA HAHA HAHAHA

During Christmas vacation, I'd have done anything not to have to go back to school.

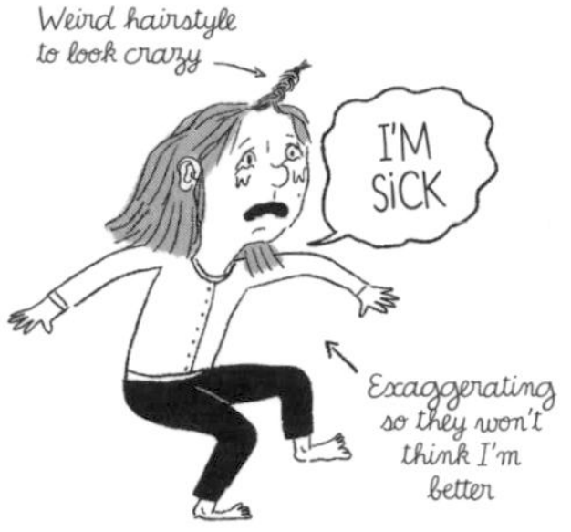
Weird hairstyle to look crazy
I'M SiCK
Exaggerating so they won't think I'm better

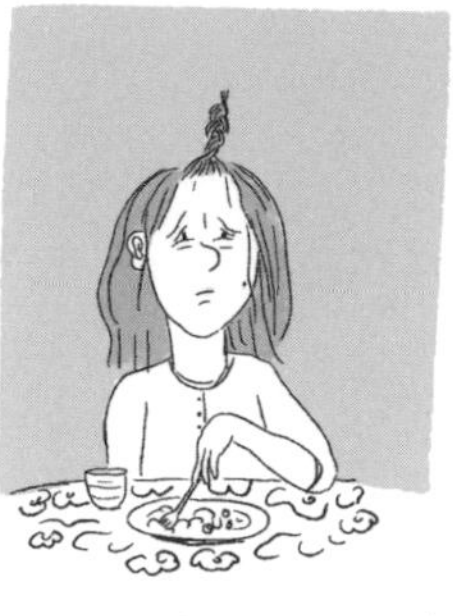

But mostly I really wasn't hungry, for real.

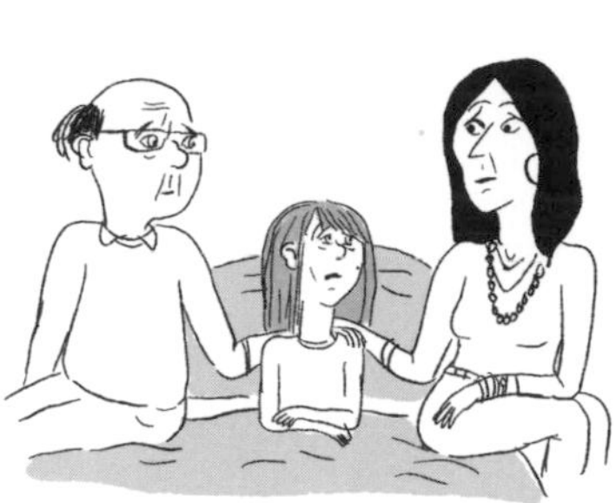

And for real, I wasn't doing well, and because of that, neither were my parents...

When school started again in January, it was official: I wasn't getting better. My parents leapt into action to save me.

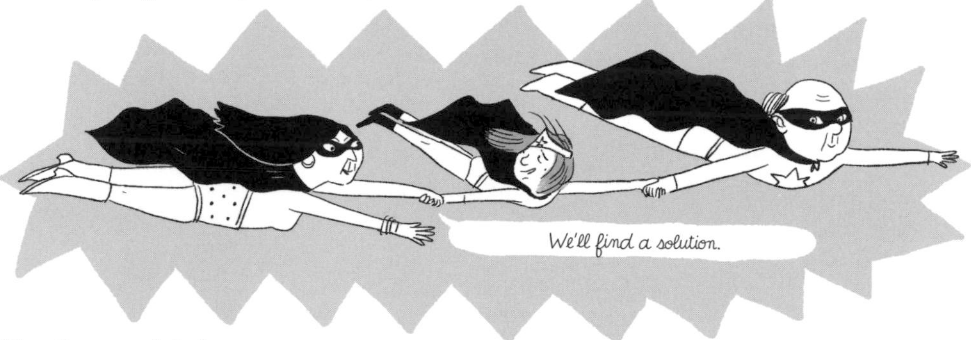
We'll find a solution.

Phase 2 accomplished: they took me to talk to a lady who could identify the problem at last.

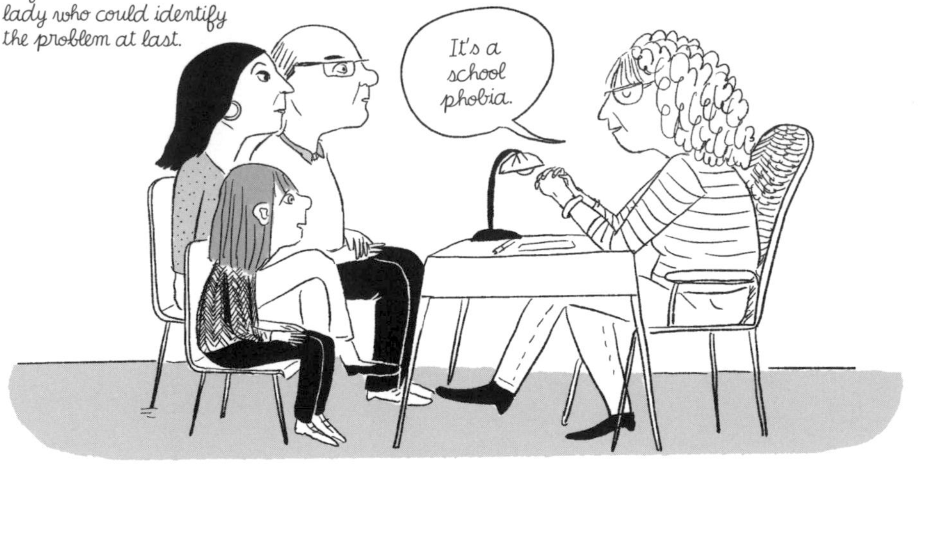
It's a school phobia.

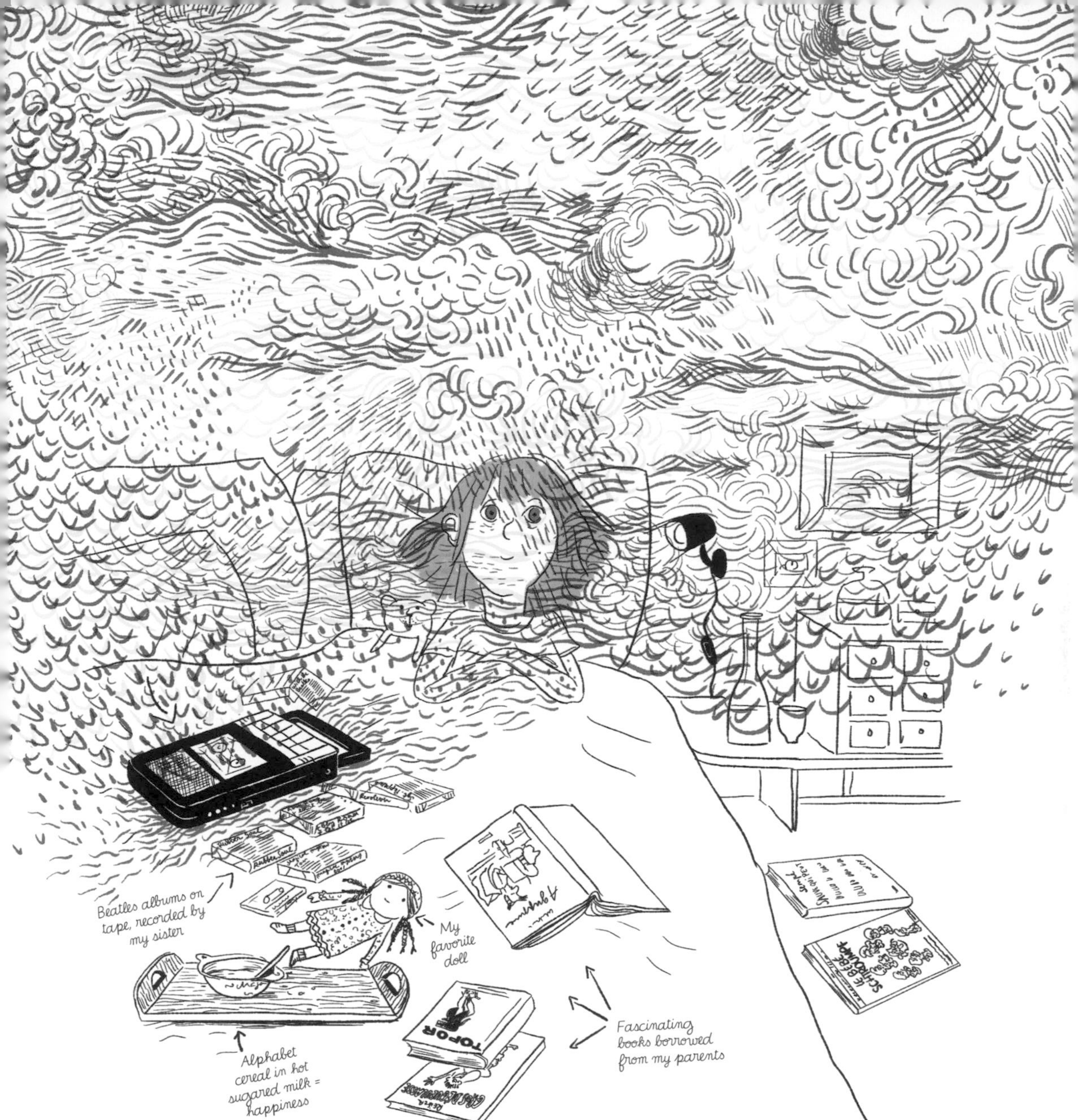
Beatles albums on tape, recorded by my sister
My favorite doll
Alphabet cereal in hot sugared milk = happiness
Fascinating books borrowed from my parents
TOPOR

So the thing I had was really real and had a name: a school phobia.
It sounded serious and a little scary.

Phase 3 accomplished:
I could finally stay home.

At first, Agatha continued bringing my schoolwork to the house.

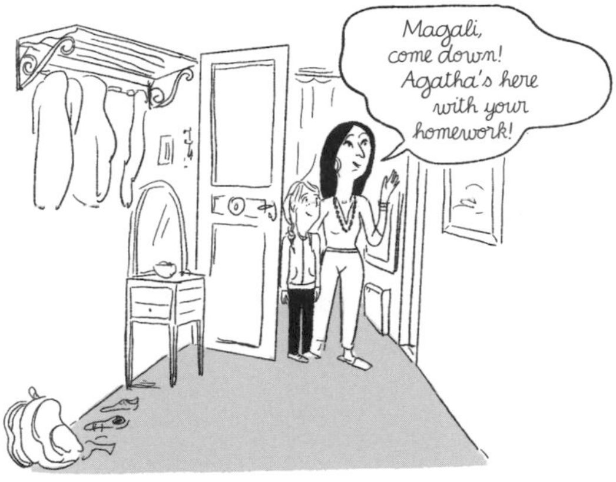
Magali, come down! Agatha's here with your homework!

Sometimes I was too ashamed to come out and say hello. I felt like I'd abandoned her. I thought she must be mad at me.

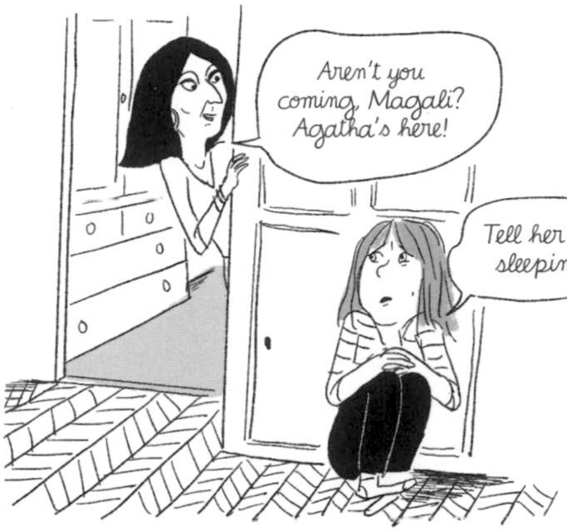
Aren't you coming, Magali? Agatha's here!
Tell her I'm sleeping.

Soon, I started going to a new school.

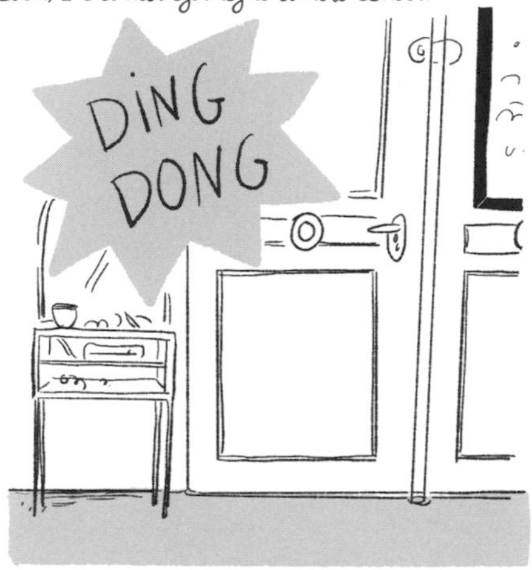
DING DONG

My schoolwork came in the mail.

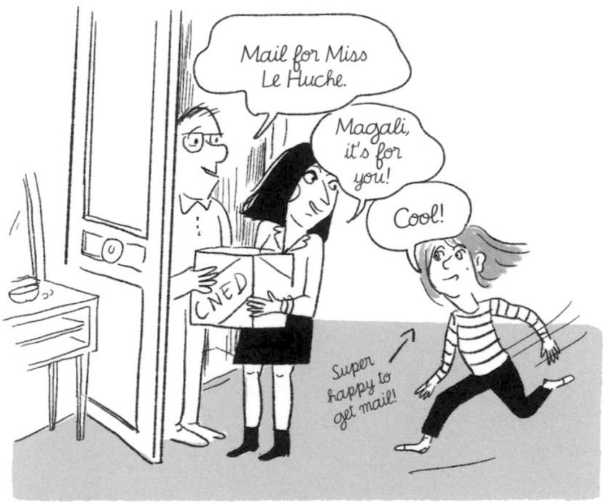
Mail for Miss Le Huche.
Magali, it's for you!
Cool!
CNED
Super happy to get mail!

And I did everything from home.

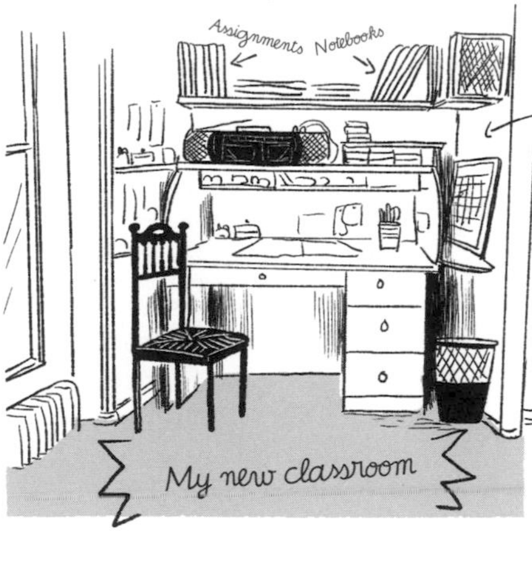
Assignments
Notebooks
Super full planner
My new classroom

But I didn't want to jump ship without giving my friends an explanation.

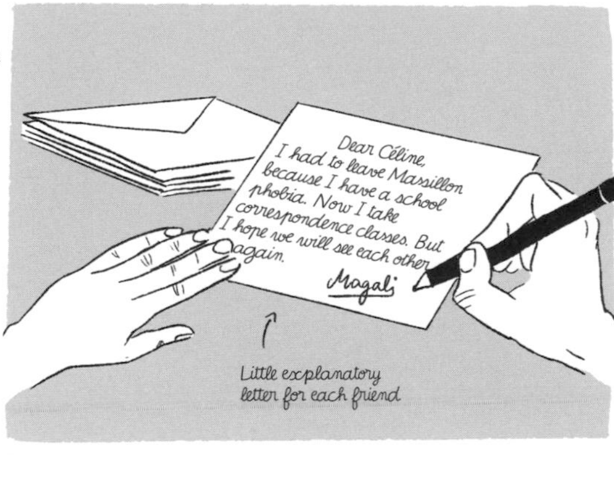
Dear Céline,
I had to leave Massillon because I have a school phobia. Now I take correspondence classes. But I hope we will see each other again.
Magali
Little explanatory letter for each friend

Monday mornings, Sandra
would come and help me study.

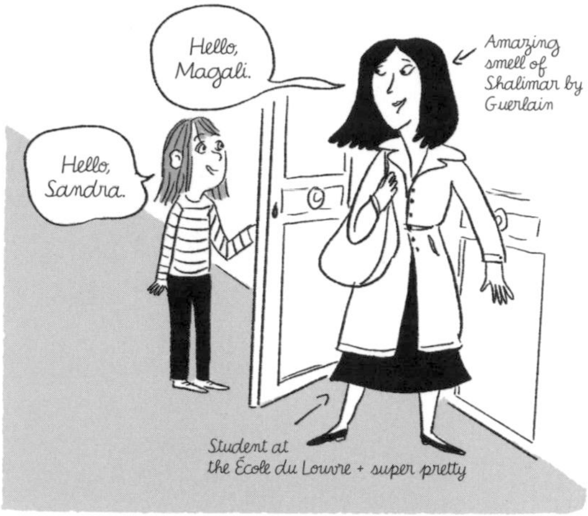
Hello, Magali.
Hello, Sandra.
Amazing smell of Shalimar by Guerlain
Student at the École du Louvre + super pretty

We worked and also had a lot of fun.

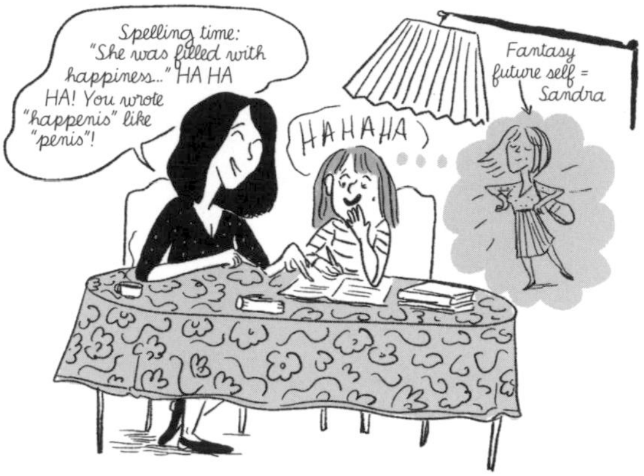
Spelling time: "She was filled with happiness..." HA HA HA! You wrote "happenis" like "penis"!
HAHAHA
Fantasy future self = Sandra

The other days, I worked alone.
I was very organized.

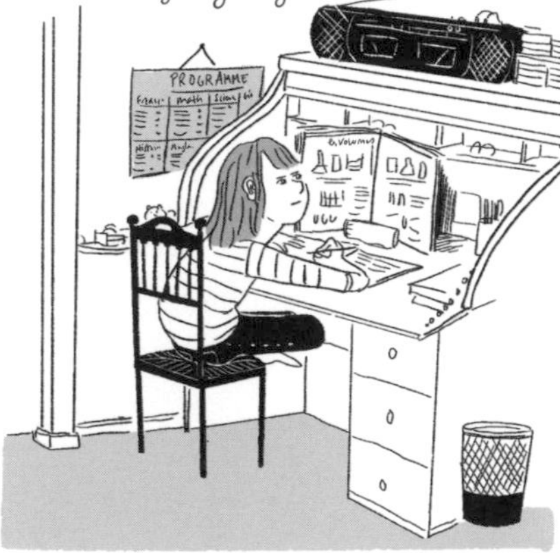
PROGRAMME

On Tuesdays, I went to see the same
lady who diagnosed my phobia.

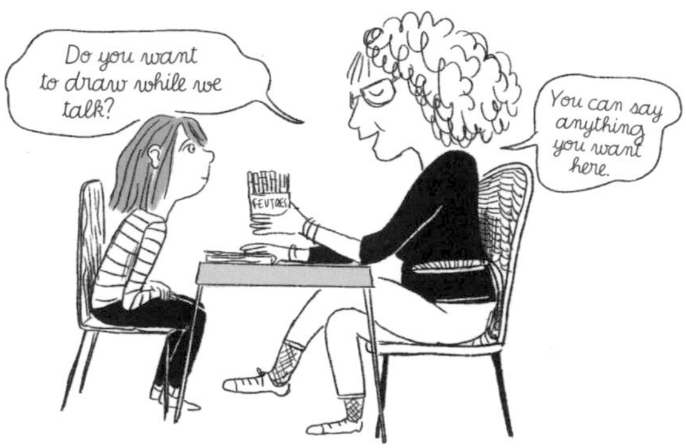
Do you want to draw while we talk?
You can say anything you want here.
FEUTRES

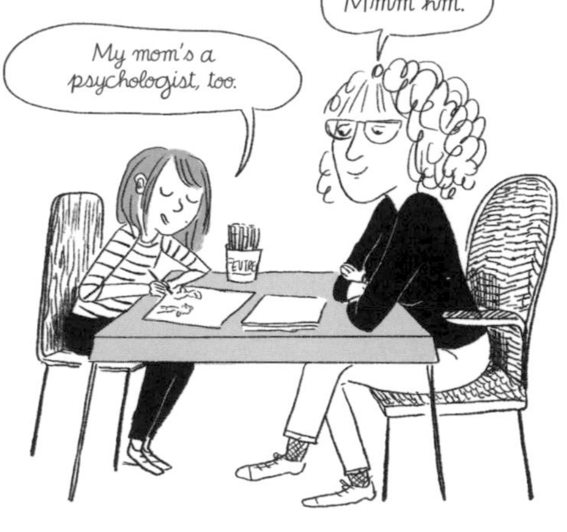
My mom's a psychologist, too.
Mmm hm.
FEUTRES

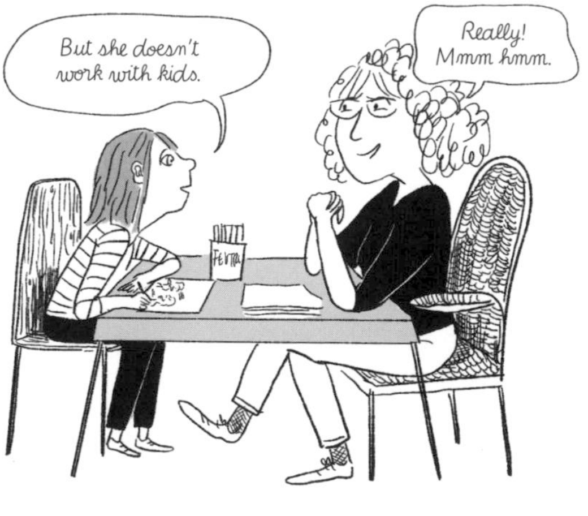
But she doesn't work with kids.
Really! Mmm hmm.
FEUTRES

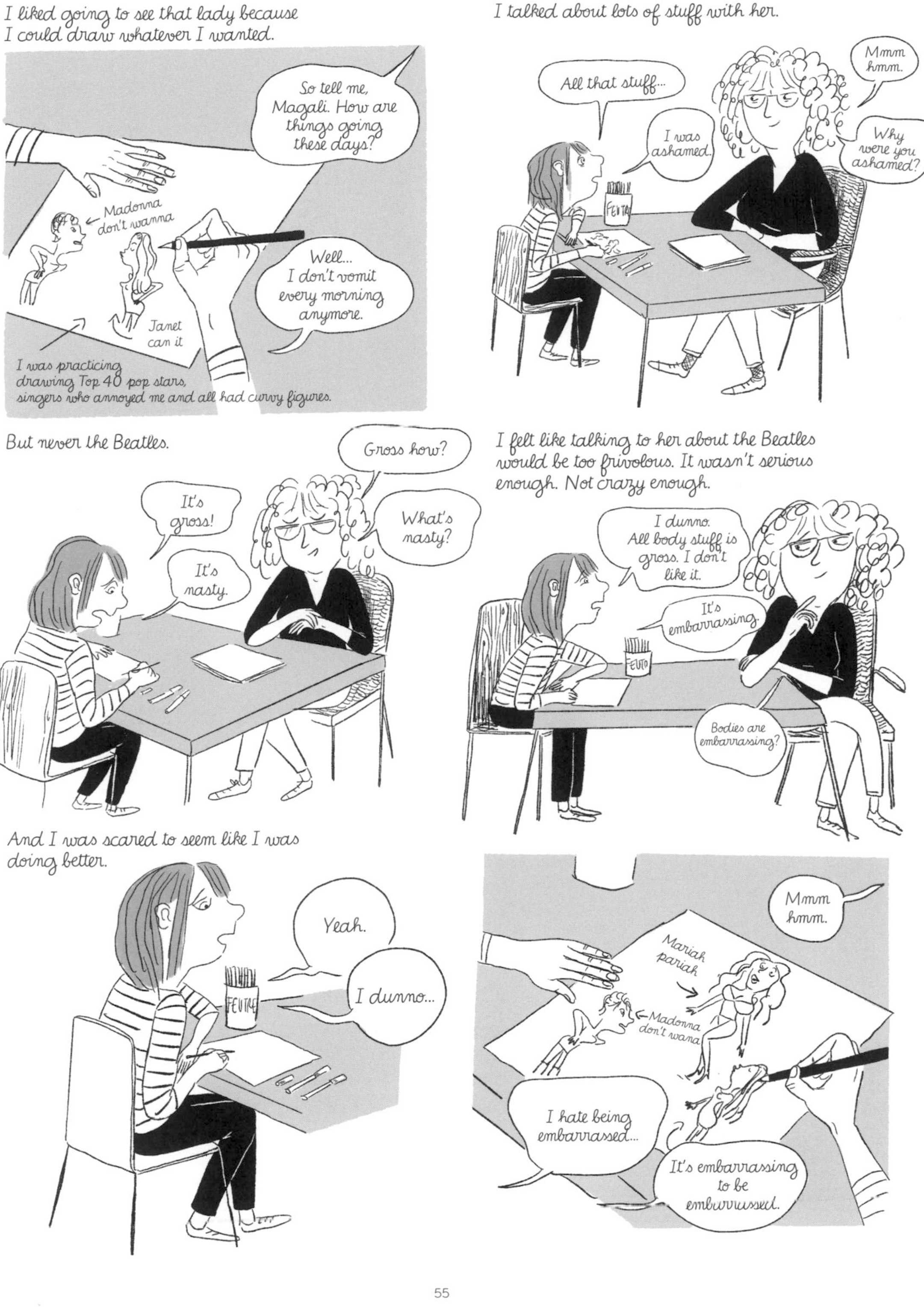
I liked going to see that lady because I could draw whatever I wanted.
So tell me, Magali. How are things going these days?
Madonna don't wanna
Well... I don't vomit every morning anymore.
Janet can it
I was practicing drawing Top 40 pop stars, singers who annoyed me and all had curvy figures.
I talked about lots of stuff with her.
All that stuff...
Mmm hmm.
I was ashamed.
Why were you ashamed?
But never the Beatles.
It's gross!
Gross how?
It's nasty.
What's nasty?
I felt like talking to her about the Beatles would be too frivolous. It wasn't serious enough. Not crazy enough.
I dunno. All body stuff is gross. I don't like it.
It's embarrassing.
Bodies are embarrassing?
And I was scared to seem like I was doing better.
Yeah.
I dunno...
Mmm hmm.
Mariah pariah
Madonna don't wana
I hate being embarrassed...
It's embarrassing to be embarrassed.

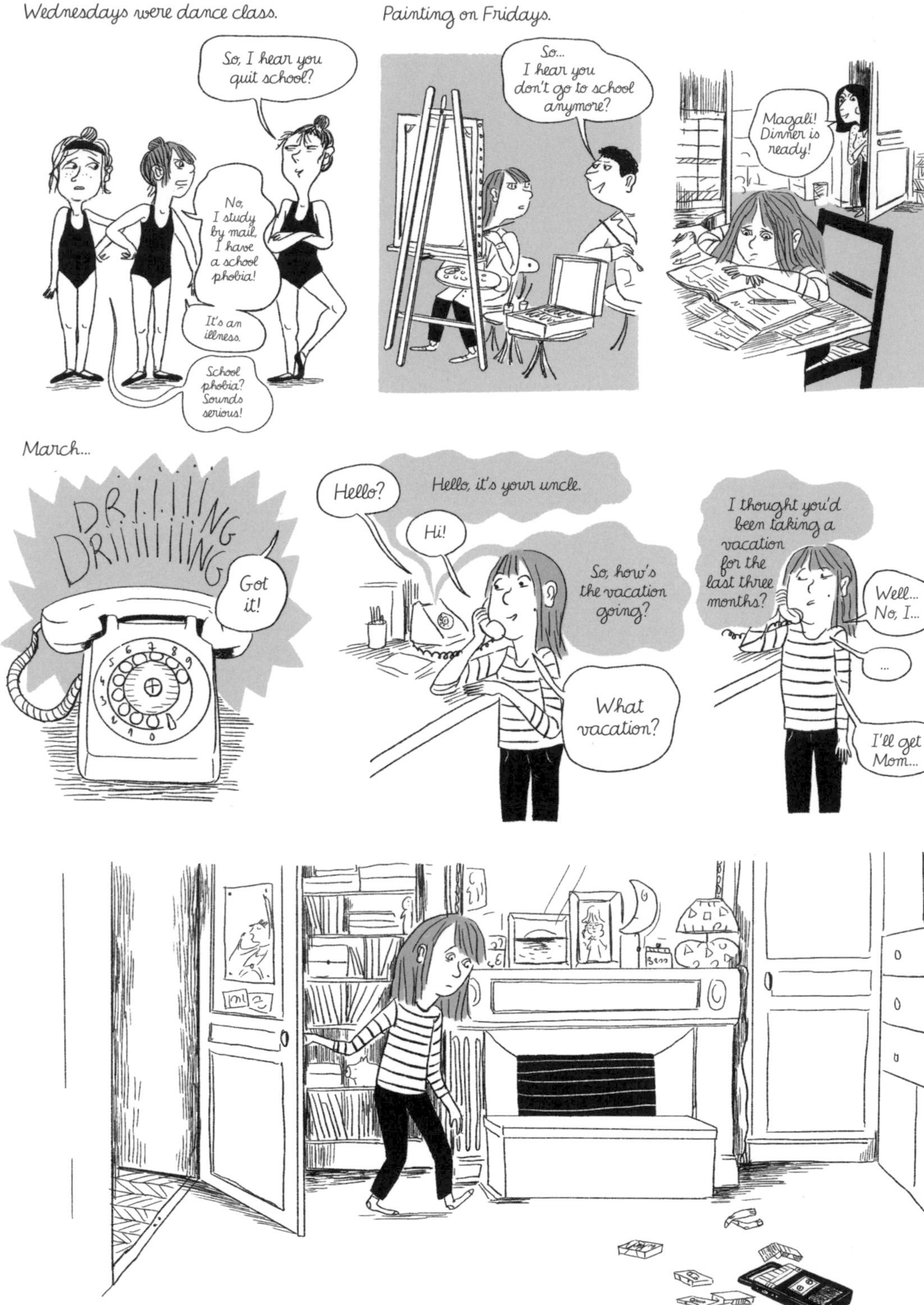

Wednesdays were dance class.
So, I hear you quit school?
No, I study by mail, I have a school phobia!
It's an illness.
School phobia? Sounds serious!
Painting on Fridays.
So... I hear you don't go to school anymore?
Magali! Dinner is ready!
March...
DRIIIIING DRIIIIIIING
Got it!
Hello?
Hello, it's your uncle.
Hi!
So, how's the vacation going?
What vacation?
I thought you'd been taking a vacation for the last three months?
Well... No, I...
...
I'll get Mom...

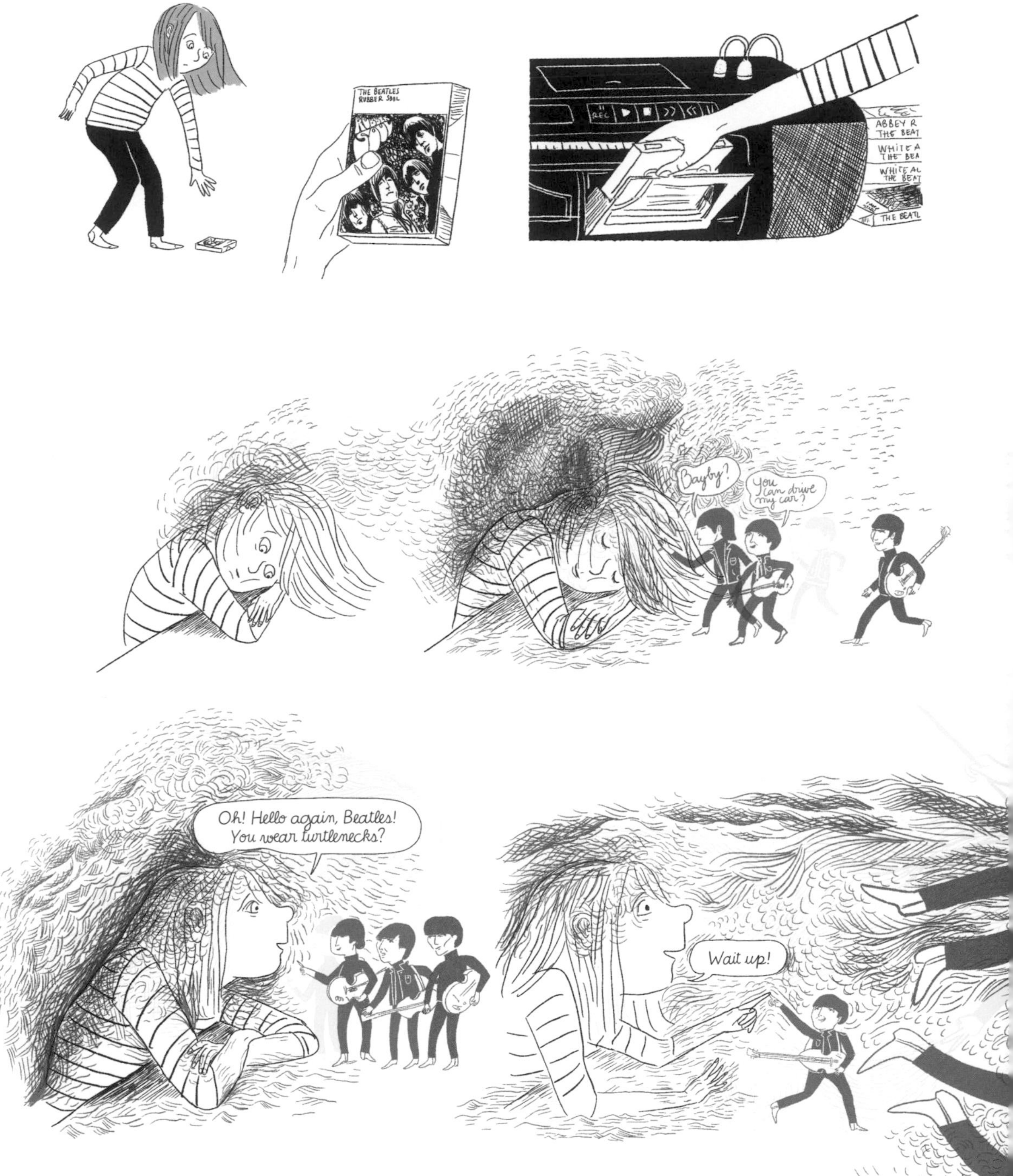
THE BEATLES
RUBBER SOUL
REC
ABBEY R
THE BEAT
WHITE A
THE BEA
WHITE AL
THE BEAT
THE BEATL
Baybry?
You can drive my car?
Oh! Hello again, Beatles! You wear turtlenecks?
Wait up!

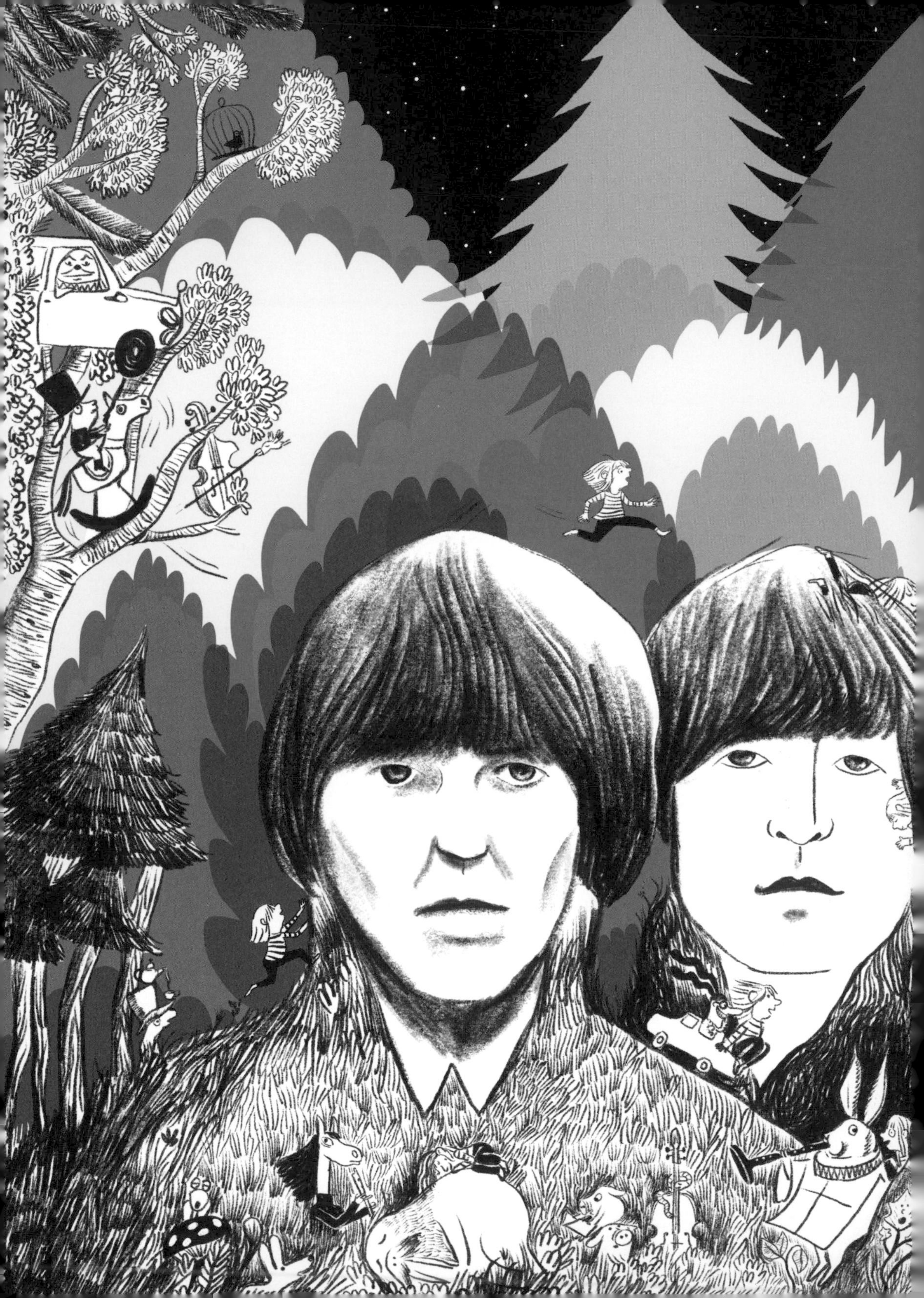

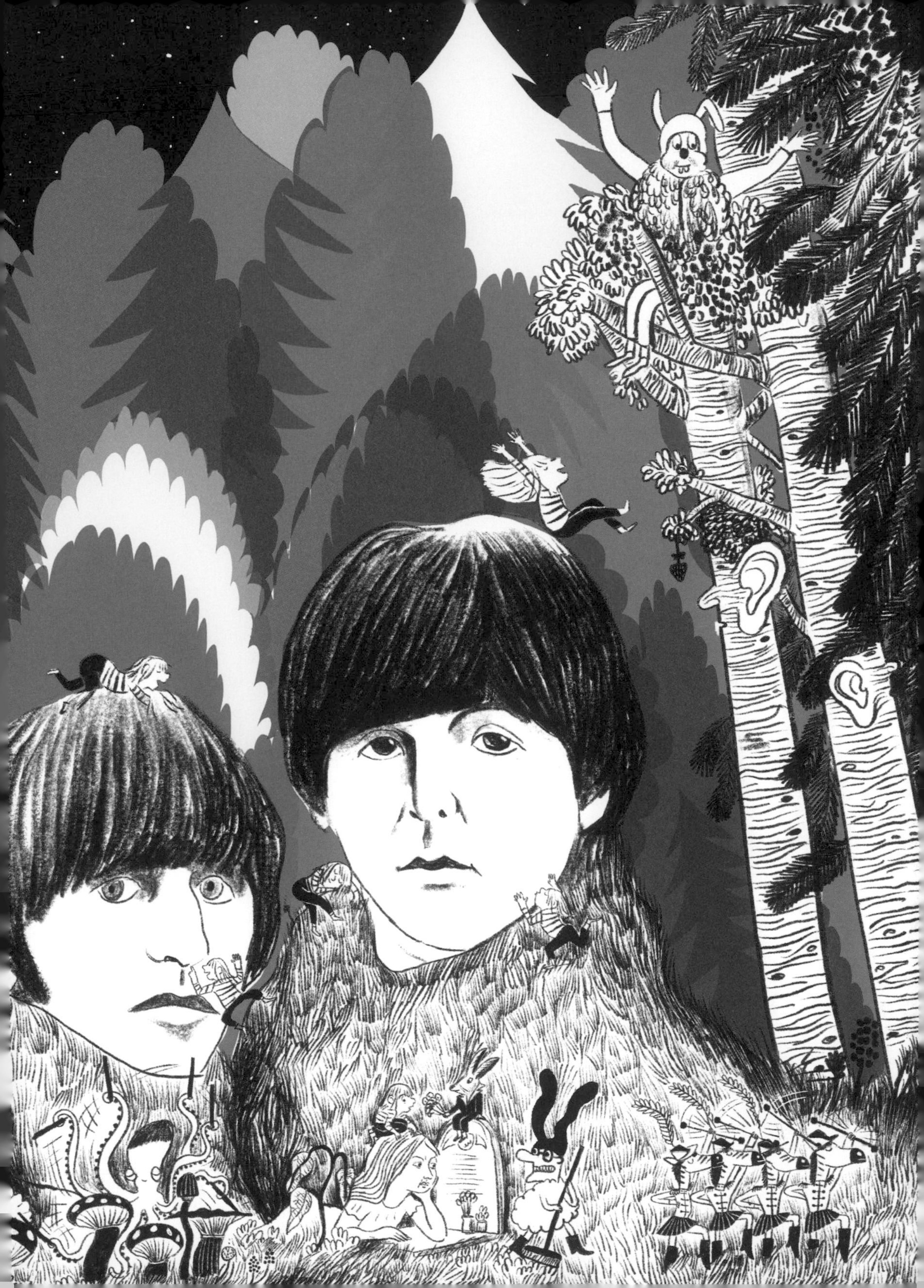

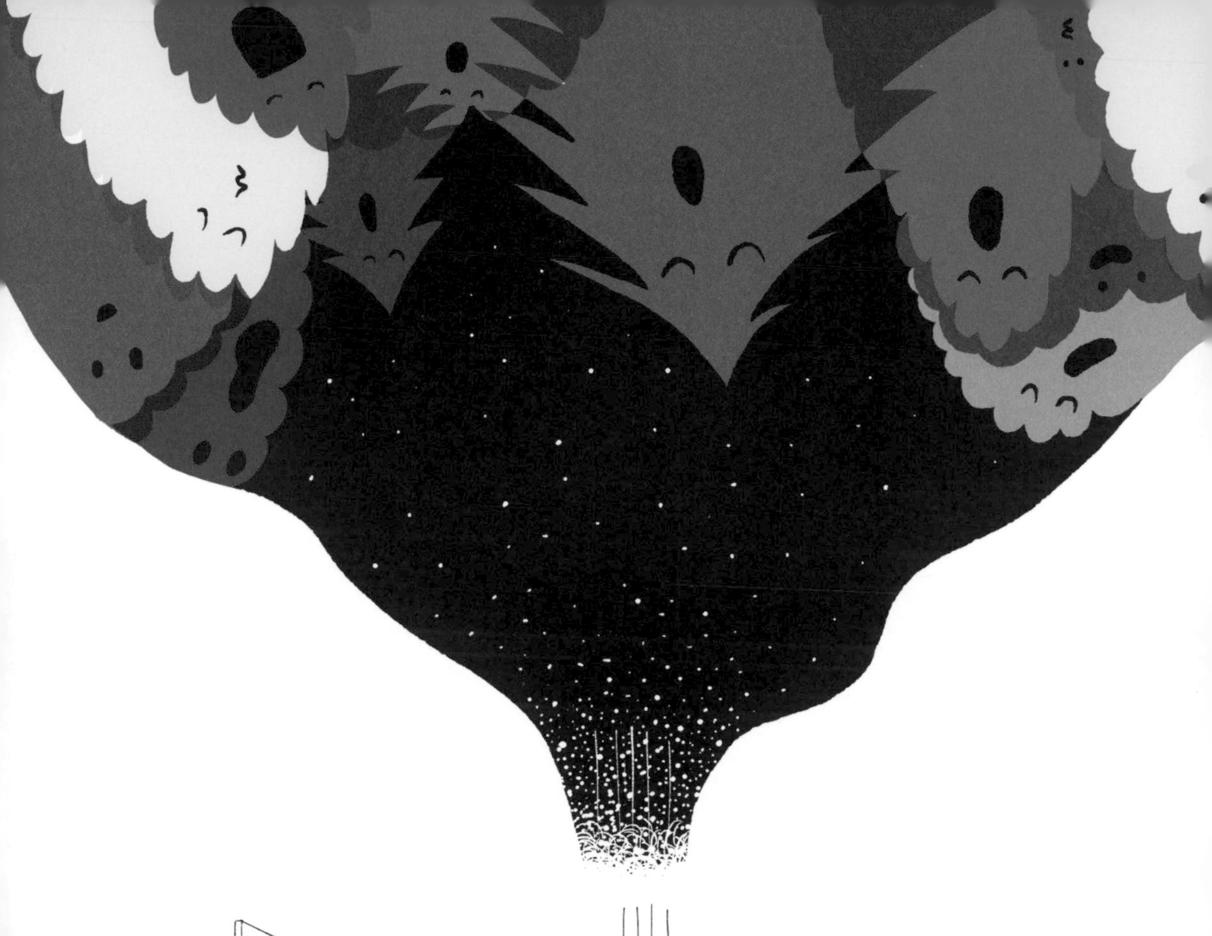
Come set the table! Dinner's almost ready.

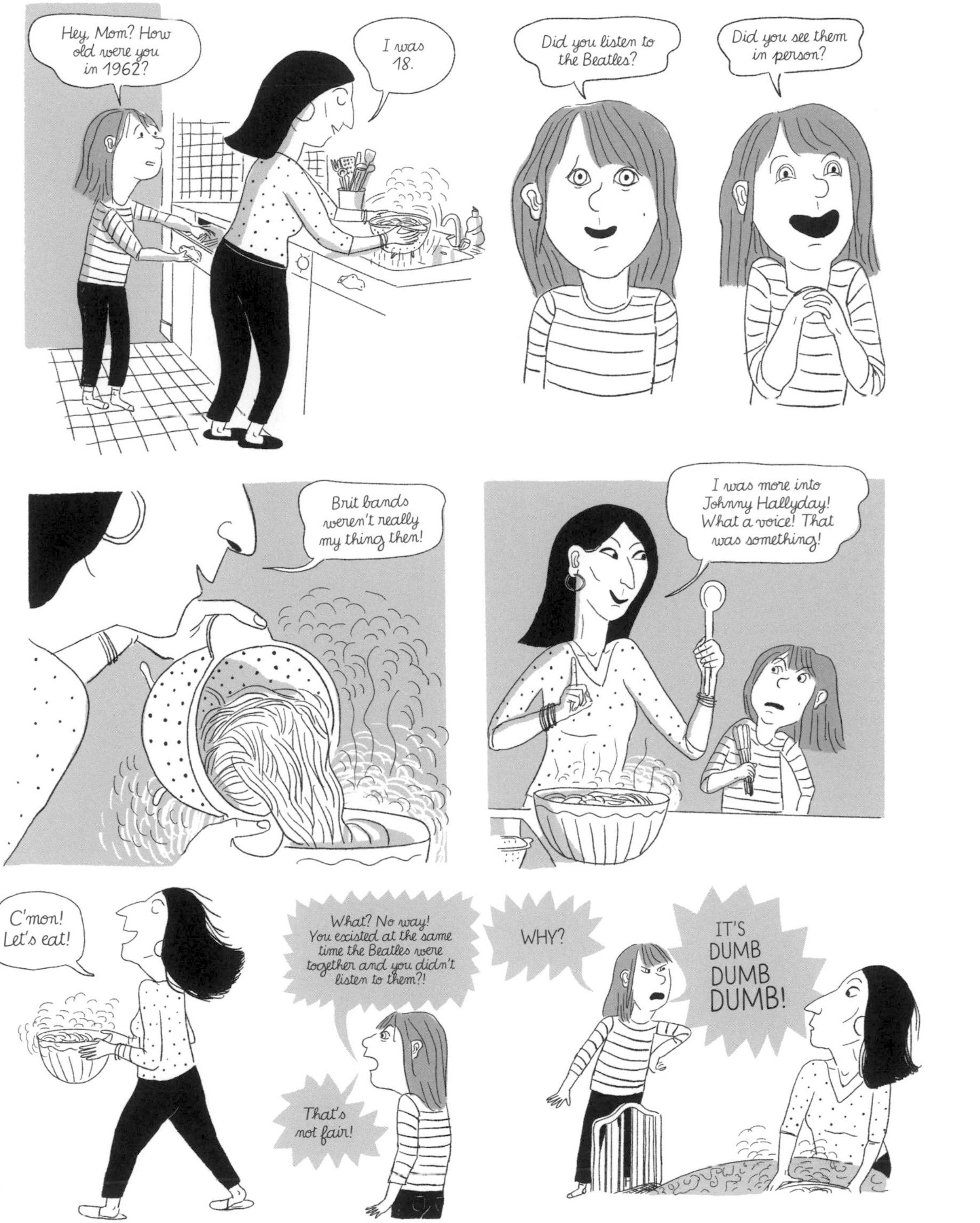
Hey, Mom? How old were you in 1962?
I was 18.
Did you listen to the Beatles?
Did you see them in person?
Brit bands weren't really my thing then!
I was more into Johnny Hallyday! What a voice! That was something!
C'mon! Let's eat!
What? No way! You existed at the same time the Beatles were together and you didn't listen to them?!
That's not fair!
WHY?
IT'S DUMB DUMB DUMB!

Everything intensified between me and the Beatles. My passion was limitless.
They became a daily obsession.

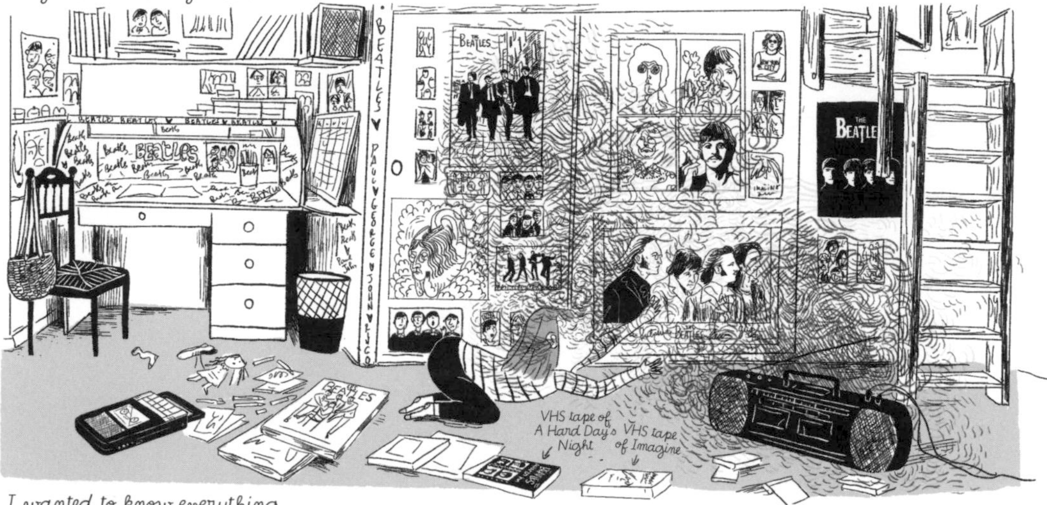
VHS tape of A Hard Day's Night
VHS tape of Imagine

I wanted to know everything.

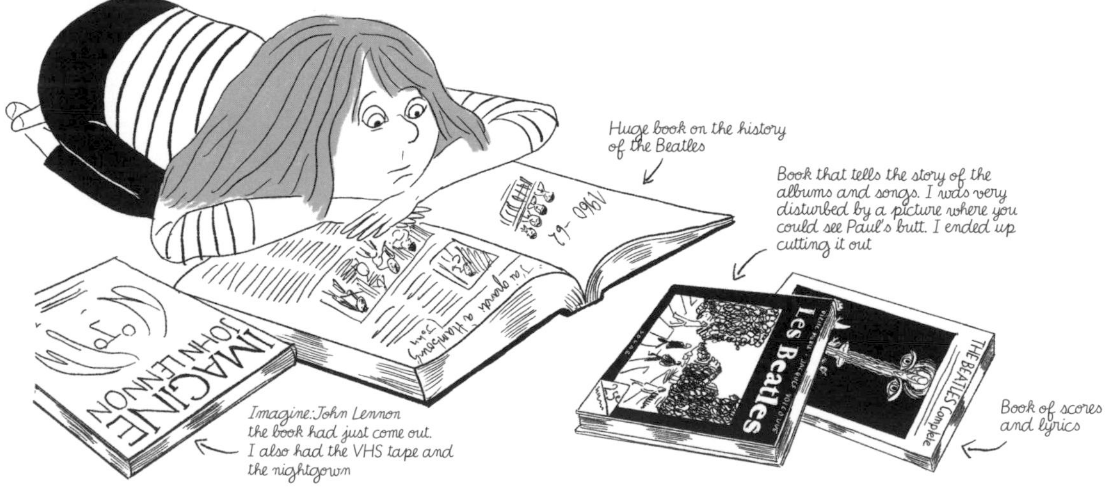
Huge book on the history of the Beatles
Book that tells the story of the albums and songs. I was very disturbed by a picture where you could see Paul's butt. I ended up cutting it out
IMAGINE JOHN LENNON
Imagine: John Lennon the book had just come out. I also had the VHS tape and the nightgown
Les Beatles
THE BEATLES Complete
Book of scores and lyrics

I practiced recognizing their voices on each song and entertained myself by doing a little in-depth analysis.

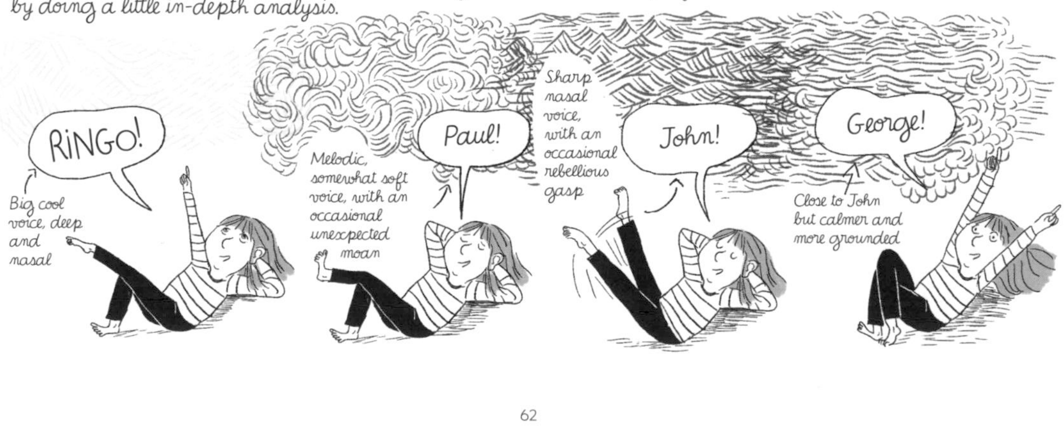
RiNGO!
Big cool voice, deep and nasal
Paul!
Melodic, somewhat soft voice, with an occasional unexpected moan
John!
Sharp nasal voice, with an occasional rebellious gasp
George!
Close to John but calmer and more grounded

I worked like crazy to memorize everything. I wanted to be precise.

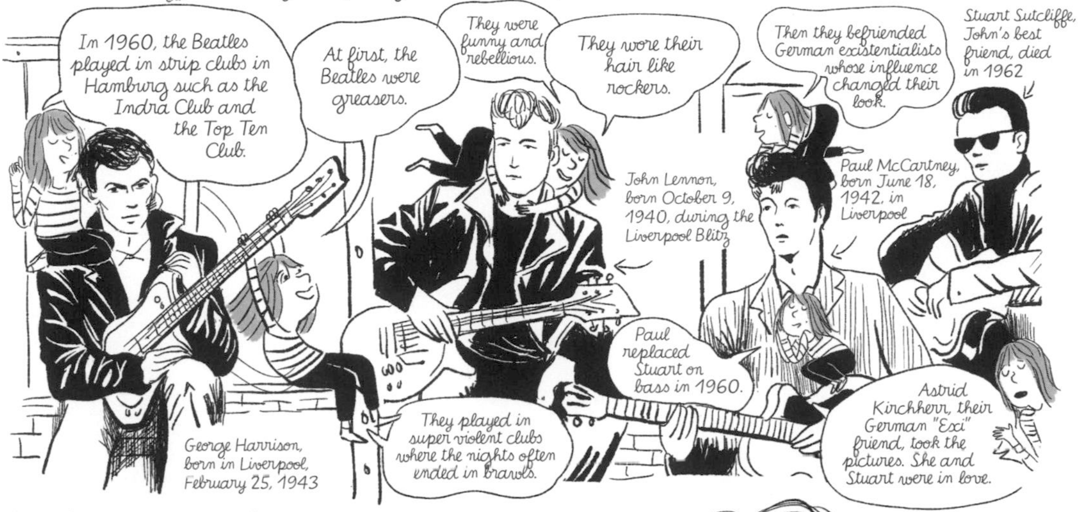
In 1960, the Beatles played in strip clubs in Hamburg such as the Indra Club and the Top Ten Club.
At first, the Beatles were greasers.
They were funny and rebellious.
They wore their hair like rockers.
Then they befriended German existentialists whose influence changed their look.
Stuart Sutcliffe, John's best friend, died in 1962
George Harrison, born in Liverpool, February 25, 1943
John Lennon, born October 9, 1940, during the Liverpool Blitz
Paul McCartney, born June 18, 1942, in Liverpool
They played in super violent clubs where the nights often ended in brawls.
Paul replaced Stuart on bass in 1960.
Astrid Kirchherr, their German "Exi" friend, took the pictures. She and Stuart were in love.

Everything was of crucial importance.

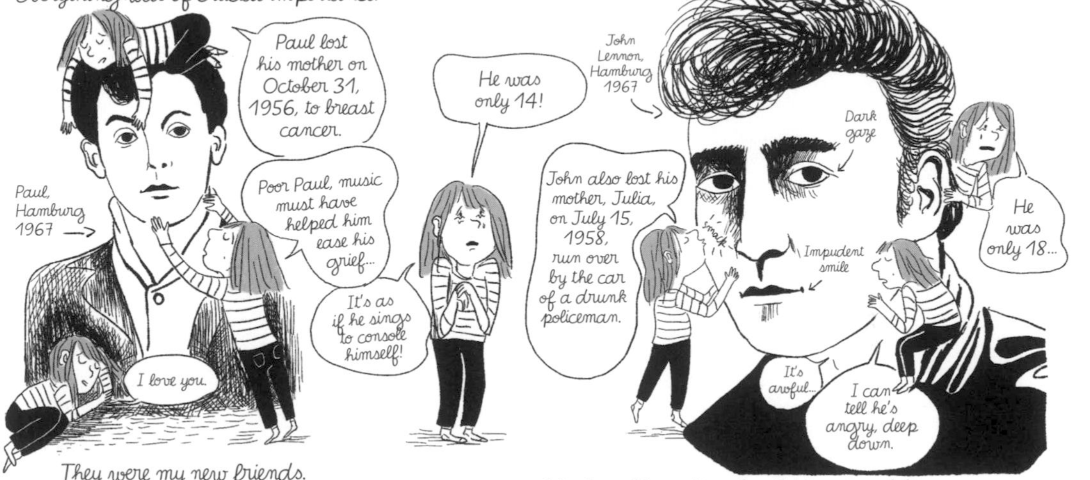
Paul lost his mother on October 31, 1956, to breast cancer.
Paul, Hamburg 1967
Poor Paul, music must have helped him ease his grief...
I love you.
It's as if he sings to console himself!
He was only 14!
John Lennon, Hamburg 1967
Dark gaze
John also lost his mother, Julia, on July 15, 1958, run over by the car of a drunk policeman.
smack
Impudent smile
He was only 18...
It's awful...
I can tell he's angry, deep down.

They were my new friends.

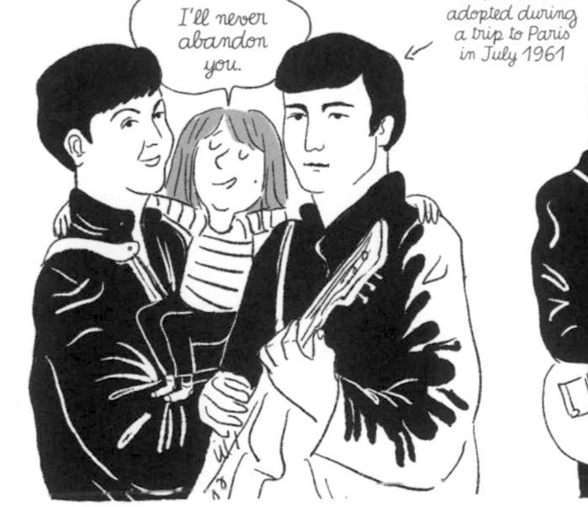
I'll never abandon you.
Bowl haircut adopted during a trip to Paris in July 1961

I had trouble reading, but I'd found my bibles: hundreds of pages that I devoured with no difficulty at all.

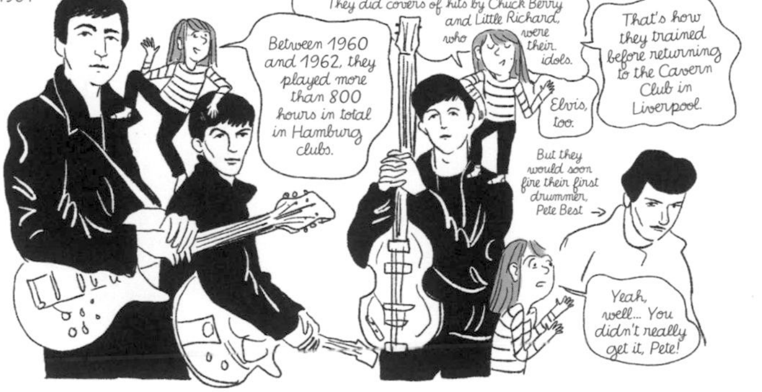
Between 1960 and 1962, they played more than 800 hours in total in Hamburg clubs.
They did covers of hits by Chuck Berry and Little Richard, who were their idols.
Elvis, too.
That's how they trained before returning to the Cavern Club in Liverpool.
But they would soon fire their first drummer, Pete Best
Yeah, well... You didn't really get it, Pete!

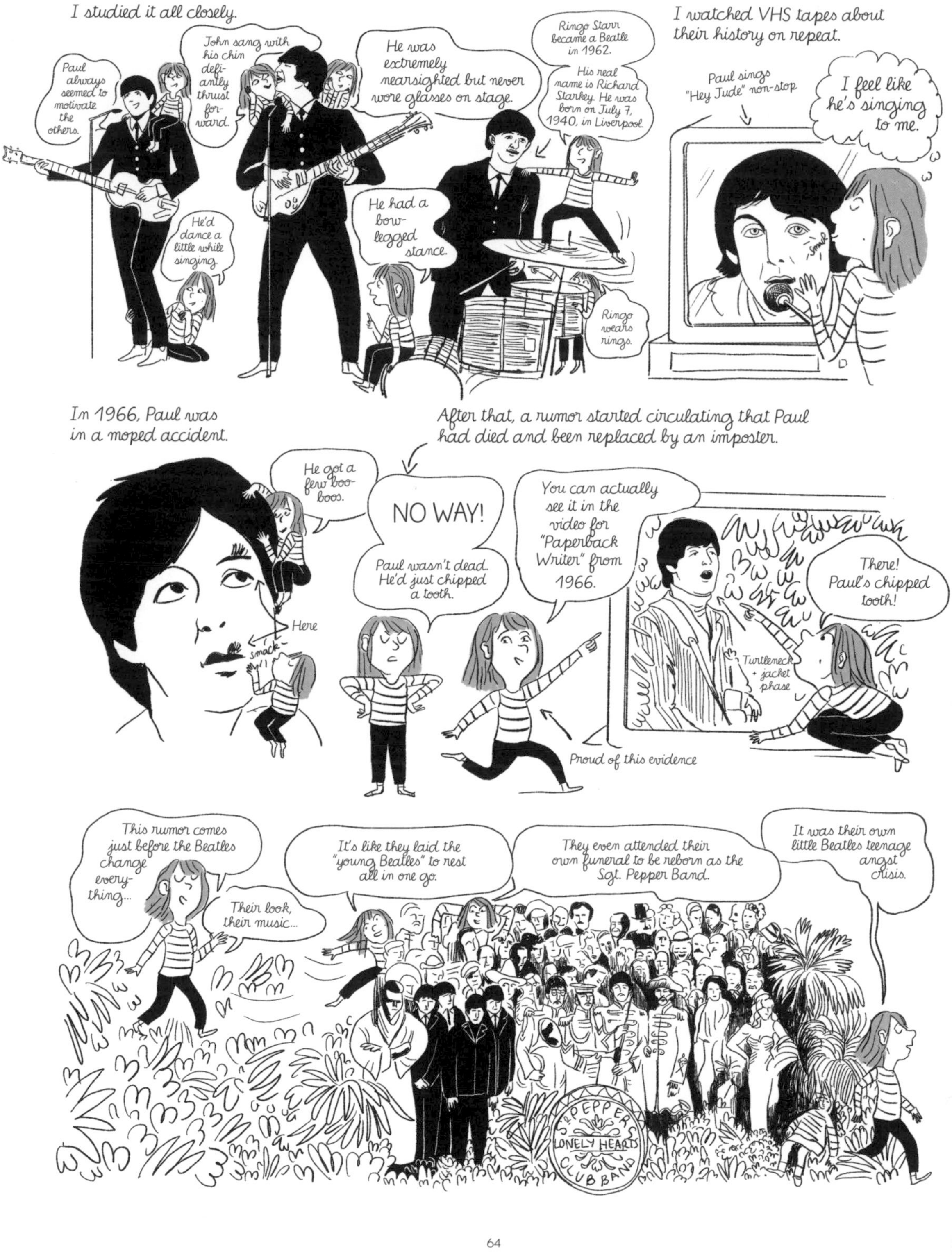

I studied it all closely.
Paul always seemed to motivate the others.
John sang with his chin defiantly thrust forward.
He'd dance a little while singing.
He was extremely nearsighted but never wore glasses on stage.
He had a bowlegged stance.
Ringo Starr became a Beatle in 1962.
His real name is Richard Starkey. He was born on July 7, 1940, in Liverpool.
Ringo wears rings.
I watched VHS tapes about their history on repeat.
Paul sings "Hey Jude" non-stop
I feel like he's singing to me.
Smack
In 1966, Paul was in a moped accident.
He got a few boo-boos.
Here
smack
After that, a rumor started circulating that Paul had died and been replaced by an imposter.
NO WAY!
Paul wasn't dead. He'd just chipped a tooth.
You can actually see it in the video for "Paperback Writer" from 1966.
There! Paul's chipped tooth!
Turtleneck + jacket phase
Proud of this evidence
This rumor comes just before the Beatles change everything...
Their look, their music...
It's like they laid the "young Beatles" to rest all in one go.
They even attended their own funeral to be reborn as the Sgt. Pepper Band.
It was their own little Beatles teenage angst crisis.
SGT. PEPPER'S LONELY HEARTS CLUB BAND

The omnipresence of death and regeneration in the Beatles' story attracted me without me really understanding why. I felt a part of me was dying, too, so I clung to them like a new security blanket.

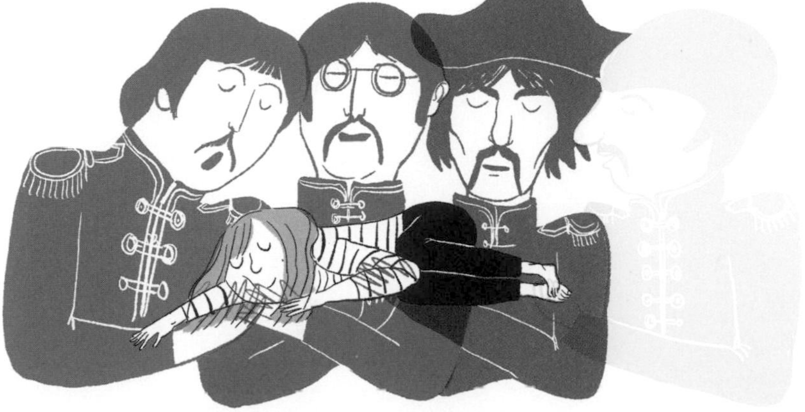

I was happy inside that off-kilter gaiety. We'd be together forever.

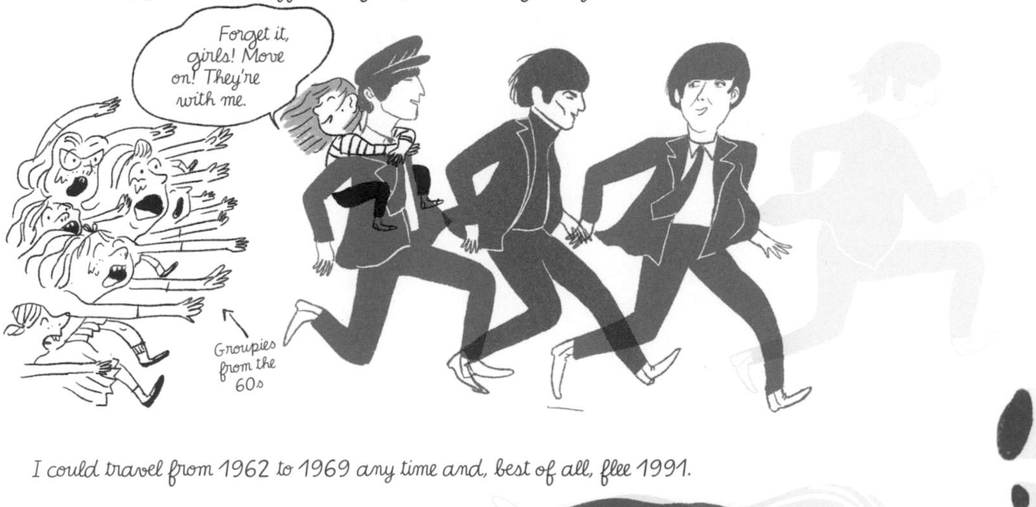
Forget it, girls! Move on! They're with me.
Groupies from the 60s

I could travel from 1962 to 1969 any time and, best of all, flee 1991.

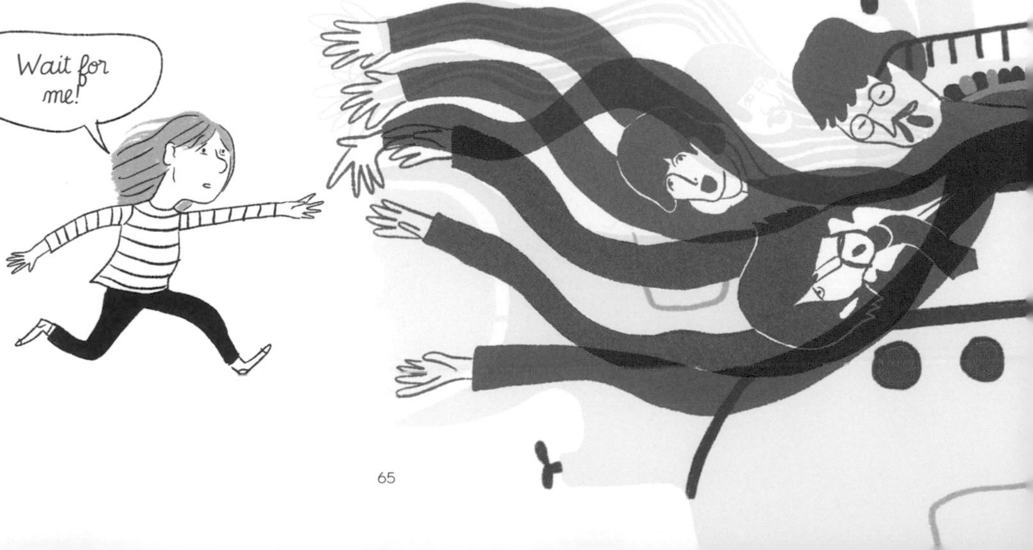
Wait for me!

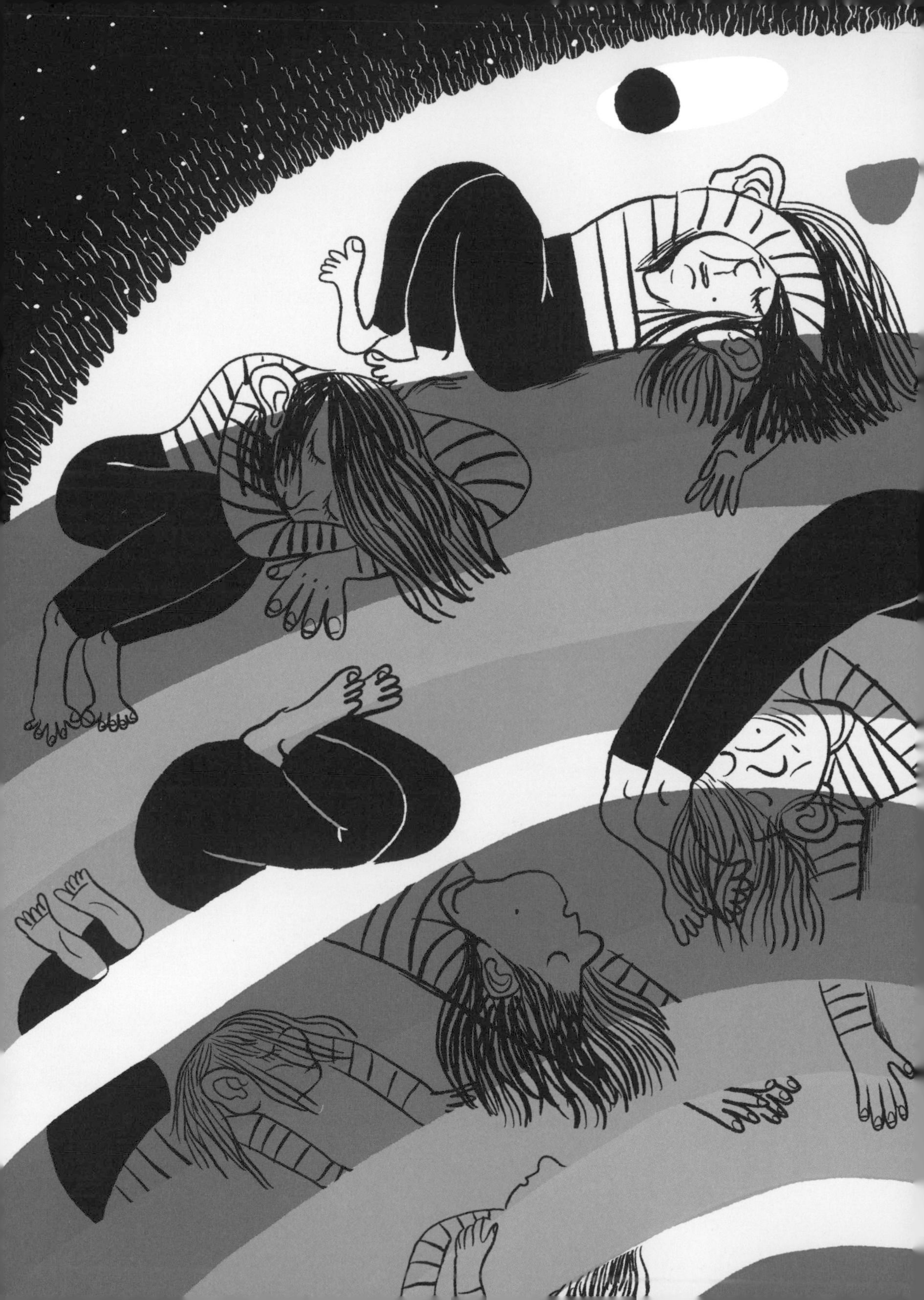

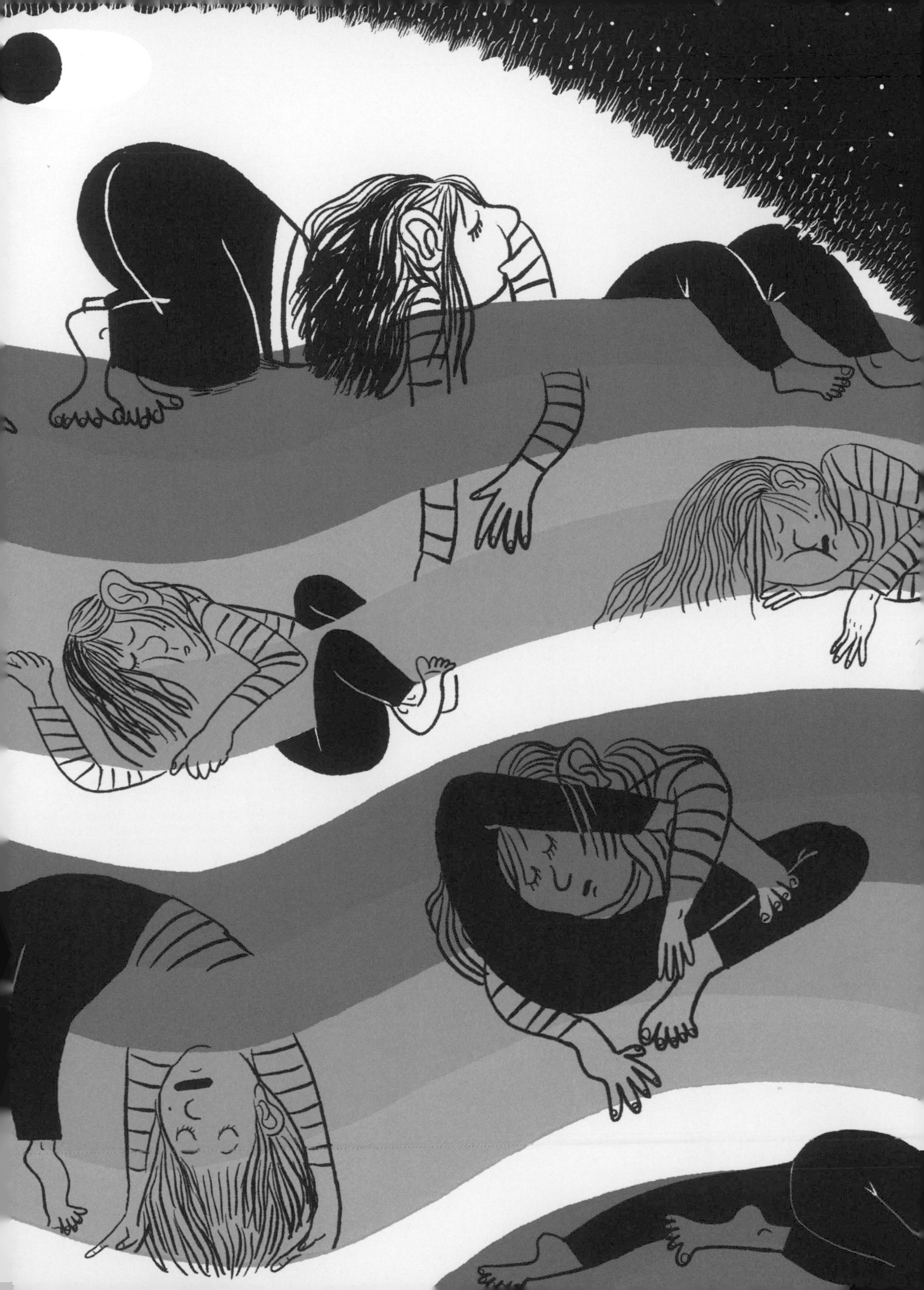

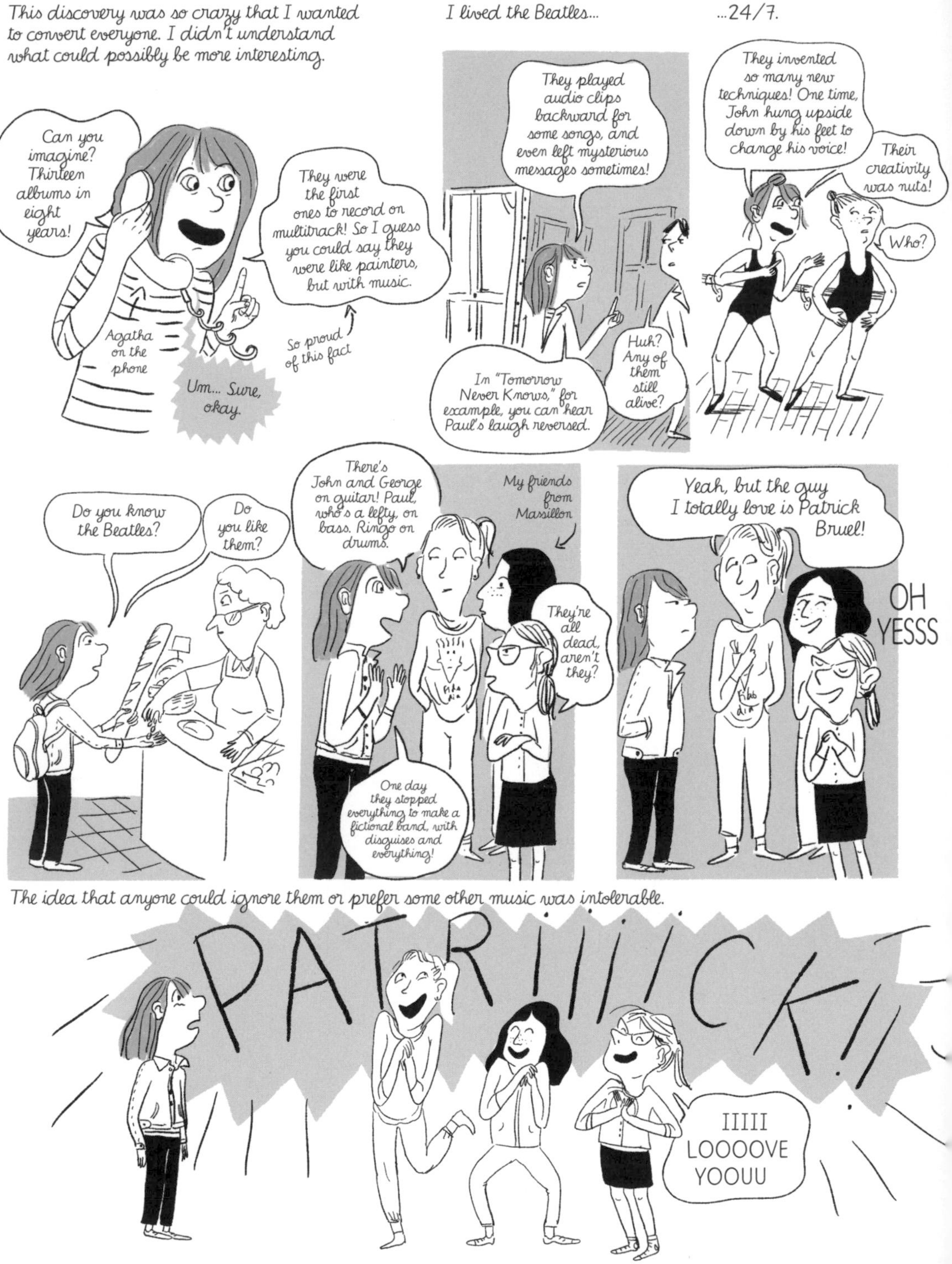
This discovery was so crazy that I wanted to convert everyone. I didn't understand what could possibly be more interesting.
Can you imagine? Thirteen albums in eight years!
They were the first ones to record on multitrack! So I guess you could say they were like painters, but with music.
Agatha on the phone
Um... Sure, okay.
So proud of this fact
I lived the Beatles...
They played audio clips backward for some songs, and even left mysterious messages sometimes!
Huh? Any of them still alive?
In "Tomorrow Never Knows," for example, you can hear Paul's laugh reversed.
...24/7.
They invented so many new techniques! One time, John hung upside down by his feet to change his voice!
Their creativity was nuts!
Who?
Do you know the Beatles?
Do you like them?
There's John and George on guitar! Paul, who's a lefty, on bass. Ringo on drums.
My friends from Massillon
They're all dead, aren't they?
One day they stopped everything to make a fictional band, with disguises and everything!
Yeah, but the guy I totally love is Patrick Bruel!
OH YESSS
The idea that anyone could ignore them or prefer some other music was intolerable.
PATRIIIICK!!
IIIII LOOOOVE YOOUU

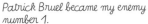

Patrick Bruel became my enemy number 1.

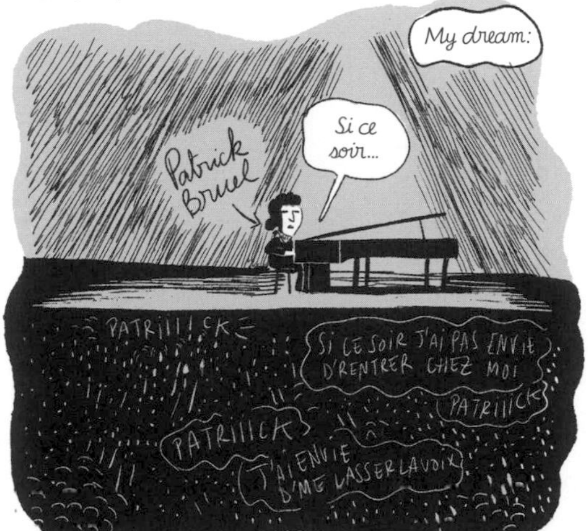

My dream:
Si ce soir...
Patrick Bruel
PATRIIIICK
SI CE SOIR J'AI PAS ENVIE D'RENTRER CHEZ MOI
PATRIIICK
PATRIIICK
J'AI ENVIE D'ME CASSER LA VOIX

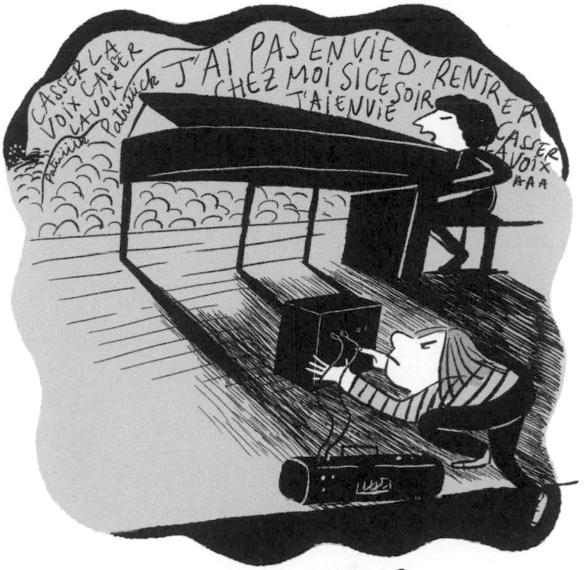

J'AI PAS ENVIE D'RENTRER CHEZ MOI SI CE SOIR J'AI ENVIE
CASSER LA VOIX CASSER LA VOIX
Patriiiick
CASSER LA VOIX AAA

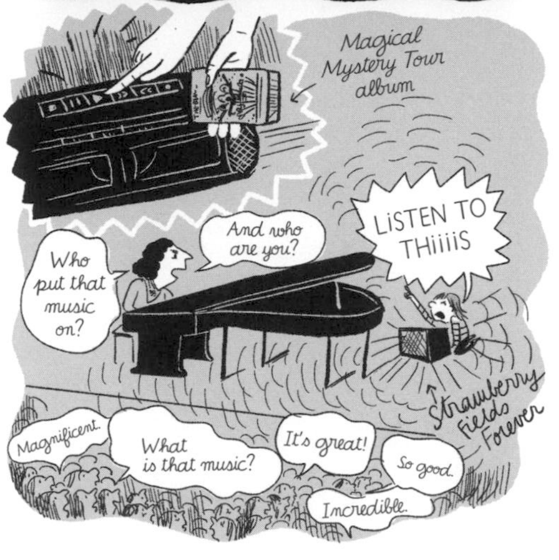

Magical Mystery Tour album
Who put that music on?
And who are you?
LISTEN TO THIiiiS
Strawberry Fields Forever
Magnificent.
What is that music?
It's great!
So good.
Incredible.

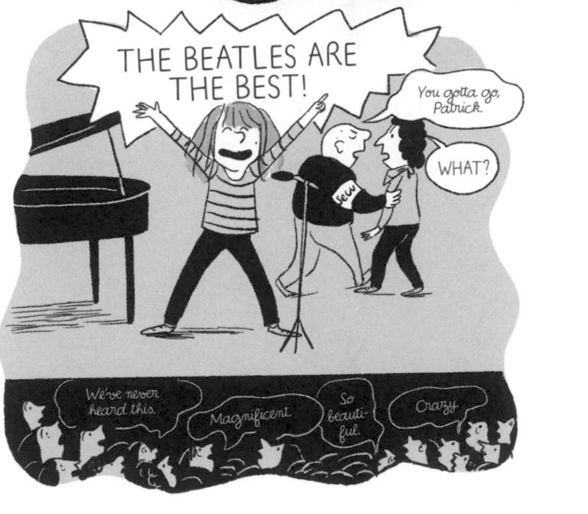

THE BEATLES ARE THE BEST!
You gotta go, Patrick.
WHAT?
We've never heard this.
Magnificent.
So beautiful.
Crazy.

I had to take immediate Beatles action.

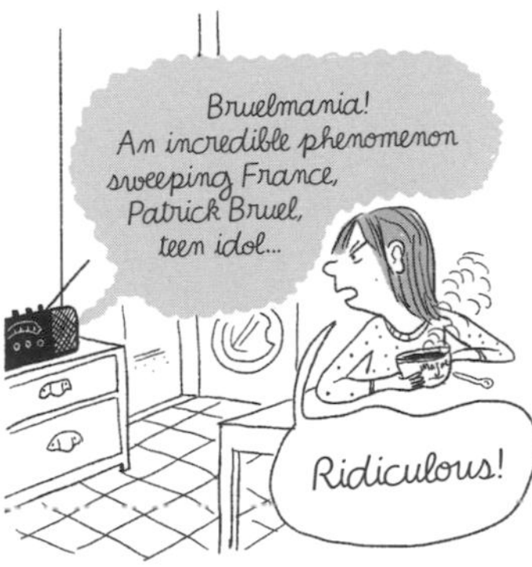

Bruelmania! An incredible phenomenon sweeping France, Patrick Bruel, teen idol...
Ridiculous!

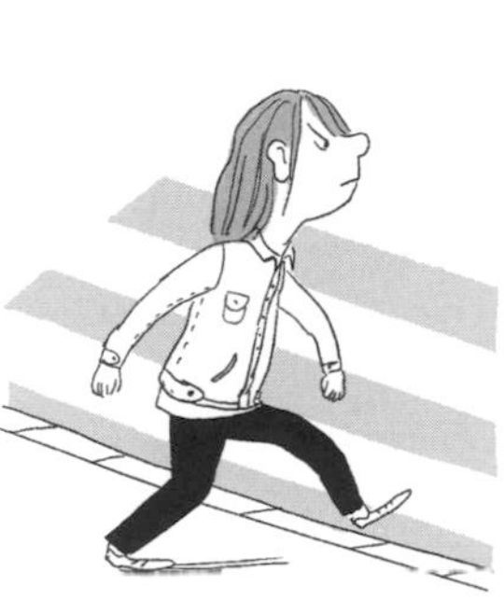

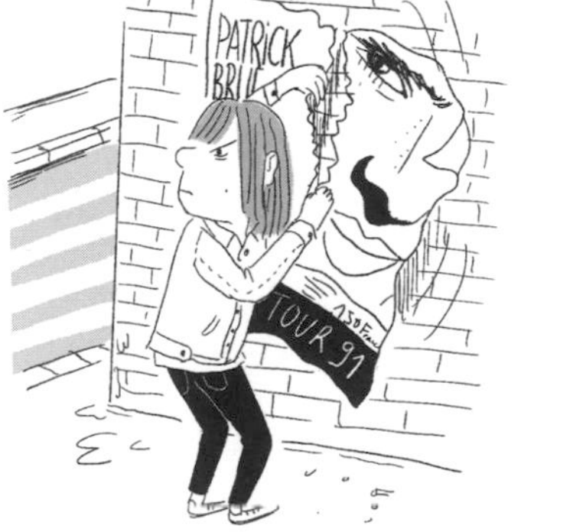

PATRICK
TOUR 91

I felt called by a serious and urgent mission: to make the Beatles known to the whole world.

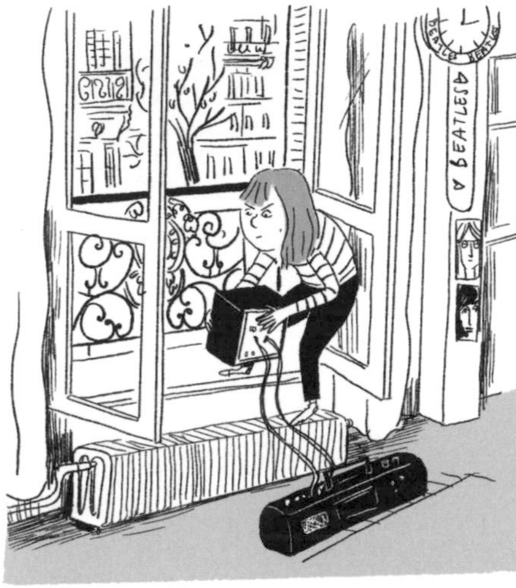
BEATLES

They could never be forgotten.

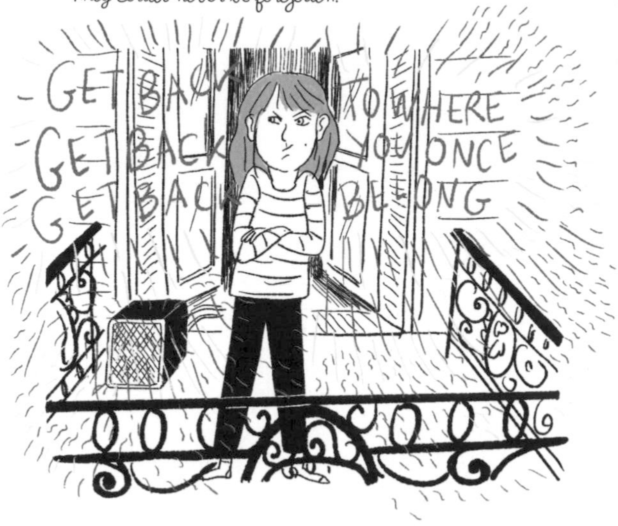
GET BACK
GET BACK
GET BACK
TO WHERE
YOU ONCE
BELONG

I had plans.

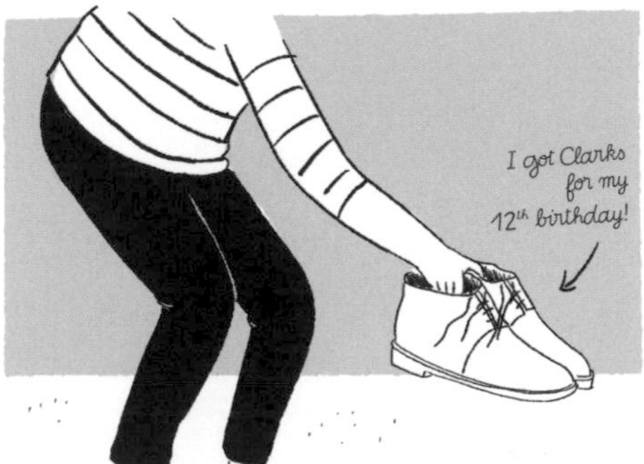
I got Clarks for my 12th birthday!

I was determined.

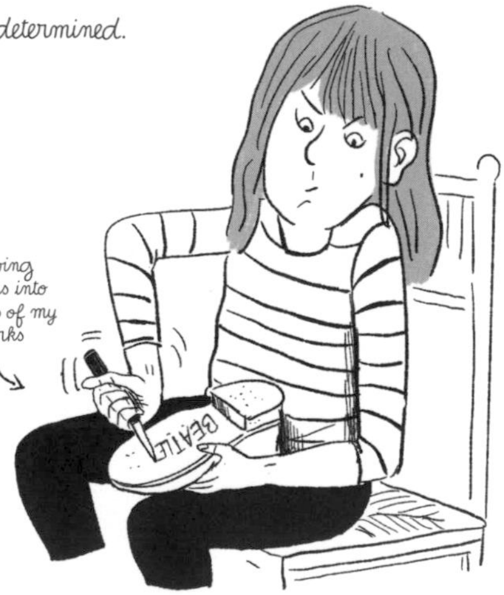
Carving stamps into the soles of my Clarks
BEATLE

I was sure I was changing the world.

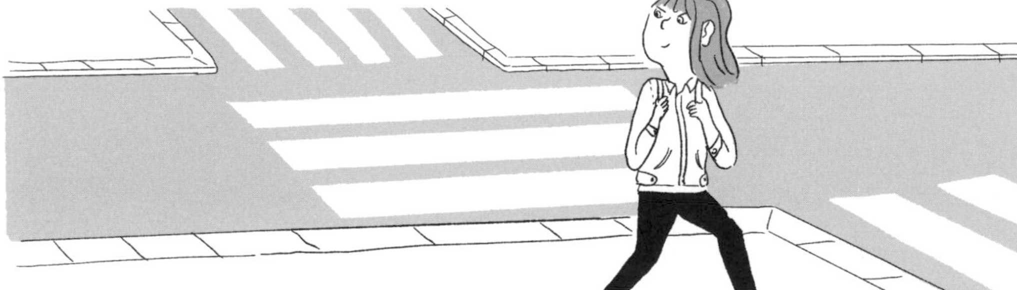

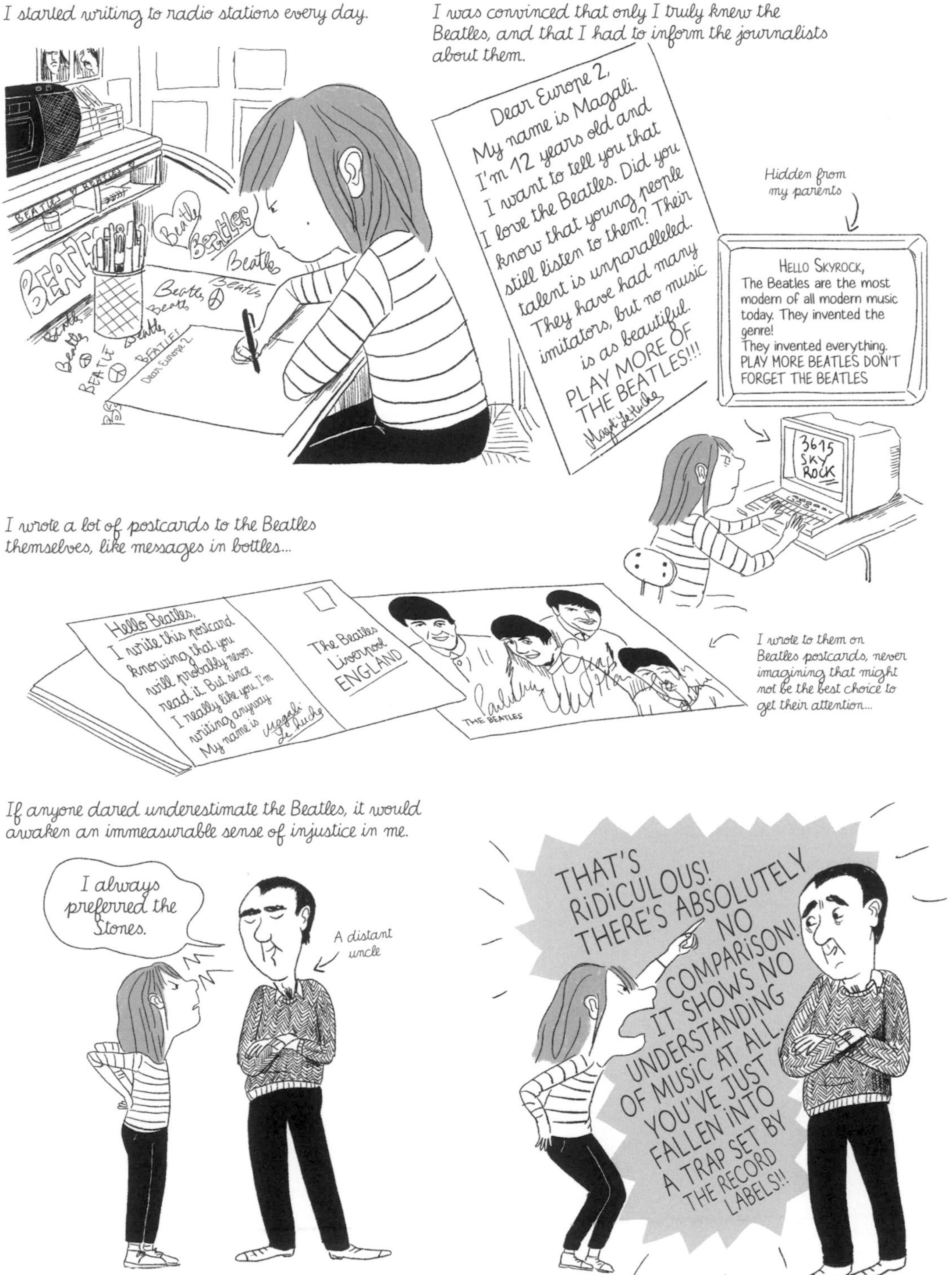
I started writing to radio stations every day.
I was convinced that only I truly knew the Beatles, and that I had to inform the journalists about them.
Dear Europe 2,
My name is Magali.
I'm 12 years old and I want to tell you that I love the Beatles. Did you know that young people still listen to them? Their talent is unparalleled. They have had many imitators, but no music is as beautiful.
PLAY MORE OF THE BEATLES!!!
Hidden from my parents
HELLO SKYROCK,
The Beatles are the most modern of all modern music today. They invented the genre!
They invented everything.
PLAY MORE BEATLES DON'T FORGET THE BEATLES
3615 SKY ROCK
I wrote a lot of postcards to the Beatles themselves, like messages in bottles...
Hello Beatles,
I write this postcard knowing that you will probably never read it. But since I really like you, I'm writing anyway.
My name is Magali Le Huche
The Beatles Liverpool ENGLAND
THE BEATLES
I wrote to them on Beatles postcards, never imagining that might not be the best choice to get their attention...
If anyone dared underestimate the Beatles, it would awaken an immeasurable sense of injustice in me.
I always preferred the Stones.
A distant uncle
THAT'S RIDICULOUS! THERE'S ABSOLUTELY NO COMPARISON! IT SHOWS NO UNDERSTANDING OF MUSIC AT ALL. YOU'VE JUST FALLEN INTO A TRAP SET BY THE RECORD LABELS!!

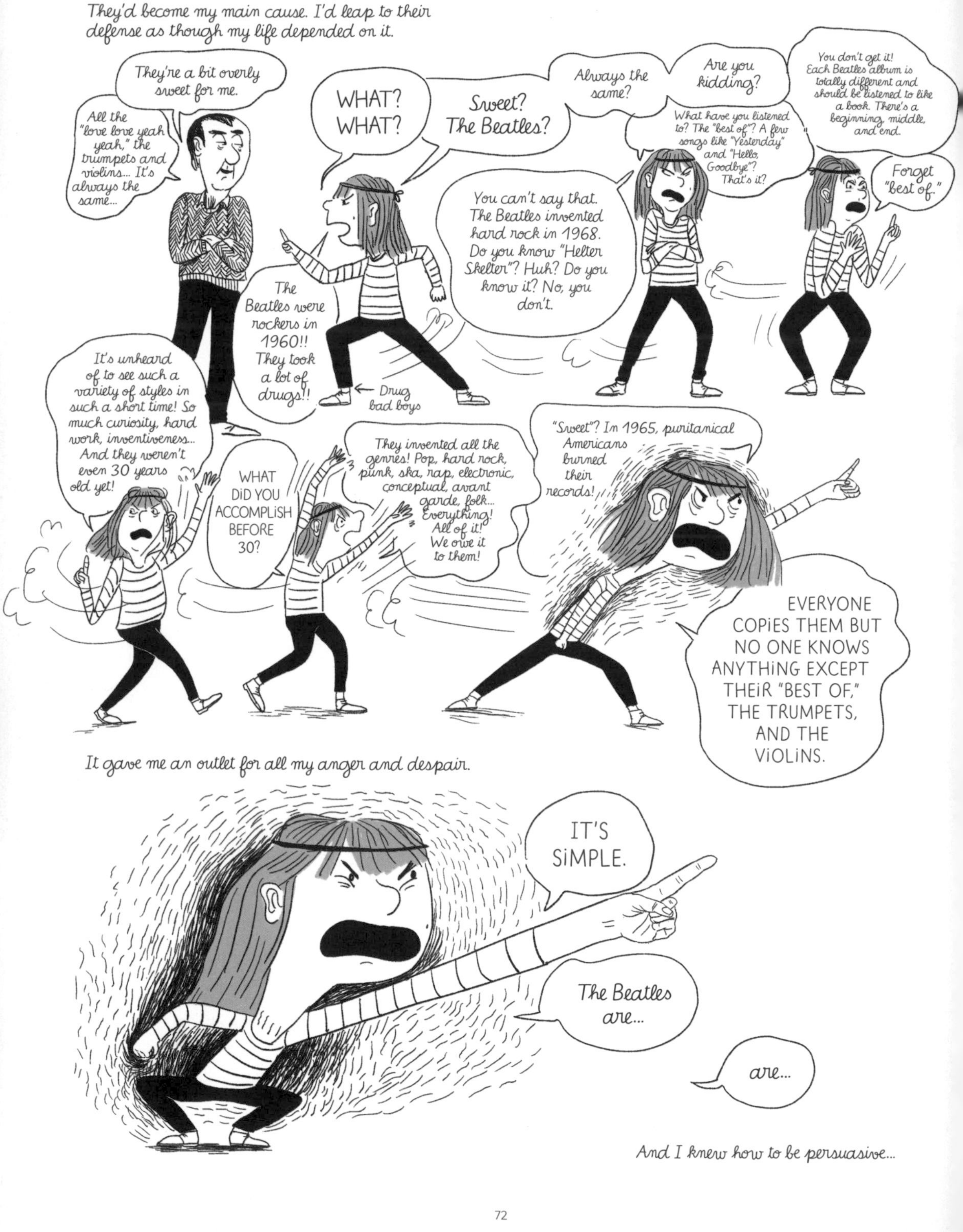
They'd become my main cause. I'd leap to their defense as though my life depended on it.
They're a bit overly sweet for me.
All the "love love yeah yeah," the trumpets and violins... It's always the same...
WHAT? WHAT?
Sweet? The Beatles?
Always the same?
Are you kidding?
What have you listened to? The "best of"? A few songs like "Yesterday" and "Hello, Goodbye"? That's it?
You don't get it! Each Beatles album is totally different and should be listened to like a book. There's a beginning, middle, and end.
Forget "best of."
You can't say that. The Beatles invented hard rock in 1968. Do you know "Helter Skelter"? Huh? Do you know it? No, you don't.
The Beatles were rockers in 1960!! They took a lot of drugs!!
Drug bad boys
It's unheard of to see such a variety of styles in such a short time! So much curiosity, hard work, inventiveness... And they weren't even 30 years old yet!
WHAT DID YOU ACCOMPLISH BEFORE 30?
They invented all the genres! Pop, hard rock, punk, ska, rap, electronic, conceptual, avant garde, folk... Everything! All of it! We owe it to them!
"Sweet"? In 1965, puritanical Americans burned their records!
EVERYONE COPIES THEM BUT NO ONE KNOWS ANYTHING EXCEPT THEIR "BEST OF," THE TRUMPETS, AND THE VIOLINS.
It gave me an outlet for all my anger and despair.
IT'S SIMPLE.
The Beatles are...
are...
And I knew how to be persuasive...

THE BEATLES ARE THE MASTERS OF THE UNIVERSE!!
...restrained, and objective.

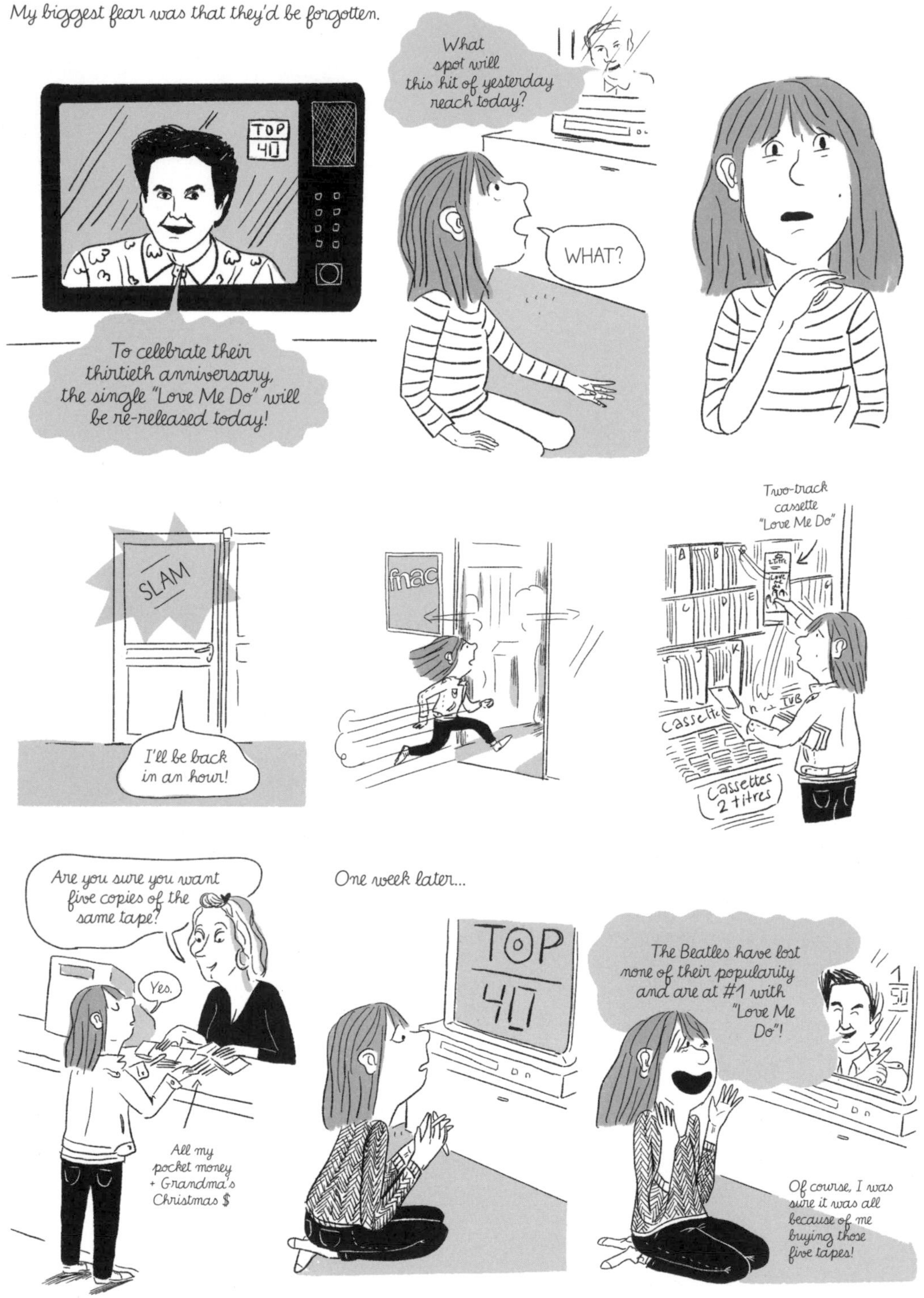
My biggest fear was that they'd be forgotten.
TOP 40
To celebrate their thirtieth anniversary, the single "Love Me Do" will be re-released today!
What spot will this hit of yesterday reach today?
WHAT?
SLAM
I'll be back in an hour!
fnac
Two-track cassette "Love Me Do"
Cassettes 2 titres
Are you sure you want five copies of the same tape?
Yes.
All my pocket money + Grandma's Christmas $
One week later...
TOP 40
The Beatles have lost none of their popularity and are at #1 with "Love Me Do"!
Of course, I was sure it was all because of me buying those five tapes!

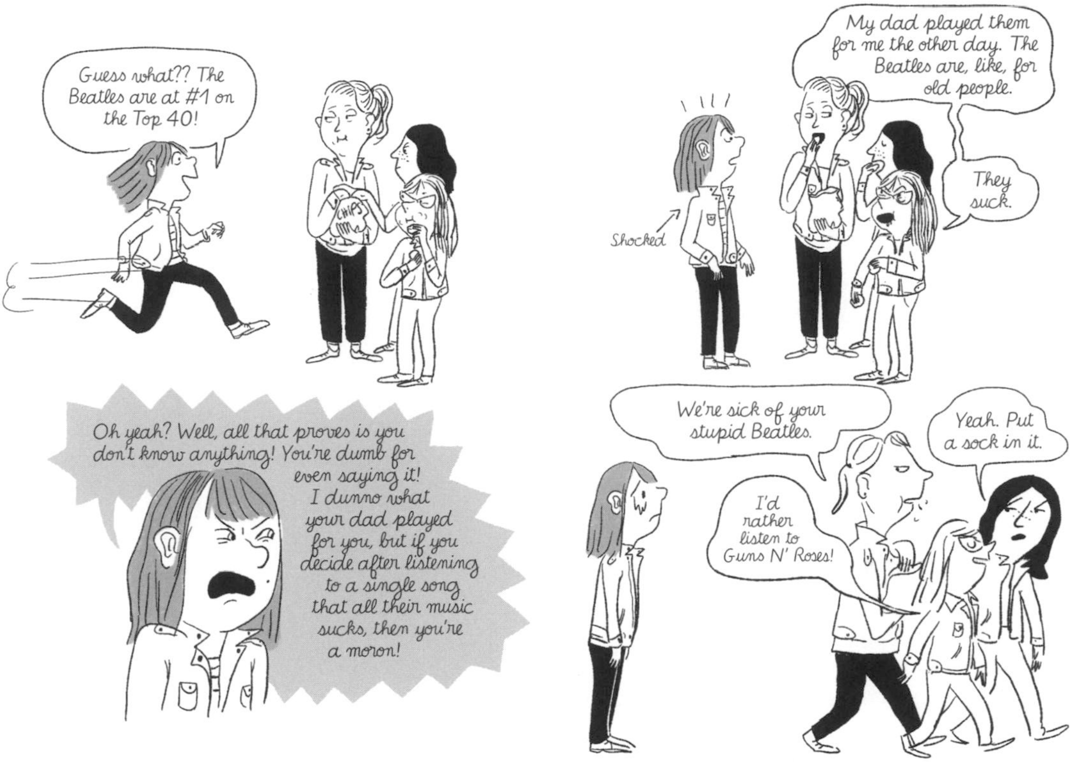
Guess what?? The Beatles are at #1 on the Top 40!
My dad played them for me the other day. The Beatles are, like, for old people.
They suck.
Shocked
Oh yeah? Well, all that proves is you don't know anything! You're dumb for even saying it! I dunno what your dad played for you, but if you decide after listening to a single song that all their music sucks, then you're a moron!
We're sick of your stupid Beatles.
Yeah. Put a sock in it.
I'd rather listen to Guns N' Roses!

The end of the school year was approaching, and I had totally shut down.

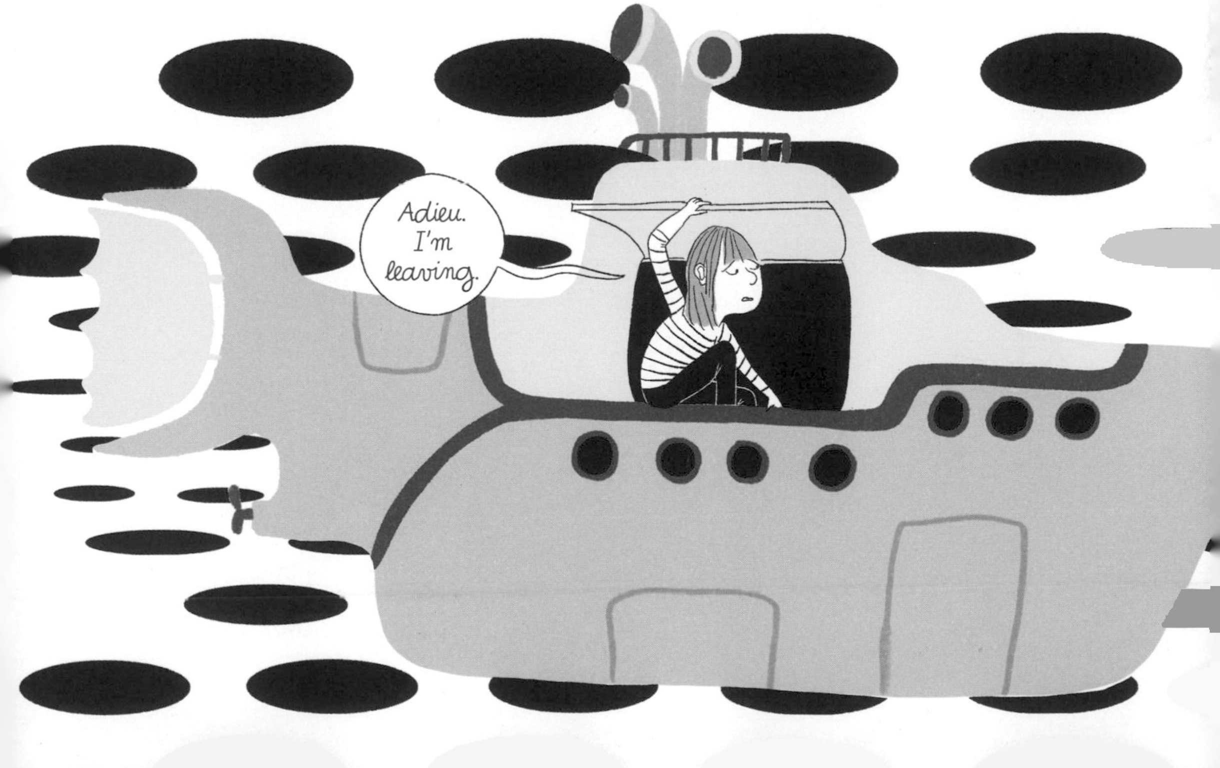
Adieu. I'm leaving.

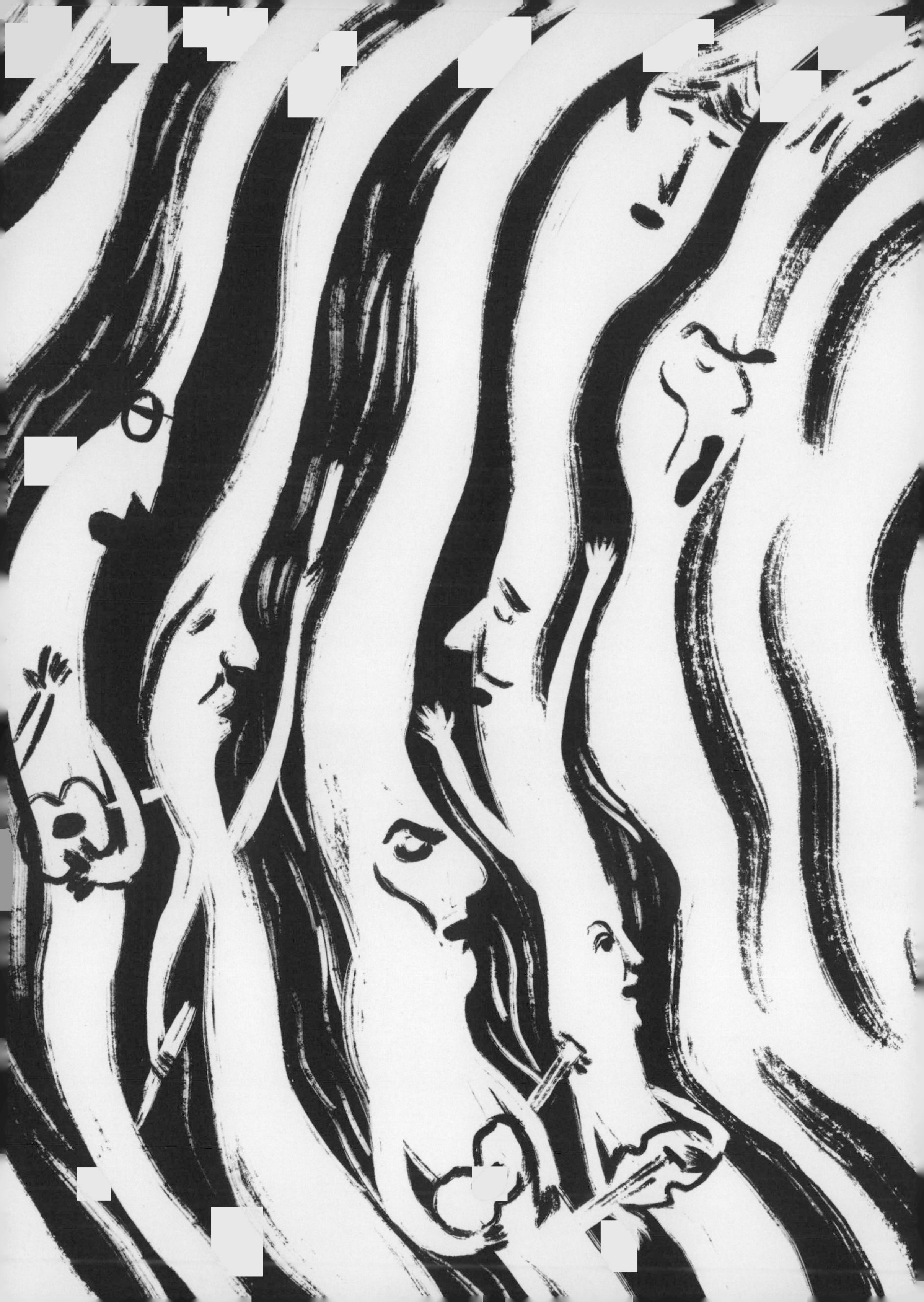

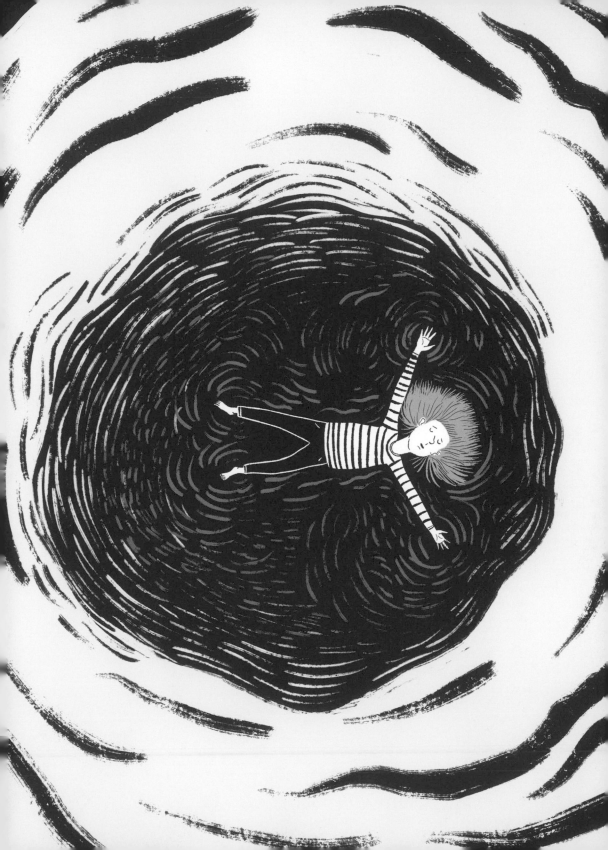

My seventh-grade year would pass quietly, in my room.

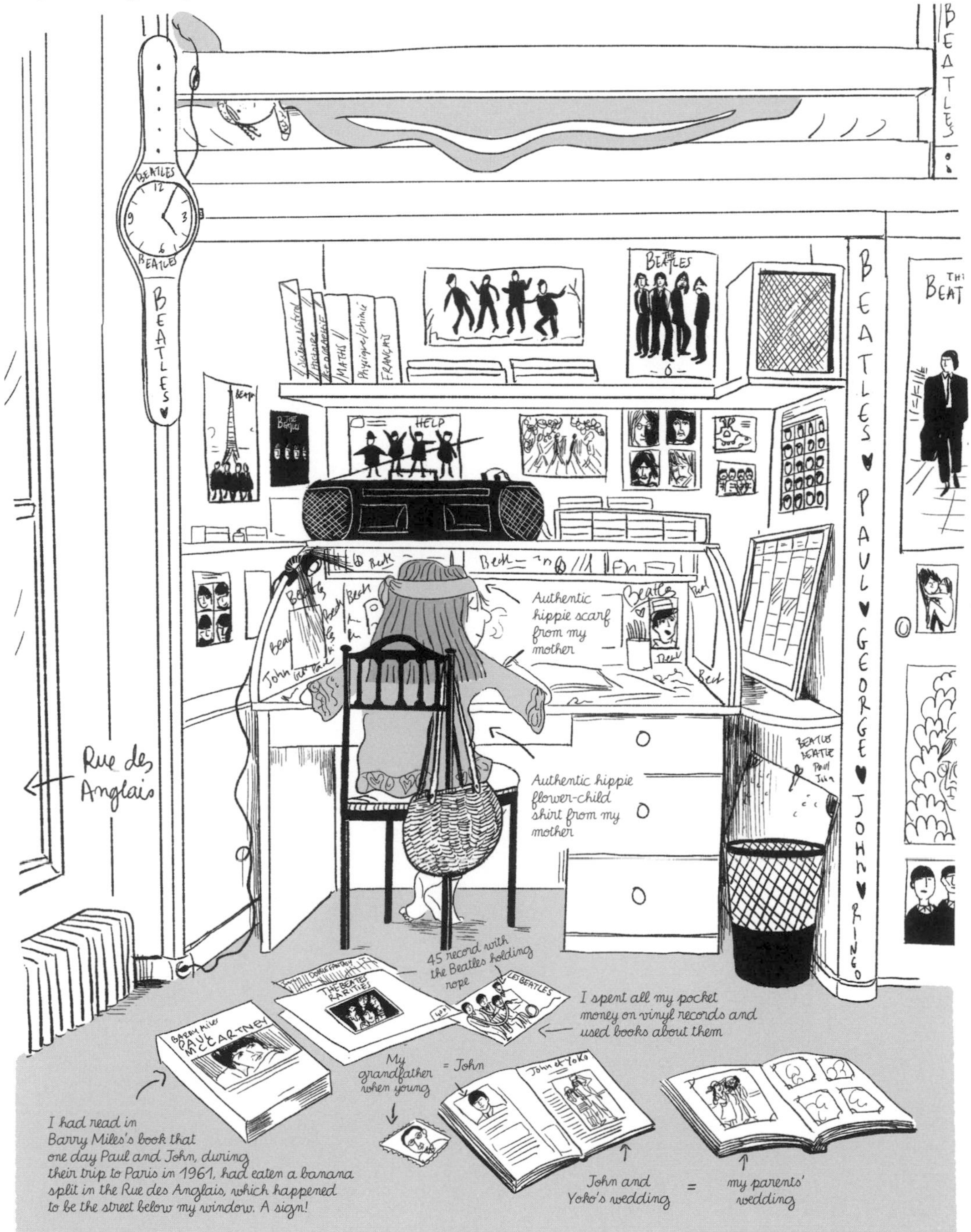
BEATLES
BEATLES
BEATLES
THE BEATLES
HELP
MATHS
Physique/chimie
FRANÇAIS
BEATLES
PAUL
GEORGE
JOHN
RINGO
Authentic hippie scarf from my mother
Authentic hippie flower-child shirt from my mother
Rue des Anglais
45 record with the Beatles holding rope
THE BEATLES RARITIES
LES BEATLES
I spent all my pocket money on vinyl records and used books about them
BARRY MILES PAUL McCARTNEY
My grandfather when young
= John
John et Yoko
I had read in Barry Miles's book that one day Paul and John, during their trip to Paris in 1961, had eaten a banana split in the Rue des Anglais, which happened to be the street below my window. A sign!
John and Yoko's wedding
=
my parents' wedding

I was inventing a Beatles family tree for myself by looking for any similarity I could find.

All my friends had changed.

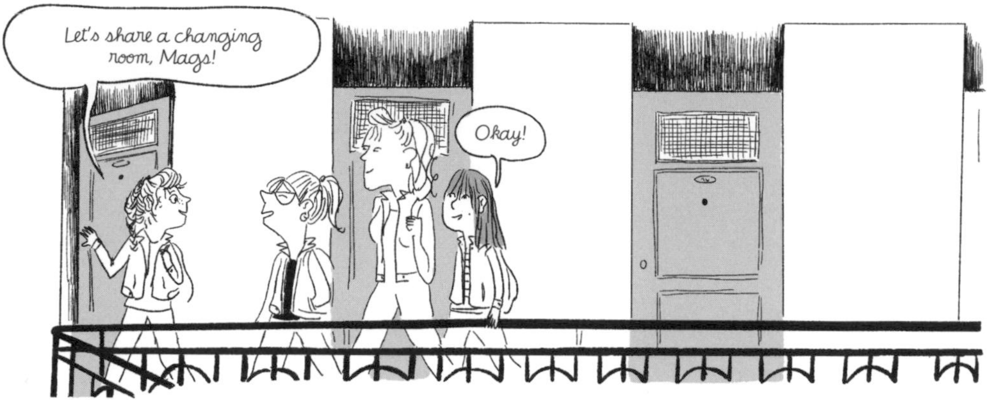
Let's share a changing room, Mags!
Okay!

Even Agatha.

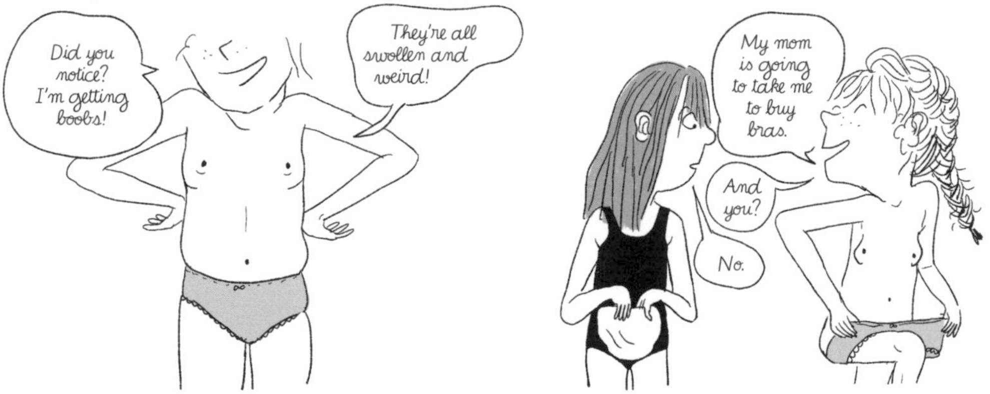
Did you notice? I'm getting boobs!
They're all swollen and weird!
My mom is going to take me to buy bras.
And you?
No.

They seemed to think it was funny.

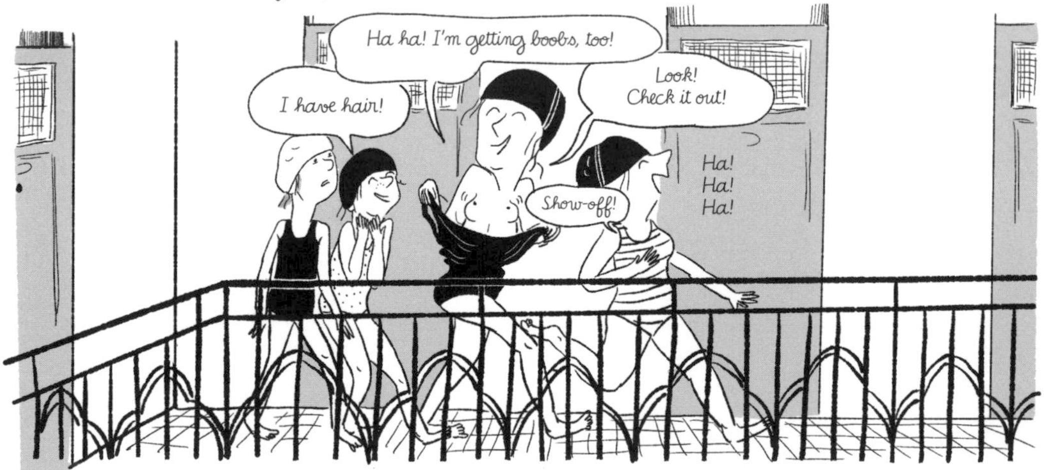
Ha ha! I'm getting boobs, too!
I have hair!
Look! Check it out!
Show-off!
Ha! Ha! Ha!

But all that stuff was out of the question for me.

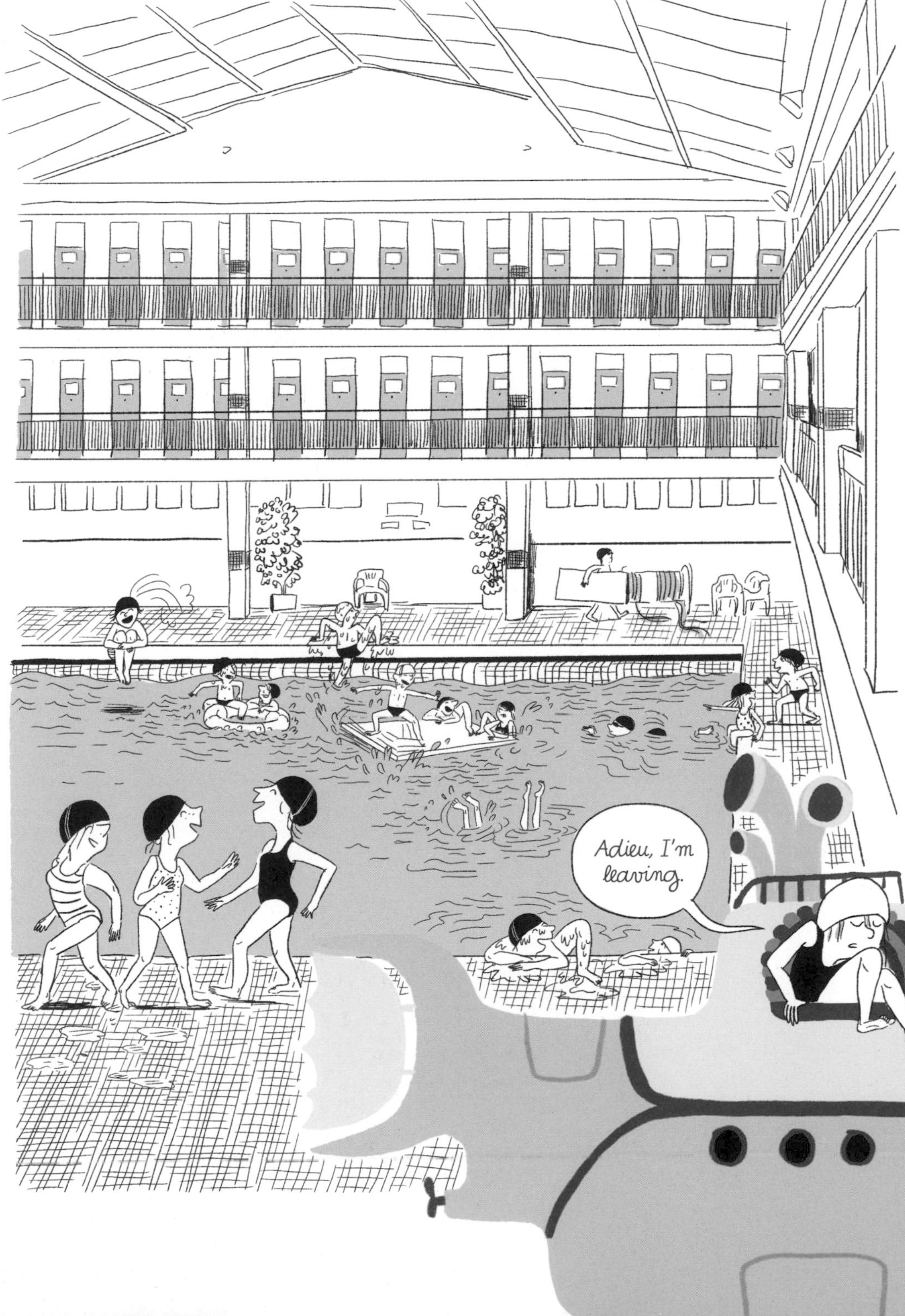
Adieu, I'm leaving.

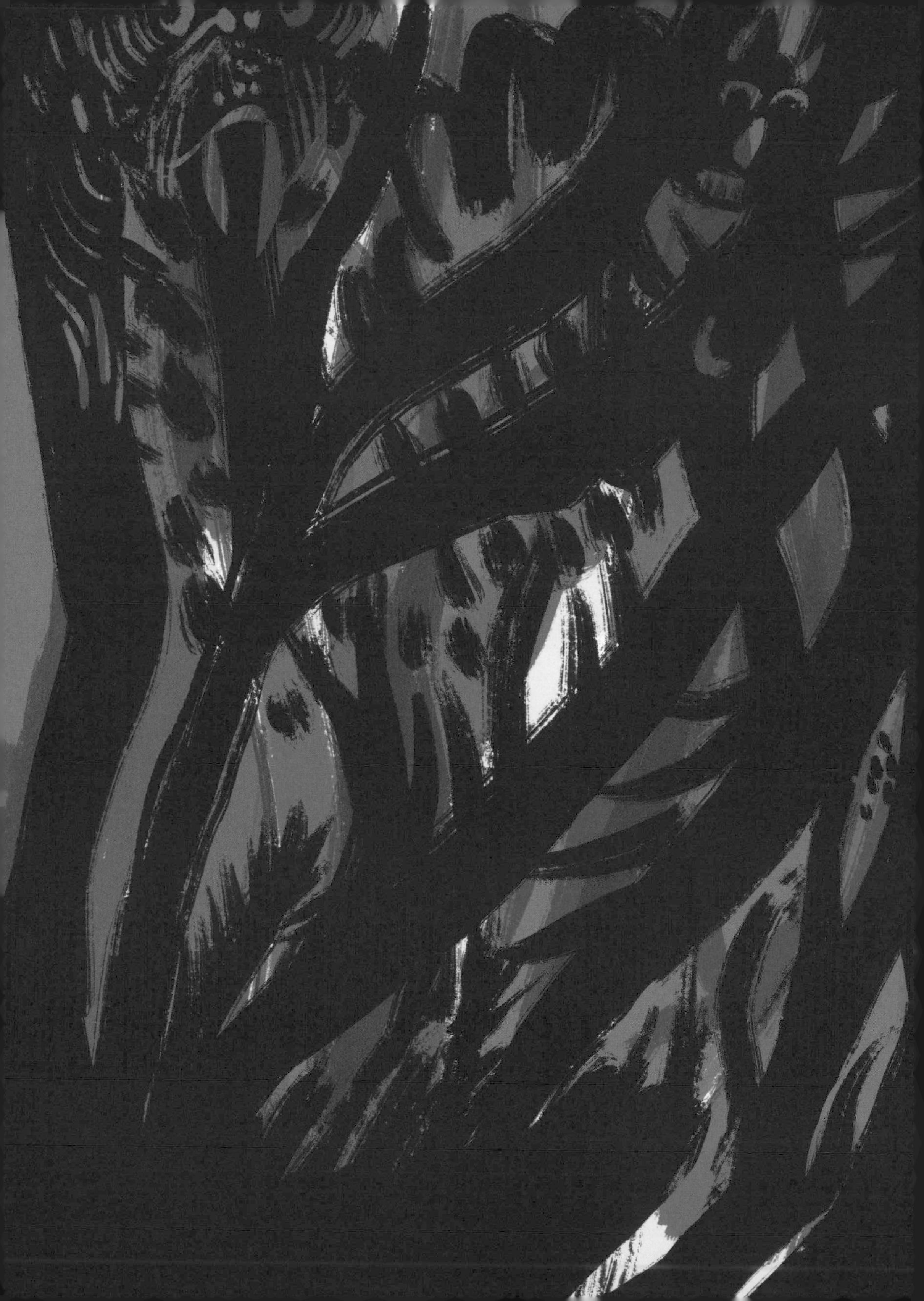

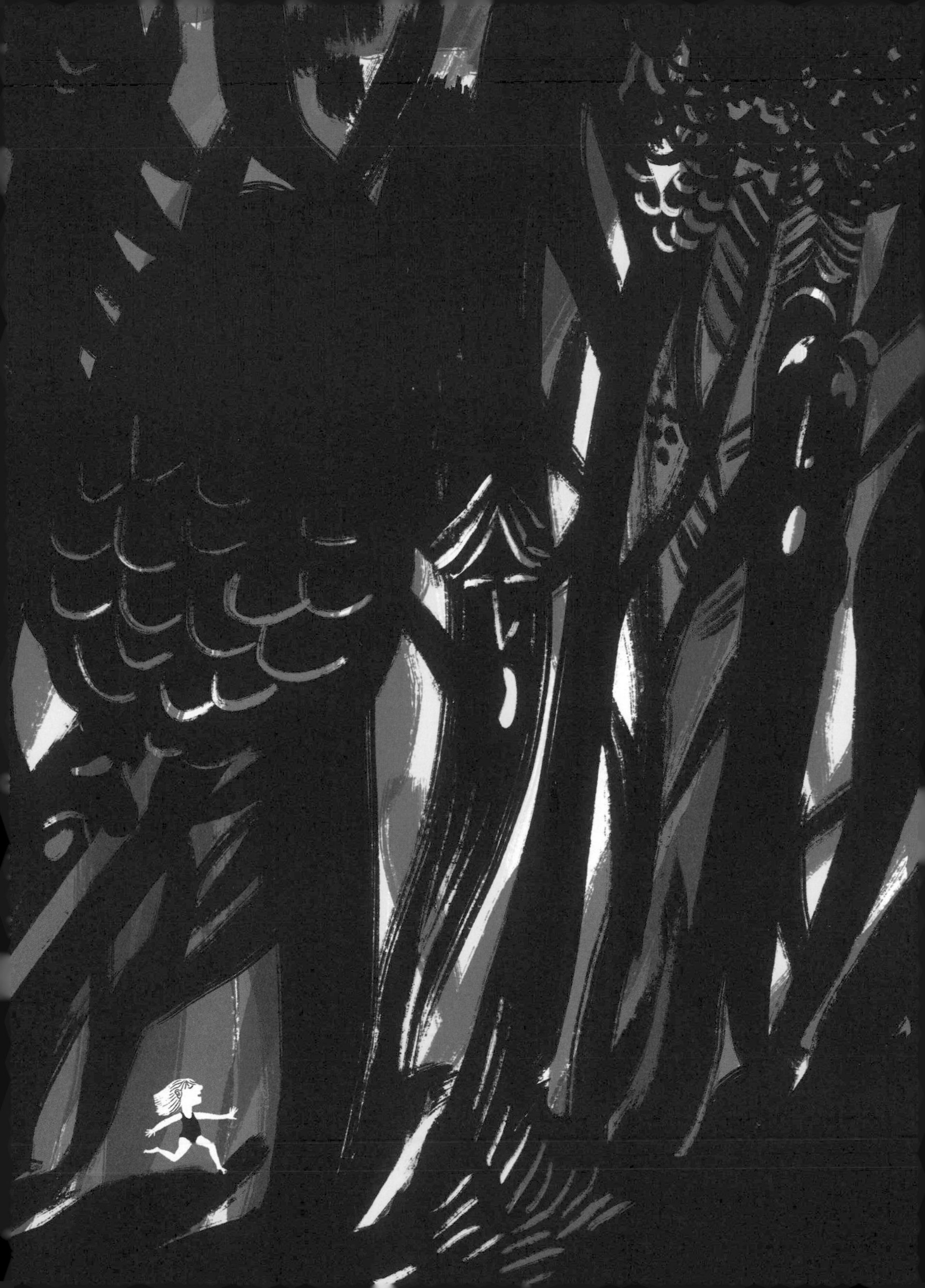

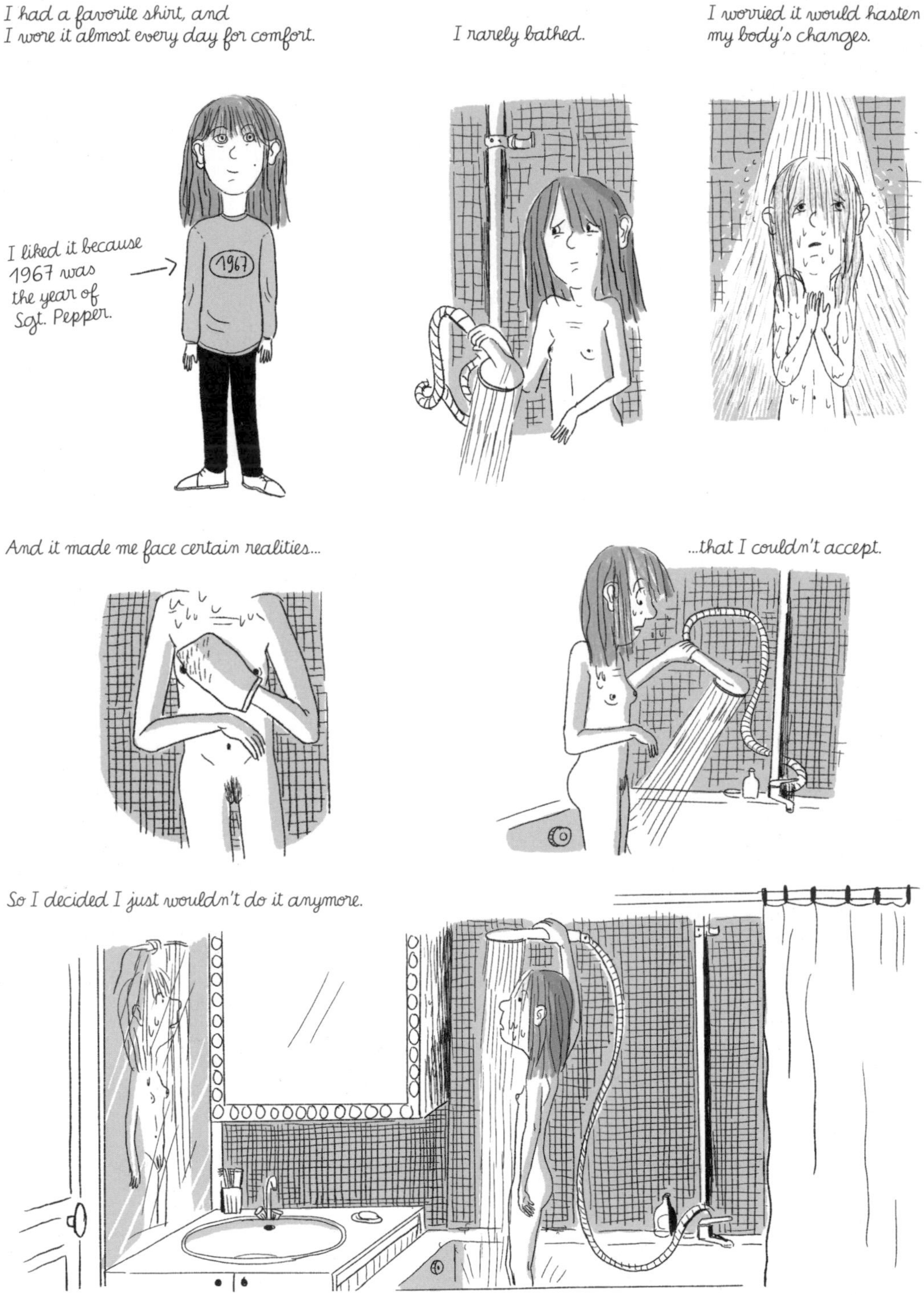
I had a favorite shirt, and
I wore it almost every day for comfort.
I liked it because 1967 was the year of Sgt. Pepper.
1967
I rarely bathed.
I worried it would hasten
my body's changes.
And it made me face certain realities...
...that I couldn't accept.
So I decided I just wouldn't do it anymore.

To make up for it, I washed my jeans every day.

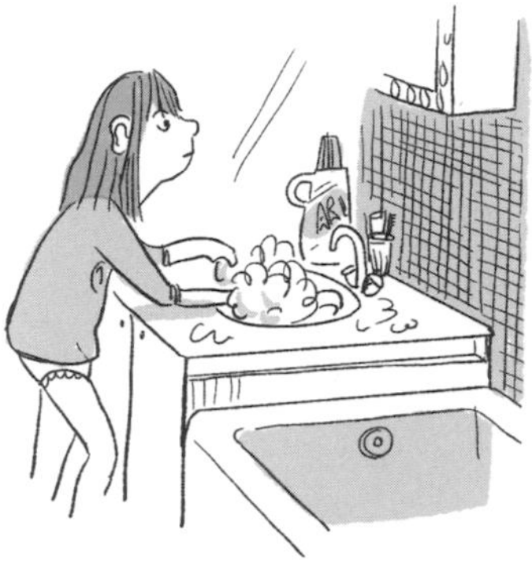

I'd dry them overnight.

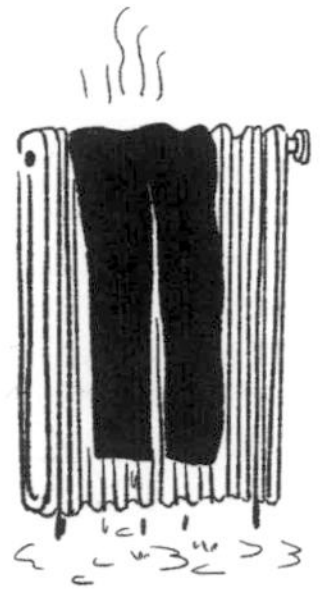

And I washed my hair every day, too.

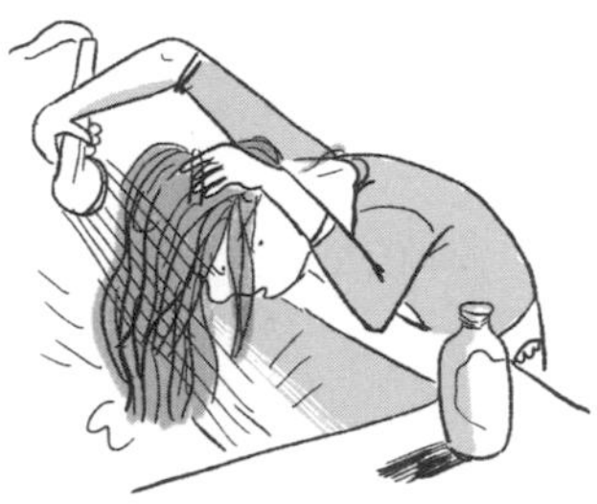

Things got complicated on December 8, 1991.

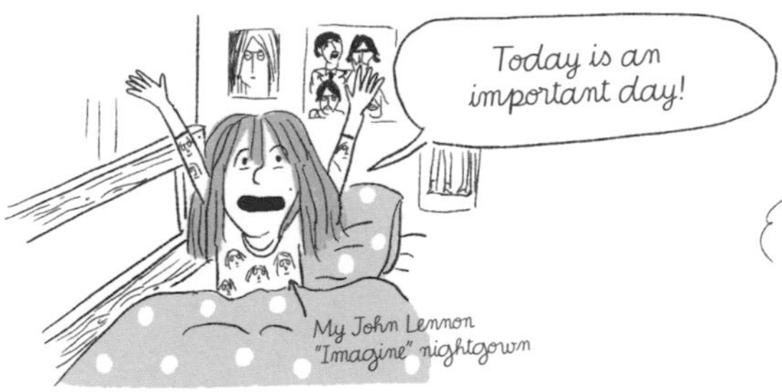
Today is an important day!
My John Lennon "Imagine" nightgown

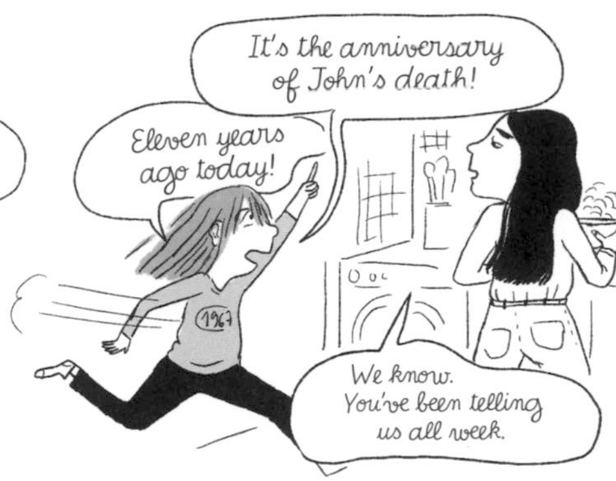
It's the anniversary of John's death!
Eleven years ago today!
1967
We know. You've been telling us all week.

I thought about John all day.

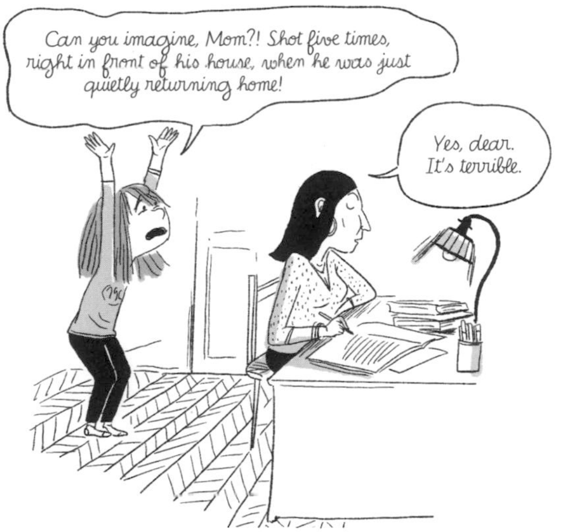
Can you imagine, Mom?! Shot five times, right in front of his house, when he was just quietly returning home!
Yes, dear. It's terrible.

All day, I waited impatiently for 11 p.m., the hour of his death, to be in total extrasensory symbiosis.

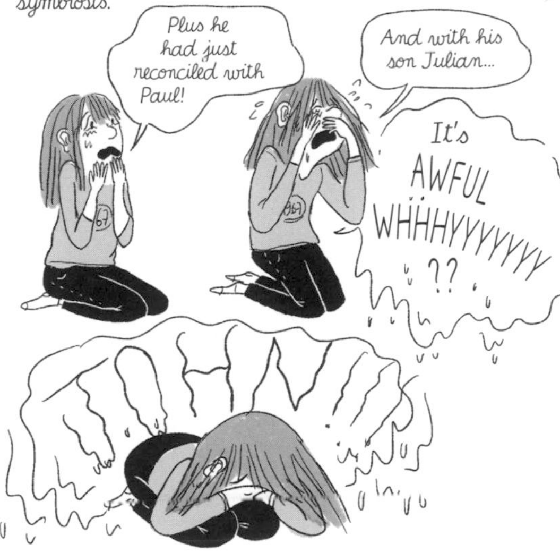
Plus he had just reconciled with Paul!
And with his son Julian...
It's AWFUL WHHHYYYYYYY ??

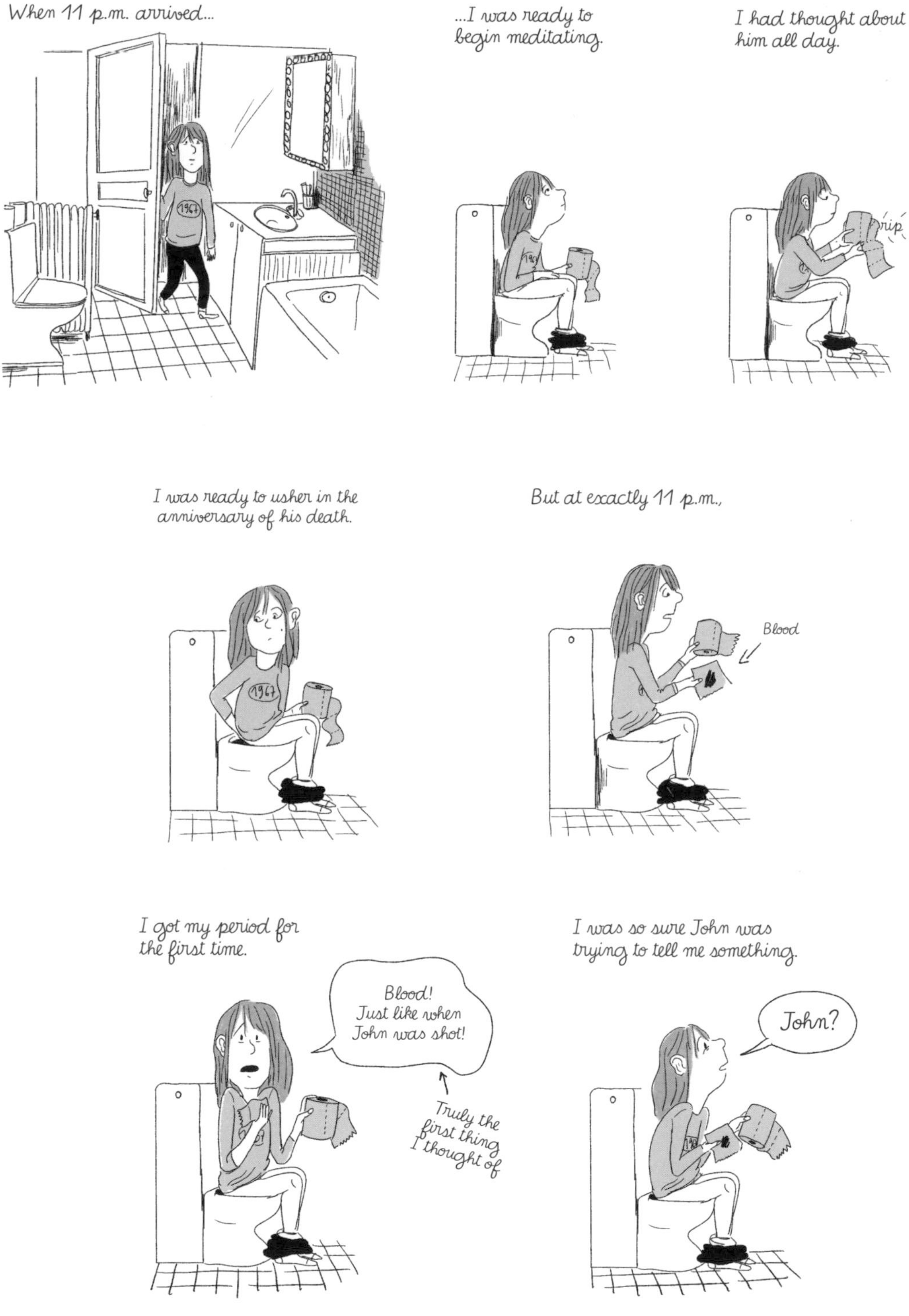
When 11 p.m. arrived...
...I was ready to begin meditating.
I had thought about him all day.
rip
I was ready to usher in the anniversary of his death.
But at exactly 11 p.m.,
Blood
I got my period for the first time.
Blood! Just like when John was shot!
Truly the first thing I thought of
I was so sure John was trying to tell me something.
John?

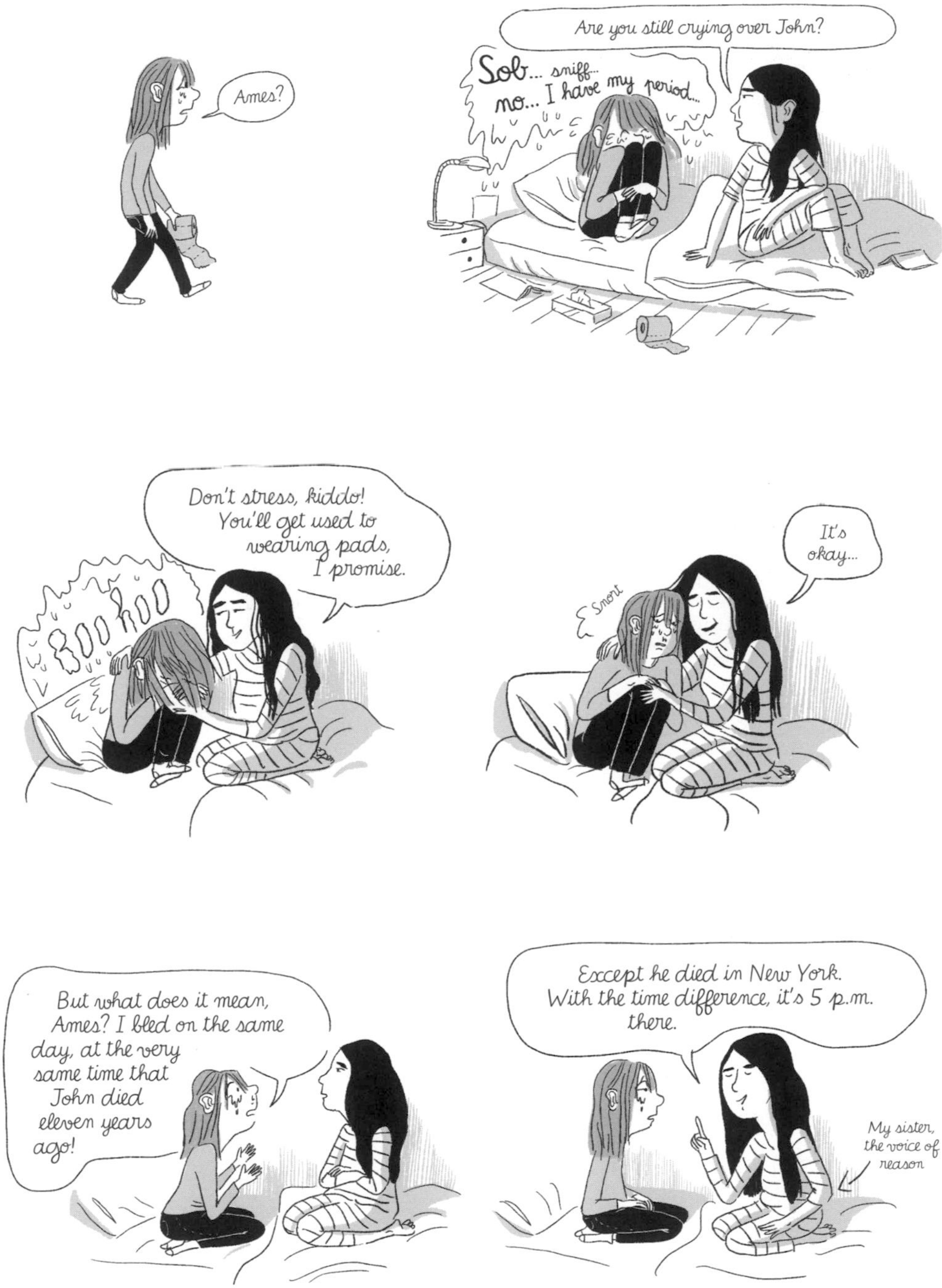

Ames?
Are you still crying over John?
Sob... sniff... no... I have my period...
BOO HOO
Don't stress, kiddo! You'll get used to wearing pads, I promise.
Snort
It's okay...
But what does it mean, Ames? I bled on the same day, at the very same time that John died eleven years ago!
Except he died in New York. With the time difference, it's 5 p.m. there.
My sister, the voice of reason

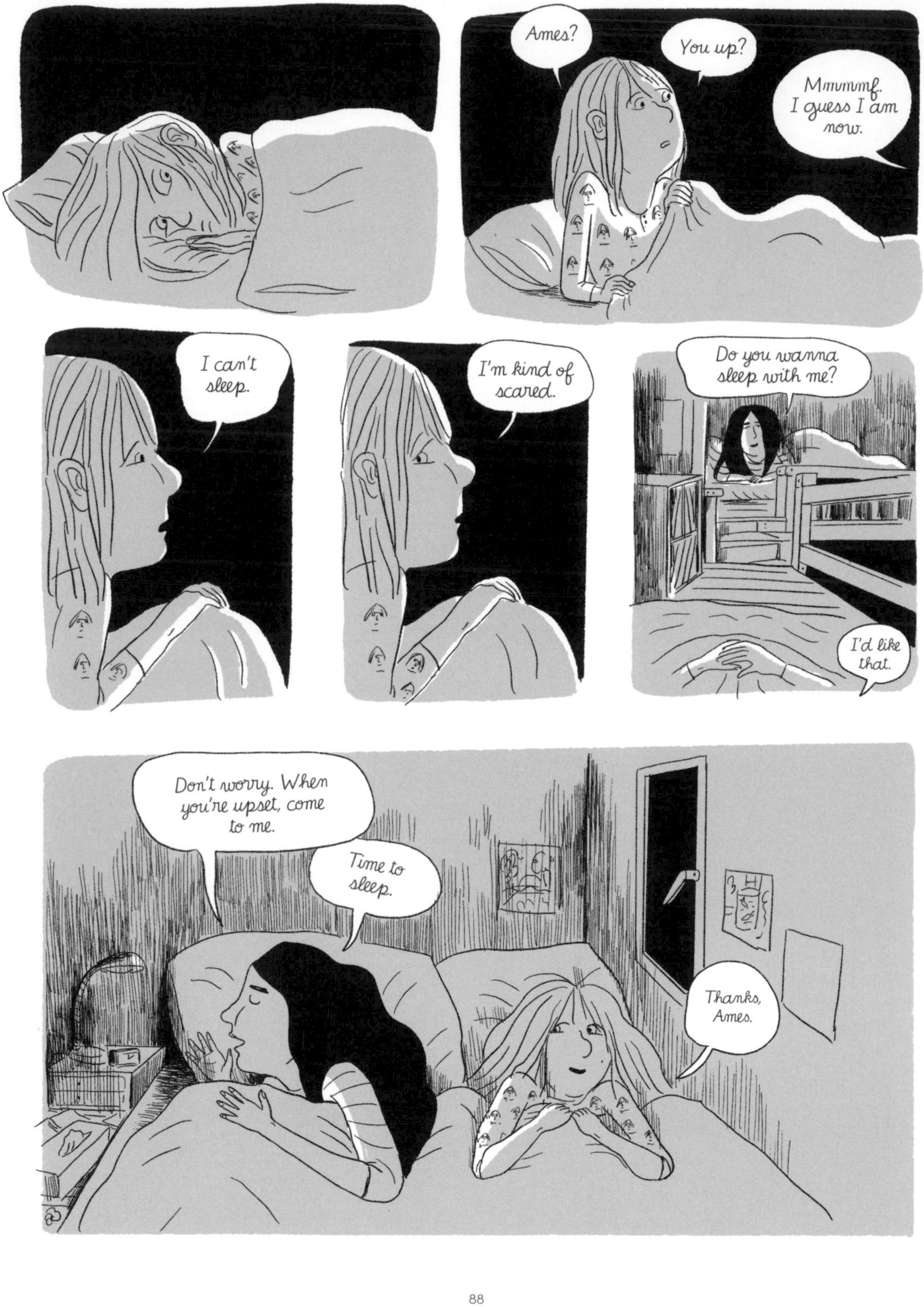
Ames?
You up?
Mmmmf. I guess I am now.
I can't sleep.
I'm kind of scared.
Do you wanna sleep with me?
I'd like that.
Don't worry. When you're upset, come to me.
Time to sleep.
Thanks, Ames.

I had to get rid of any and all evidence that my body was changing.

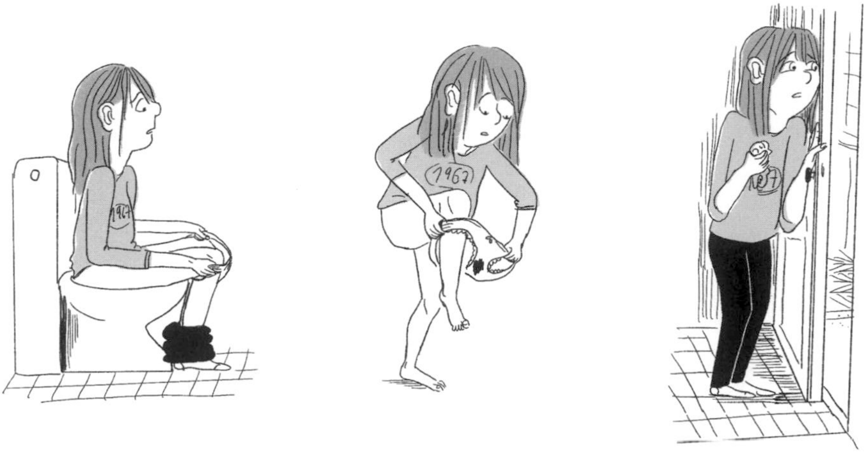

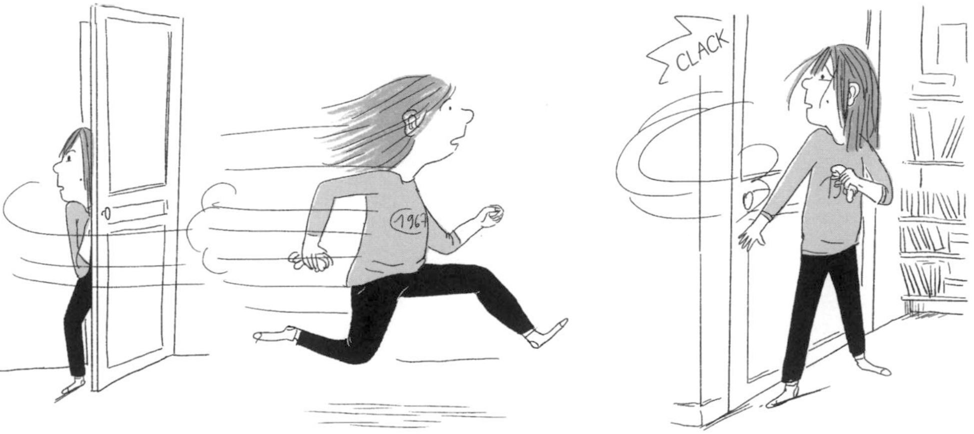
CLACK

I found a hiding place for my
blood-stained underwear.

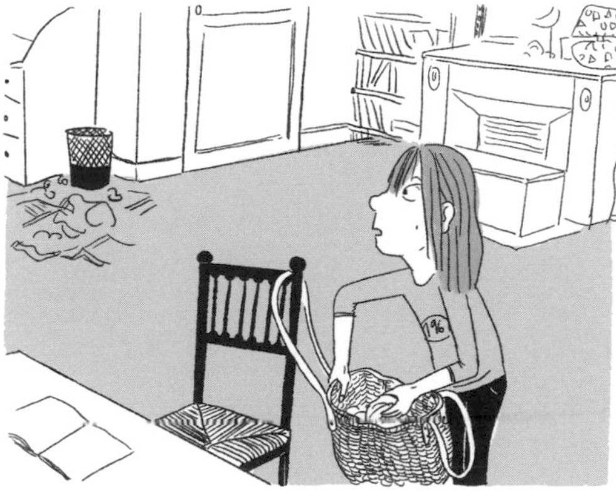

But eventually the bag filled up.
Only I knew what was inside it.

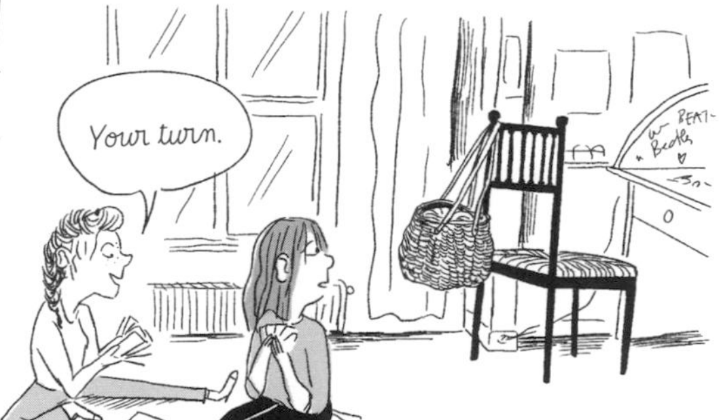
Your turn.

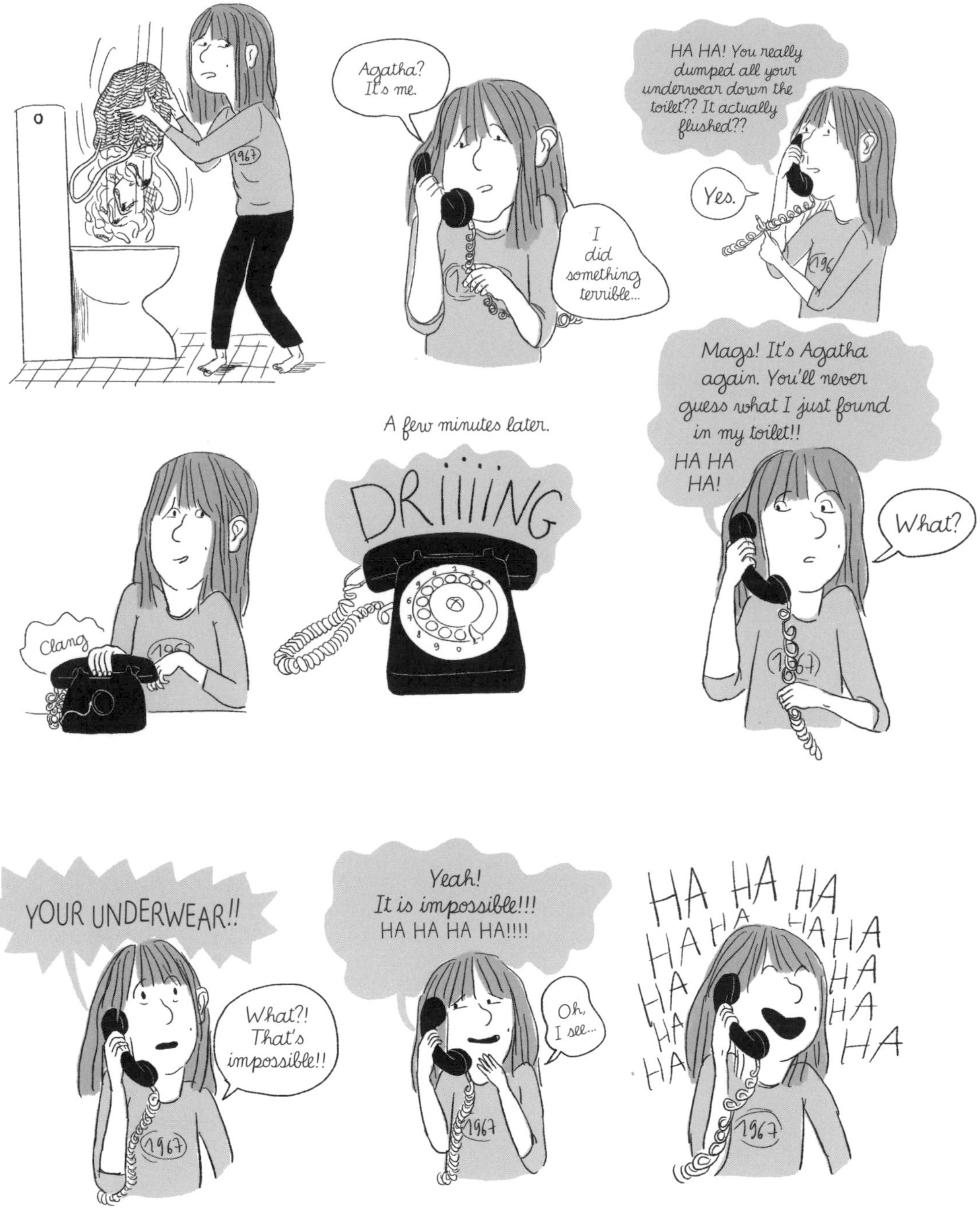
Agatha? It's me.
I did something terrible...
HA HA! You really dumped all your underwear down the toilet?? It actually flushed??
Yes.
A few minutes later.
DRIIIING
Clang
Mags! It's Agatha again. You'll never guess what I just found in my toilet!! HA HA HA!
What?
YOUR UNDERWEAR!!
What?! That's impossible!!
Yeah! It is impossible!!! HA HA HA HA!!!!
Oh, I see...
HA HA HA HA HA HA HA HA HA HA HA HA HA HA HA

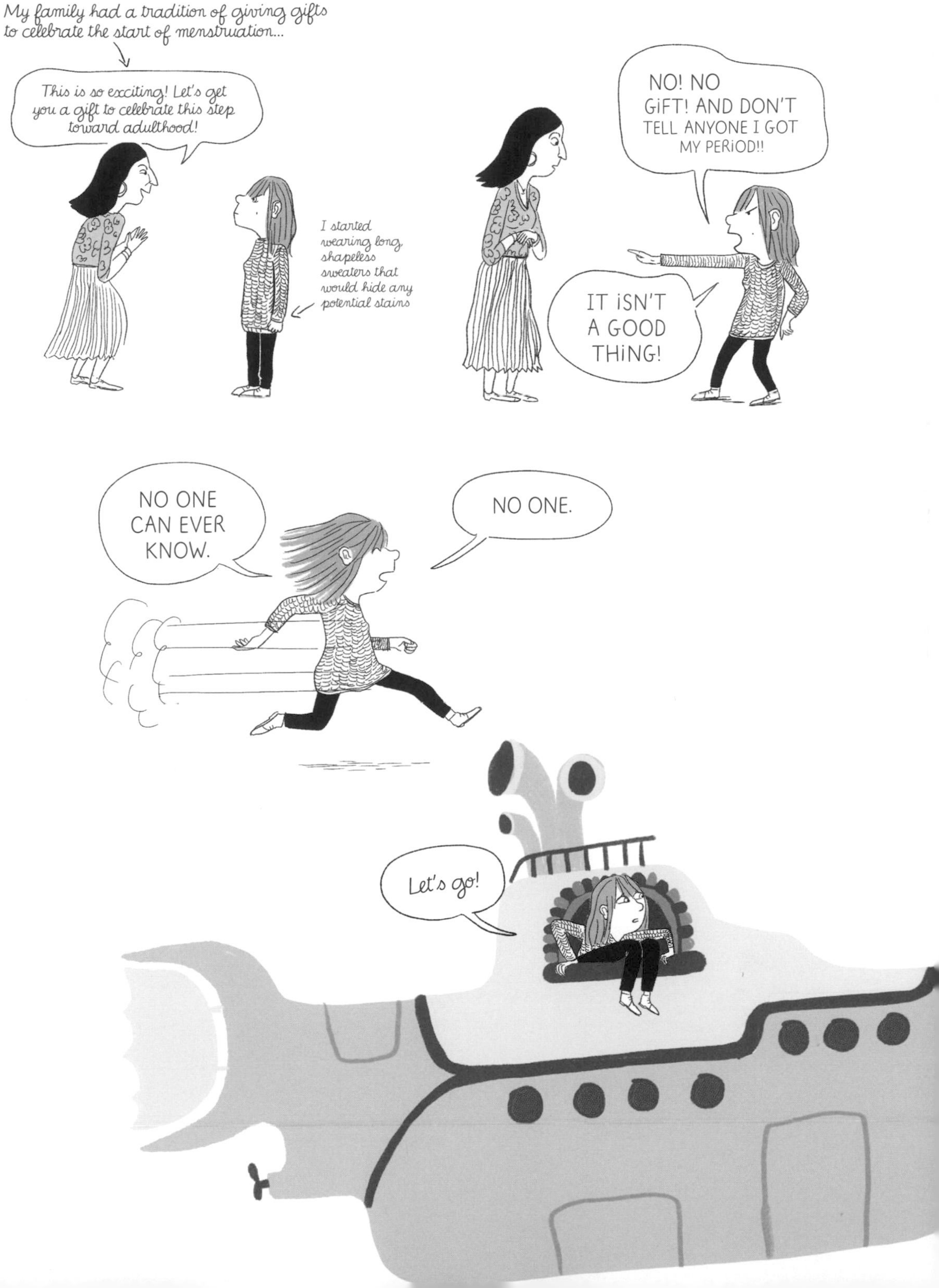
My family had a tradition of giving gifts to celebrate the start of menstruation...
This is so exciting! Let's get you a gift to celebrate this step toward adulthood!
I started wearing long shapeless sweaters that would hide any potential stains
NO! NO GIFT! AND DON'T TELL ANYONE I GOT MY PERIOD!!
IT ISN'T A GOOD THING!
NO ONE CAN EVER KNOW.
NO ONE.
Let's go!

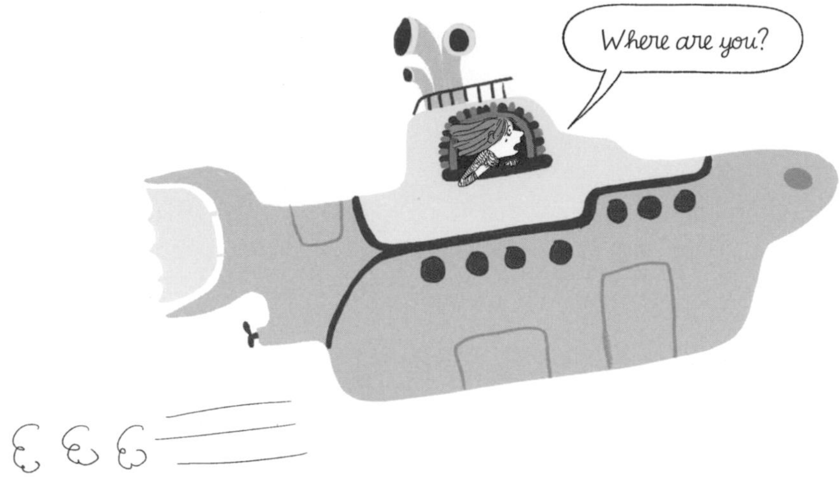
Where are you?

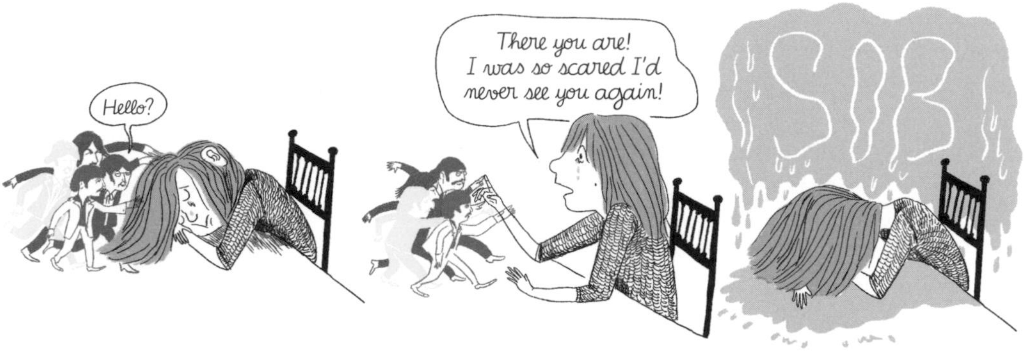
Hello?
There you are! I was so scared I'd never see you again!
SOB

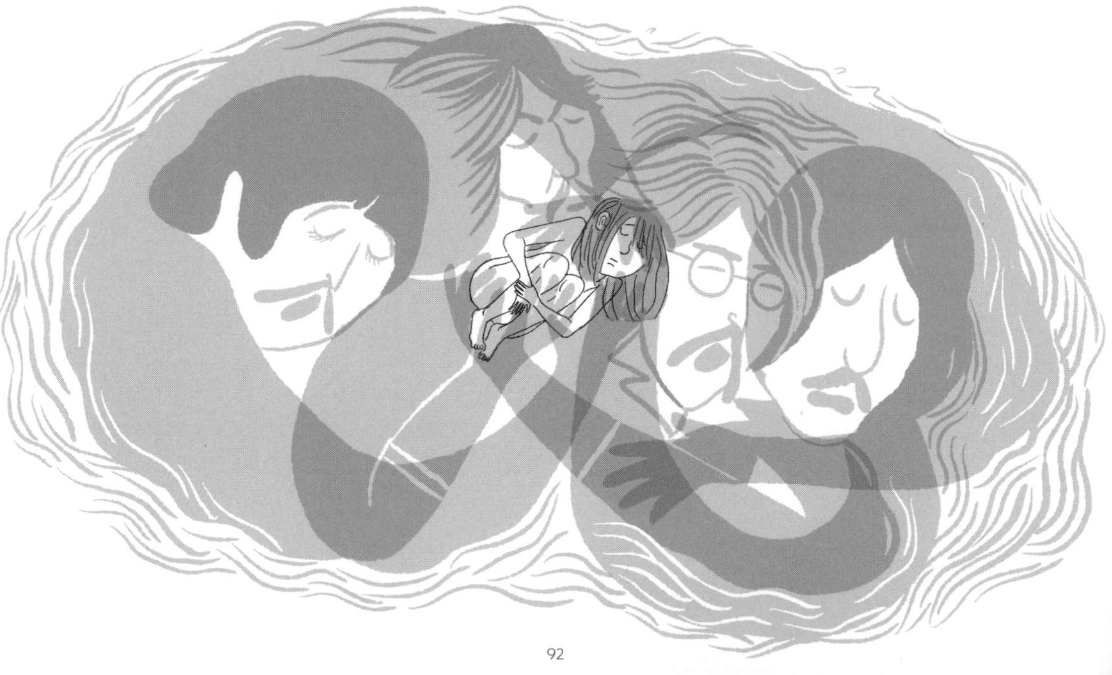

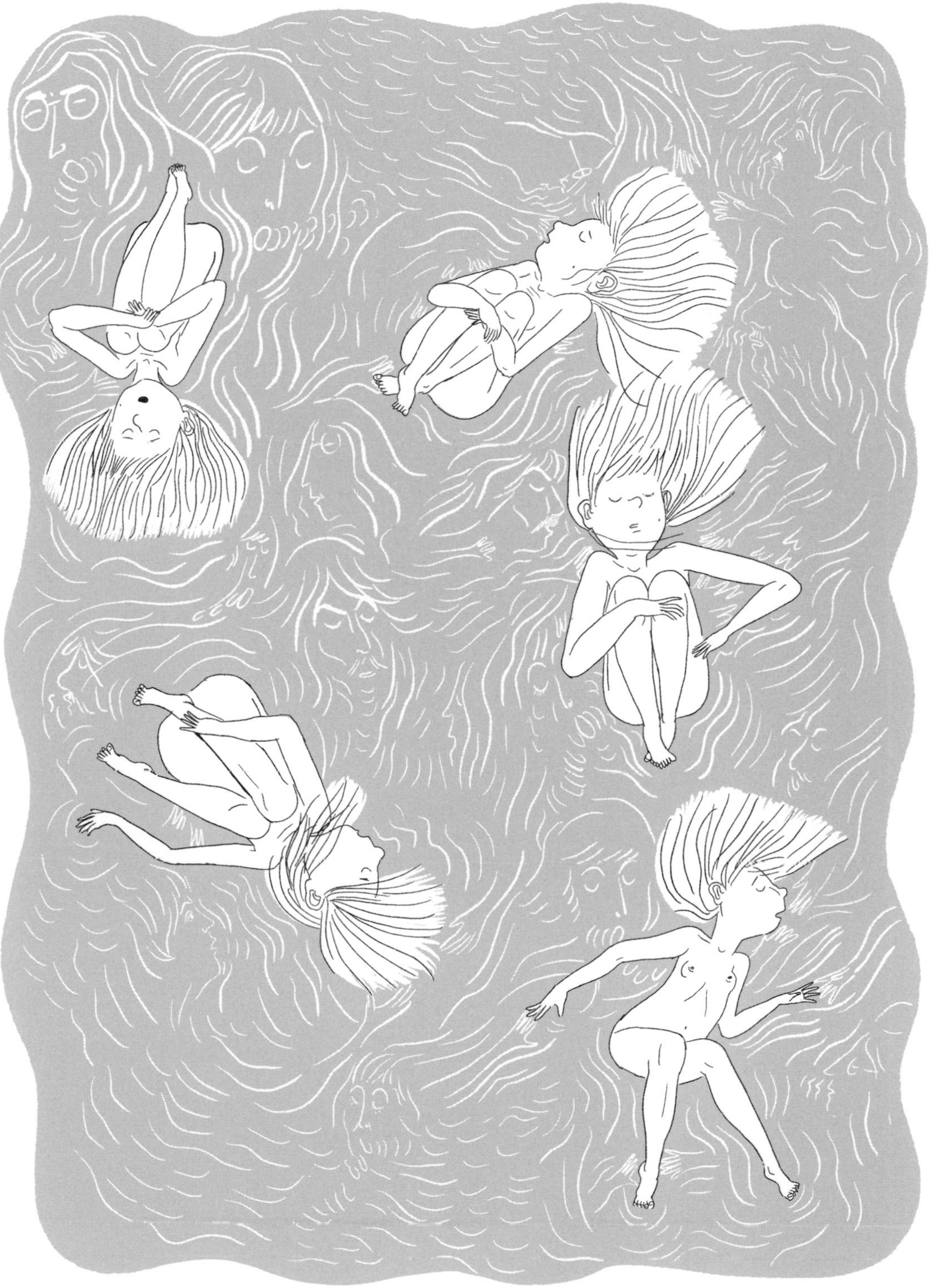

Even though my calendar was still full of activities,
I spent my seventh-grade year almost entirely alone.

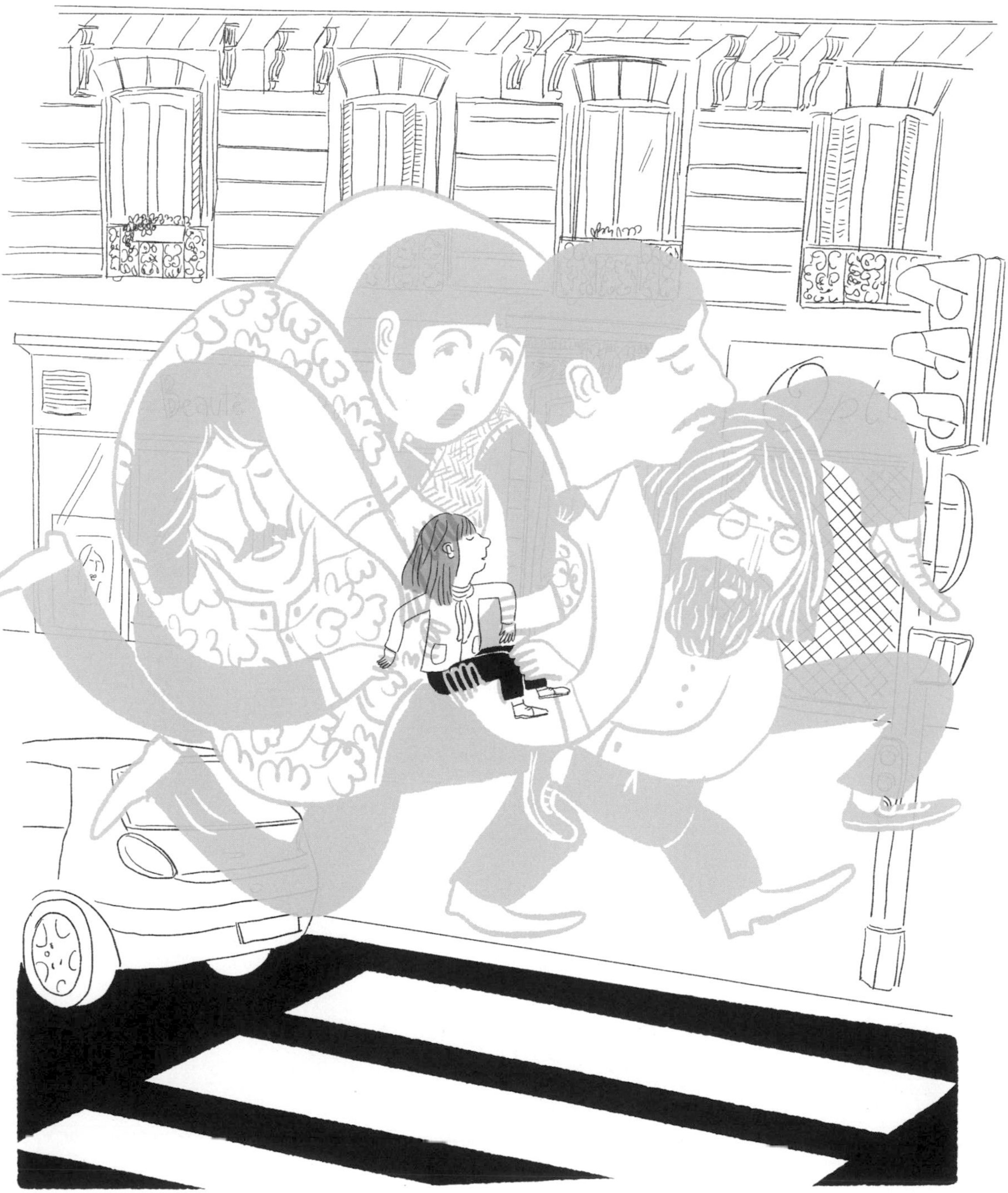
Beauté

I still went to dance class.

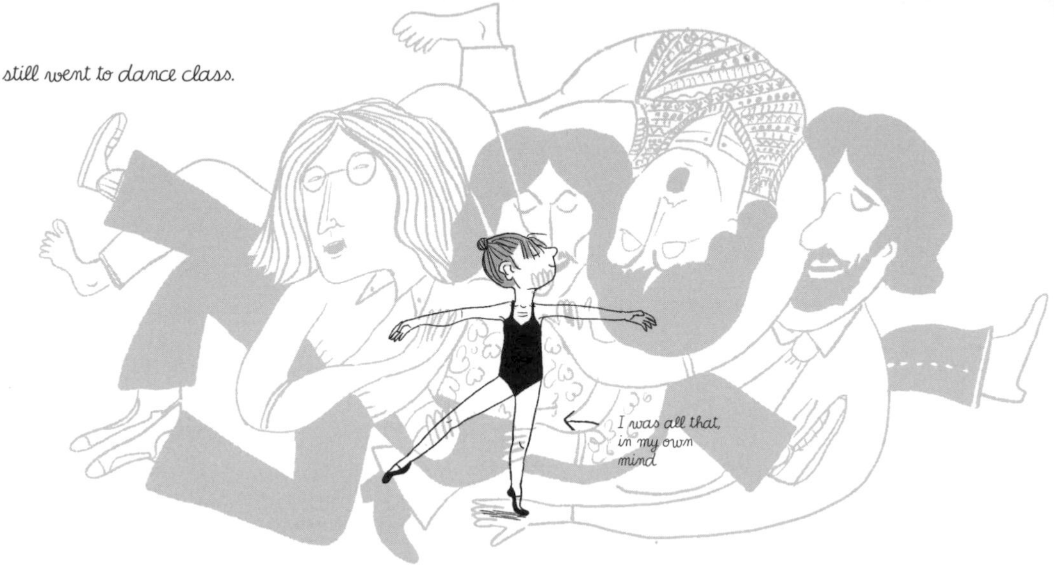
I was all that, in my own mind

I went to my painting class more than ever.

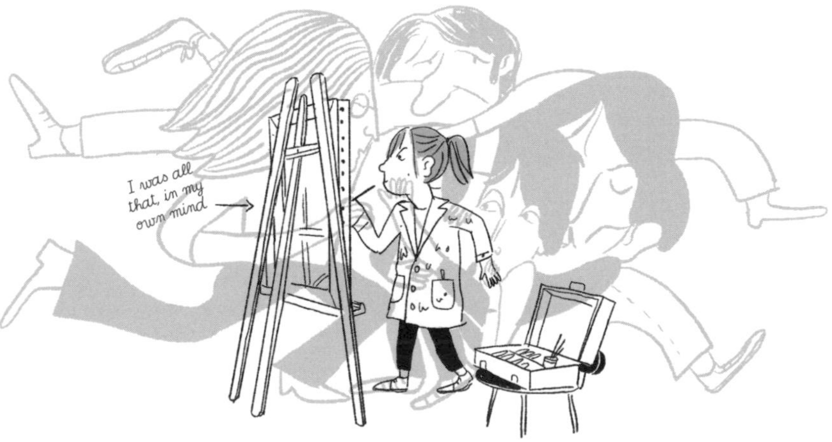
I was all that, in my own mind

And I went to acting class. There were a lot of kids there who seemed cool.

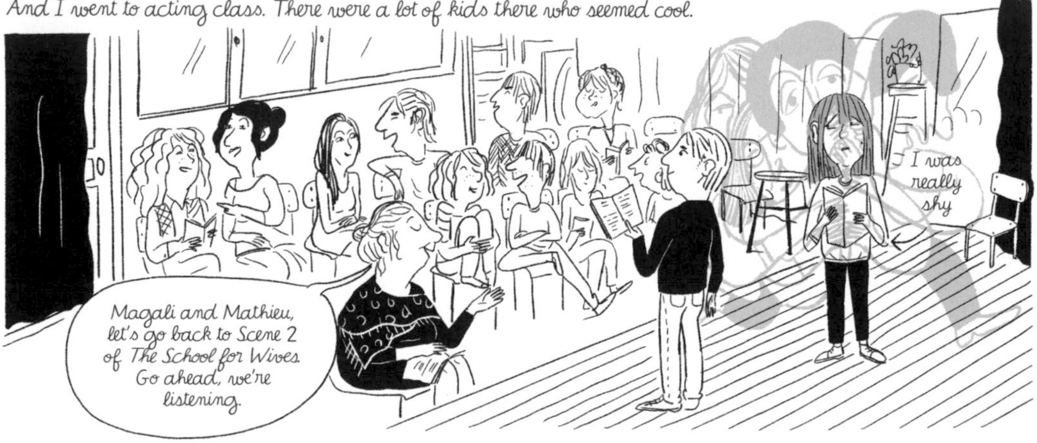
I was really shy
Magali and Mathieu, let's go back to Scene 2 of The School for Wives Go ahead, we're listening.

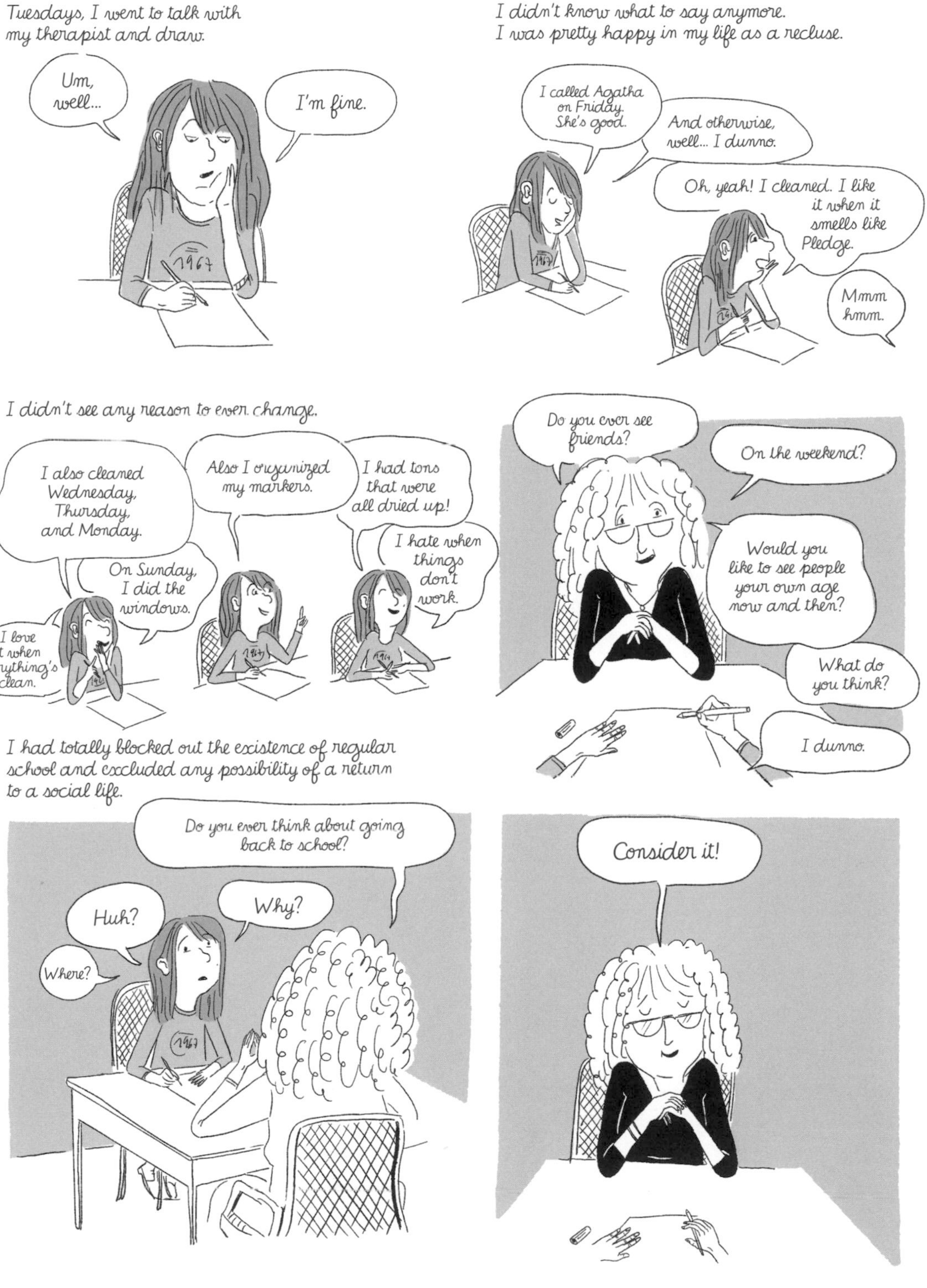
Tuesdays, I went to talk with my therapist and draw.
Um, well...
I'm fine.
I didn't know what to say anymore. I was pretty happy in my life as a recluse.
I called Agatha on Friday. She's good.
And otherwise, well... I dunno.
Oh, yeah! I cleaned. I like it when it smells like Pledge.
Mmm hmm.
I didn't see any reason to ever change.
I also cleaned Wednesday, Thursday, and Monday.
On Sunday, I did the windows.
I love it when everything's clean.
Also I organized my markers.
I had tons that were all dried up!
I hate when things don't work.
Do you ever see friends?
On the weekend?
Would you like to see people your own age now and then?
What do you think?
I dunno.
I had totally blocked out the existence of regular school and excluded any possibility of a return to a social life.
Do you ever think about going back to school?
Huh?
Why?
Where?
Consider it!

In the spring, we were set to do a performance at the Cité Universitaire theater.

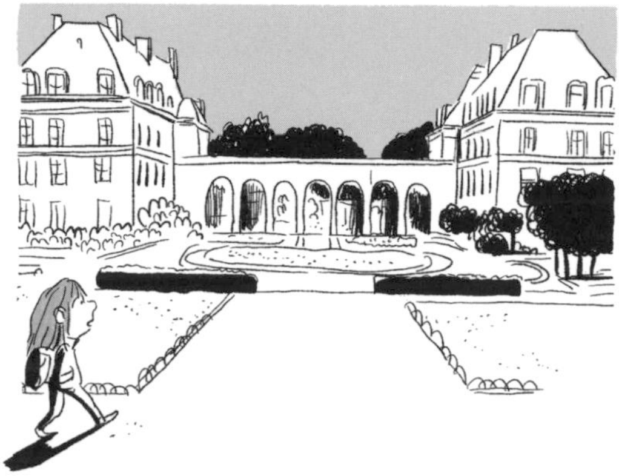

I was gonna act for real, on a stage in front of an audience, with all the cool kids from class. The day before, there was a dress rehearsal.

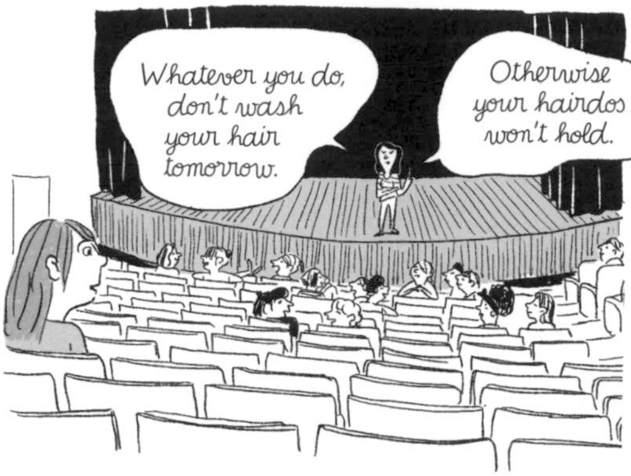

Whatever you do, don't wash your hair tomorrow.
Otherwise your hairdos won't hold.

We rehearsed in costume, with our hair done. Everyone was laughing and acting like good friends.

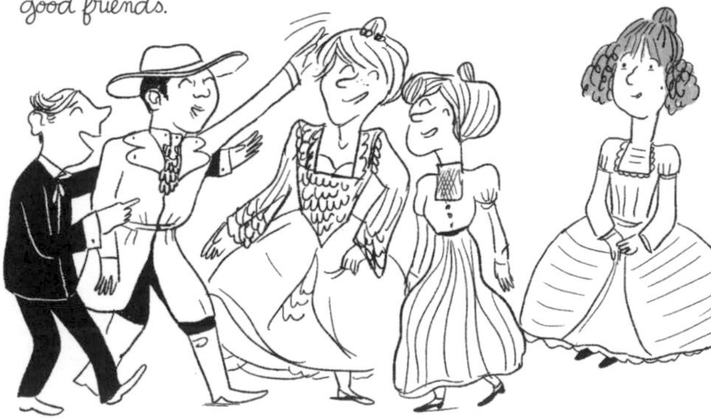

I knew my lines by heart.

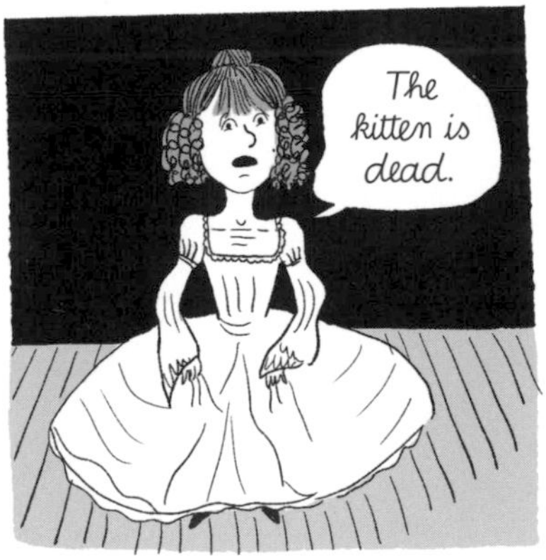

The kitten is dead.

At lunch, everyone formed groups to eat together. Since I didn't dare go up to anyone, I just stood frozen by the vending machine, alone, telling myself a soft drink would be an adequate lunch.

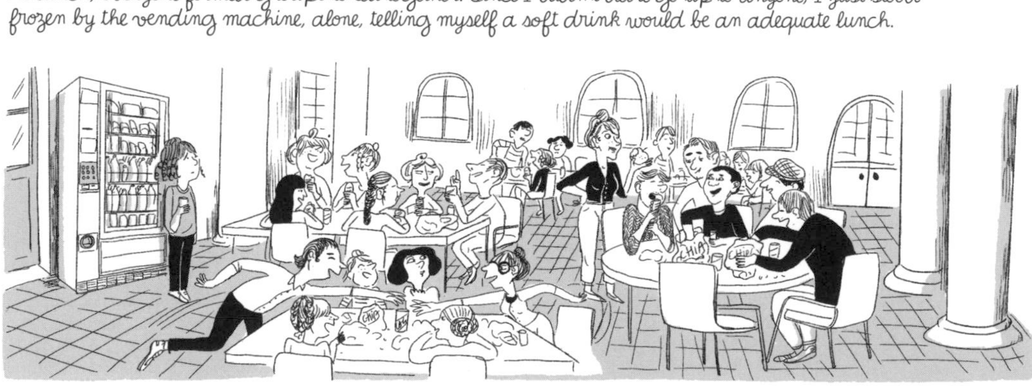

That day I realized something:

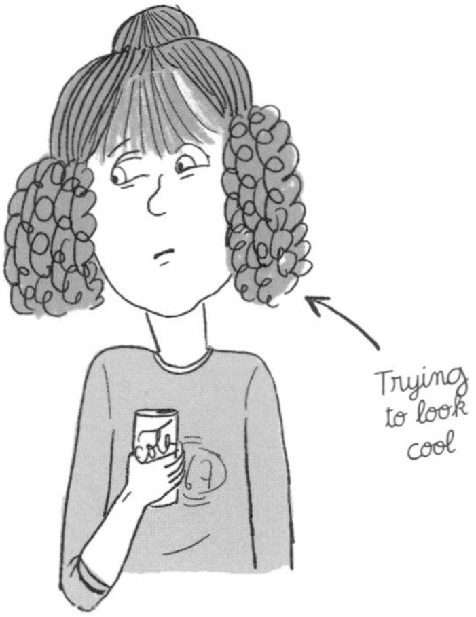
Trying to look cool

I had succeeded perfectly...

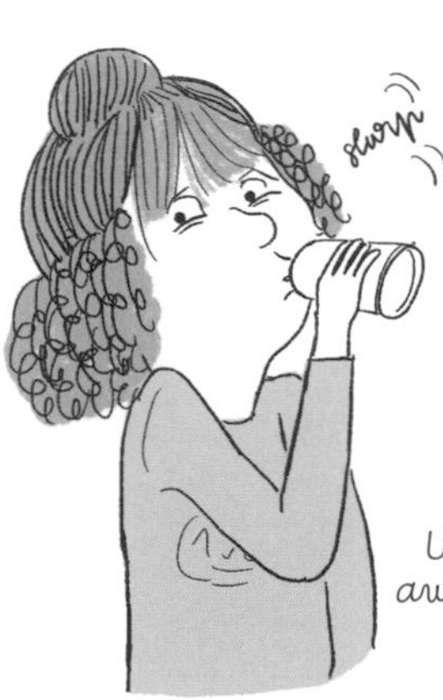

...at completely isolating myself.

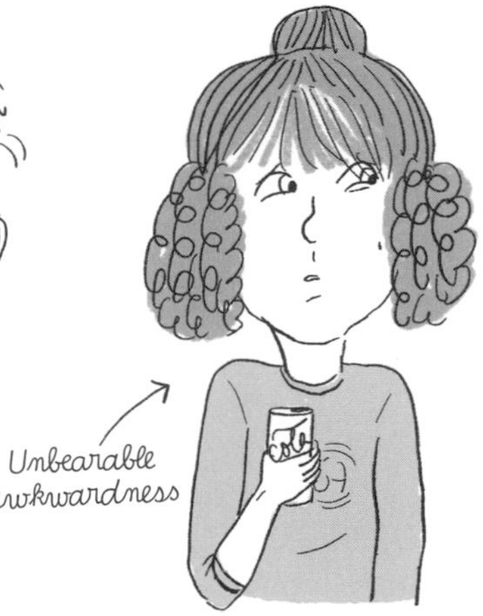
Unbearable awkwardness

I figured the Beatles hadn't been the types to stay like that, alone, standing next to a vending machine.

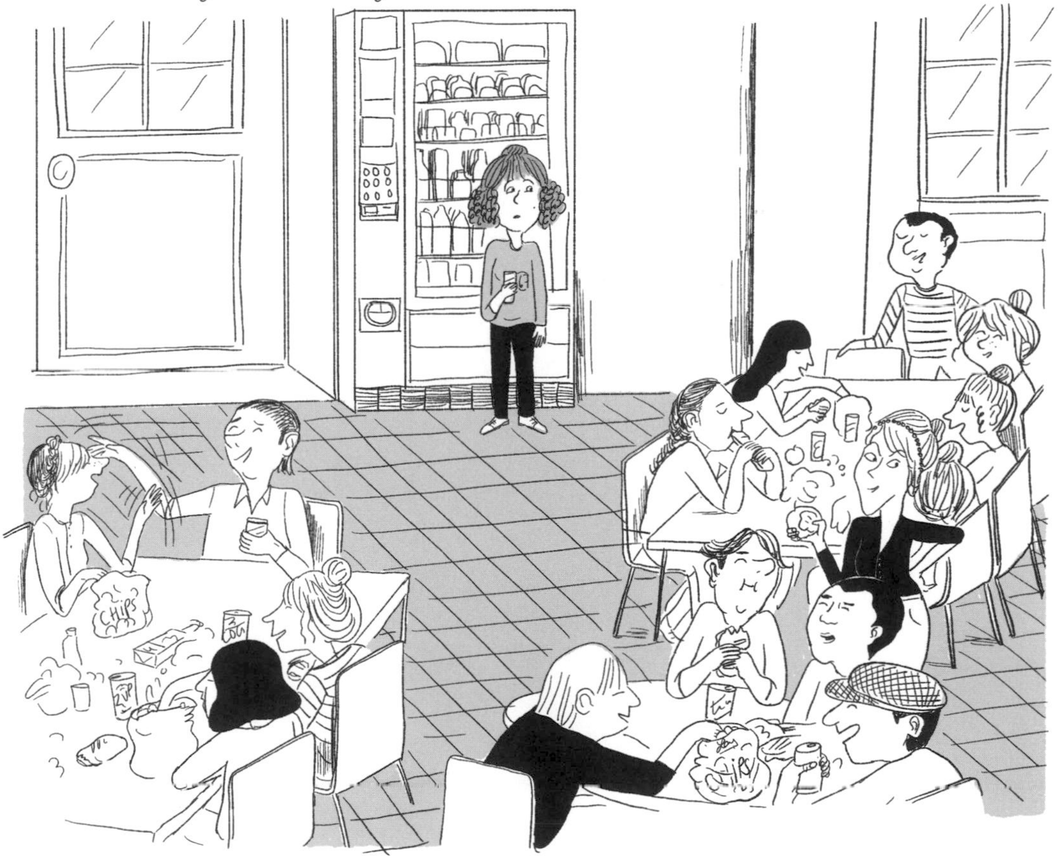
CHIPS
CHIPS

I was so good at isolating myself...

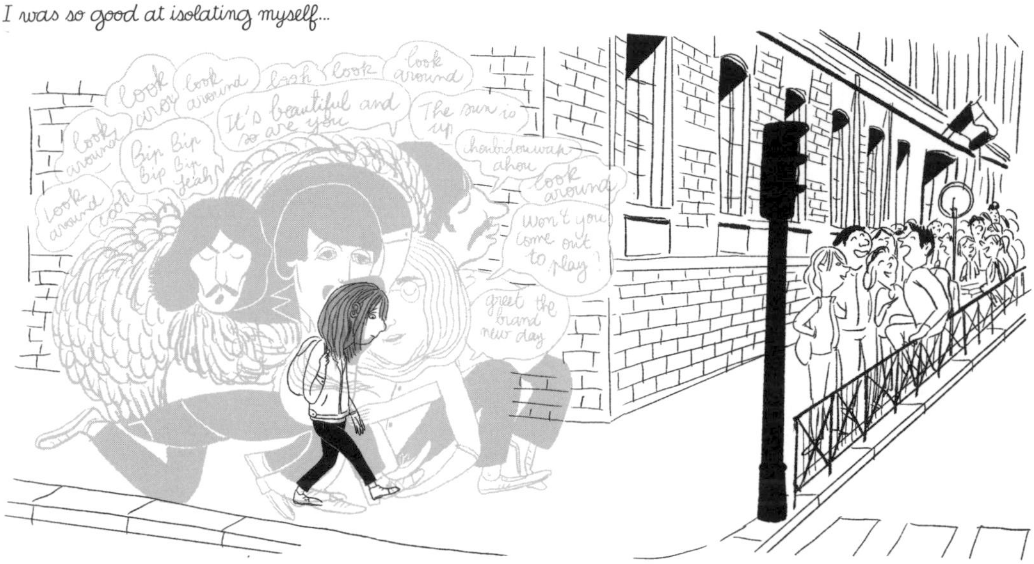
look around
look arou
look around
look look
look around
It's beautiful and so are you
The sun is up
look around
Bip Bip Bip Bip Yeah
look around
look around
Won't you come out to play!
greet the brand new day

...that I had become afraid of other people.

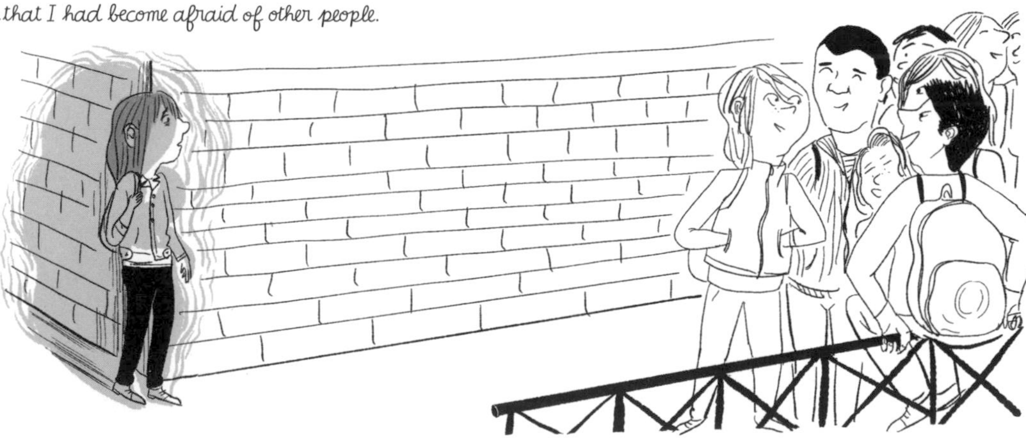

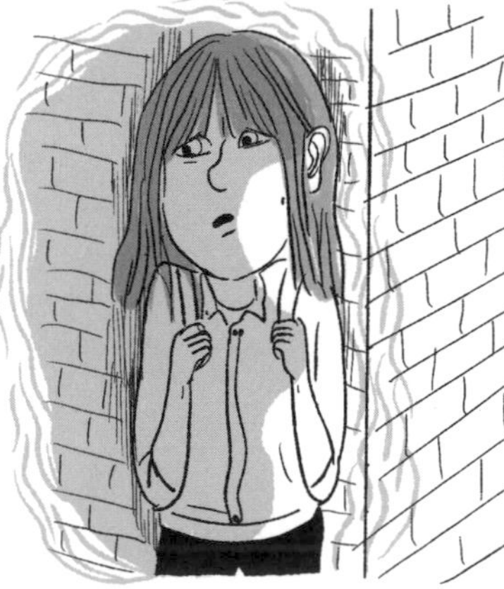

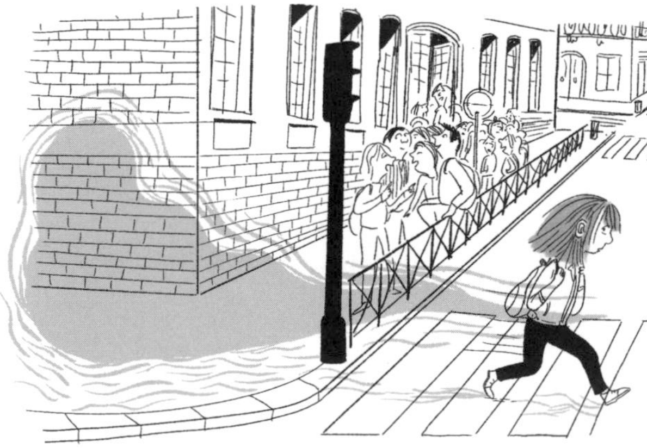

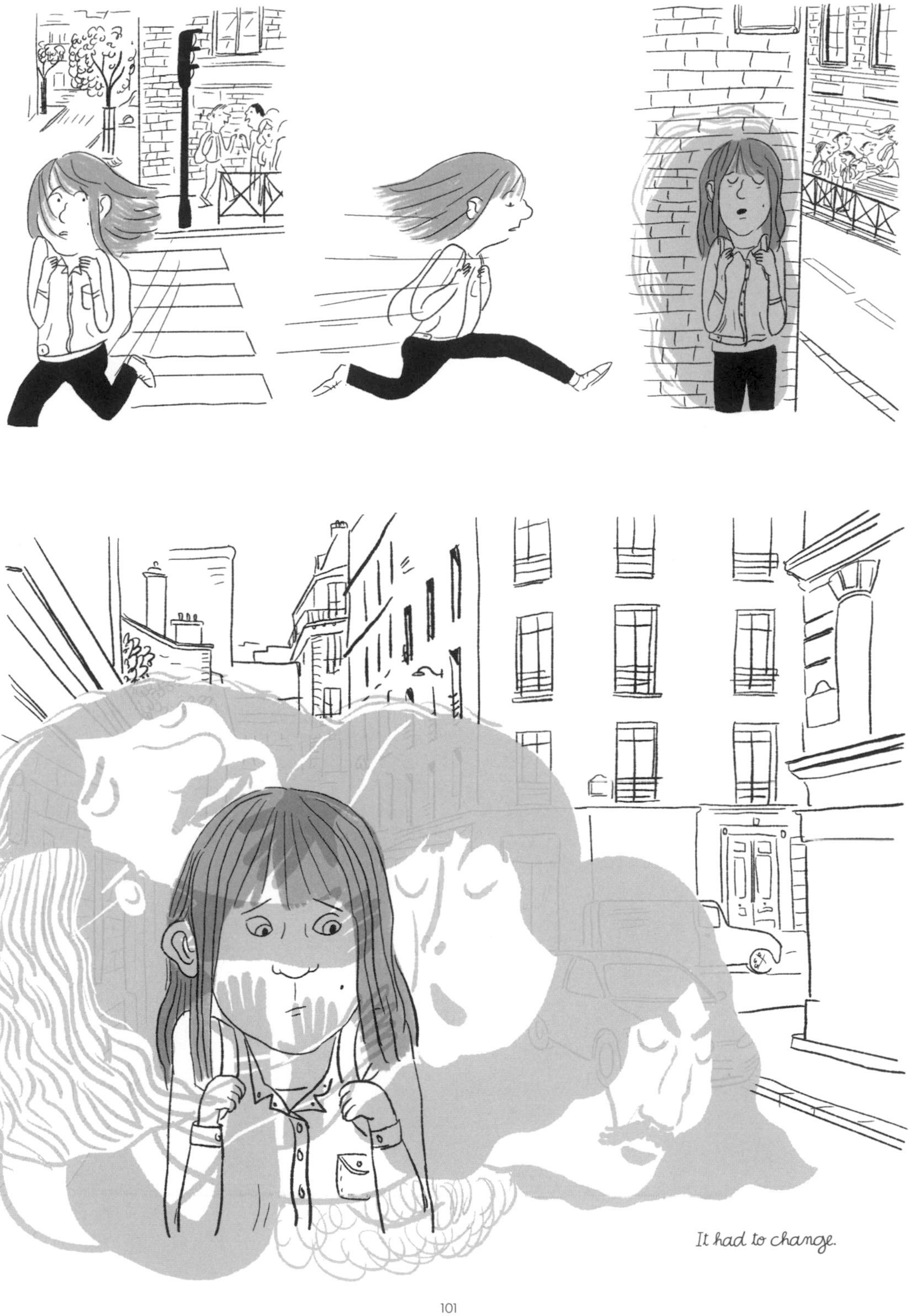
It had to change.

In my acting class, I was rehearsing a new scene, with a boy.

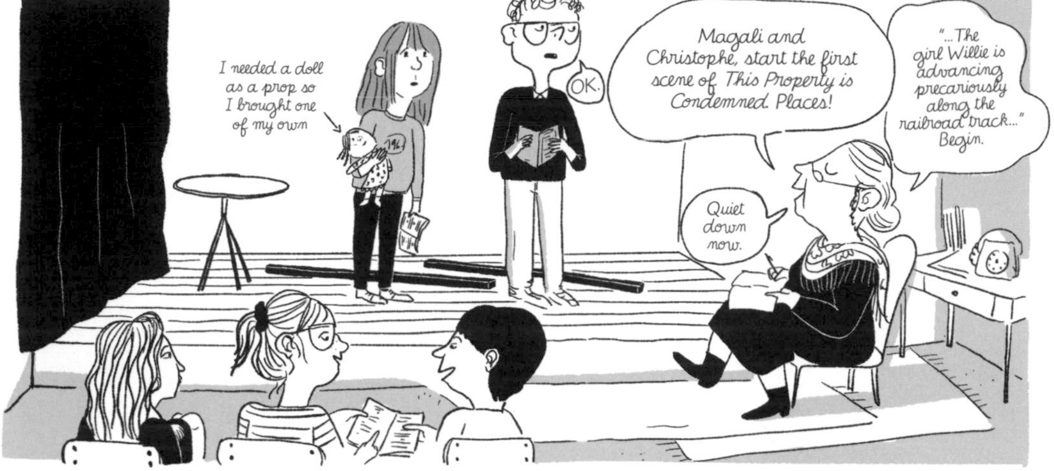
I needed a doll as a prop so I brought one of my own
OK.
Magali and Christophe, start the first scene of This Property is Condemned Places!
"...The girl Willie is advancing precariously along the railroad track..." Begin.
Quiet down now.

At one point in the scene, the two of us had to make physical contact.

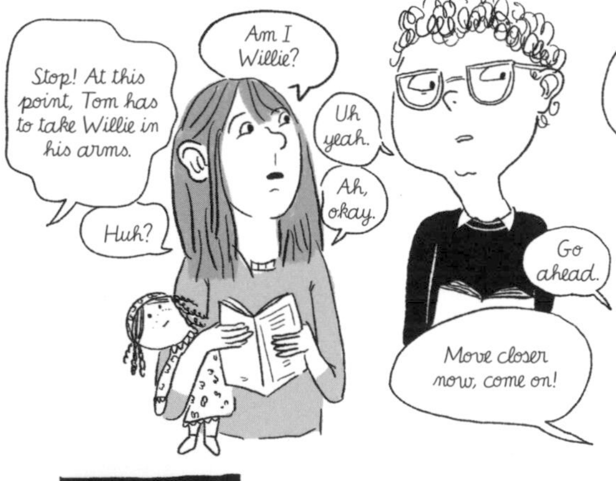
Stop! At this point, Tom has to take Willie in his arms.
Am I Willie?
Huh?
Uh yeah.
Ah, okay.
Go ahead.
Move closer now, come on!

It was embarrassing. I'd never had a reason to touch a boy with my head before.

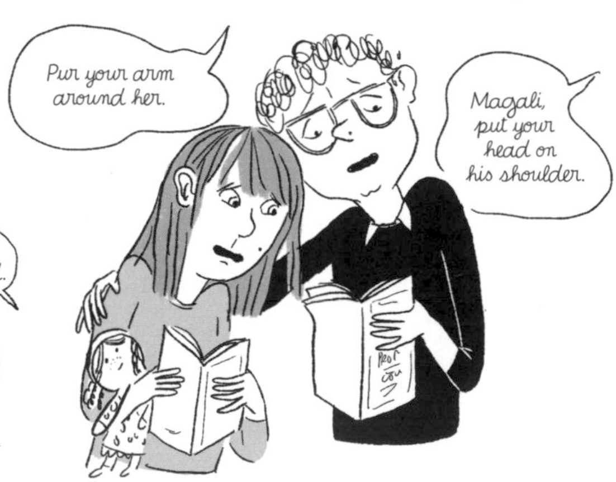
Pur your arm around her.
Magali, put your head on his shoulder.

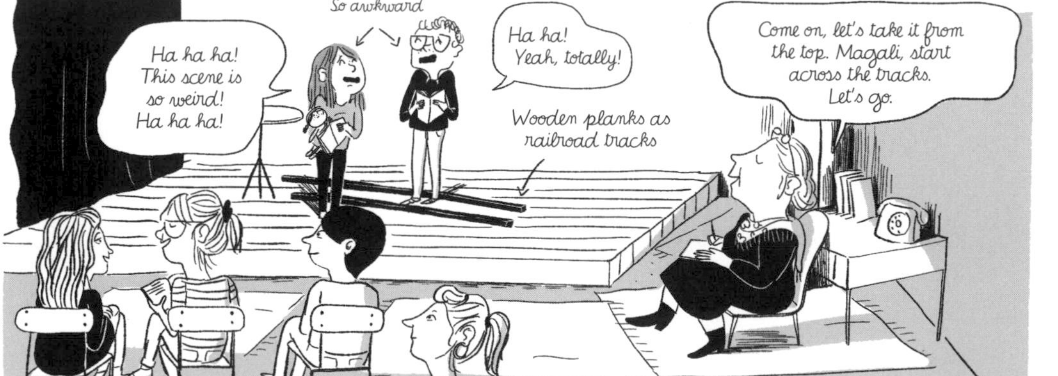
So awkward
Ha ha ha! This scene is so weird! Ha ha ha!
Ha ha! Yeah, totally!
Wooden planks as railroad tracks
Come on, let's take it from the top. Magali, start across the tracks. Let's go.

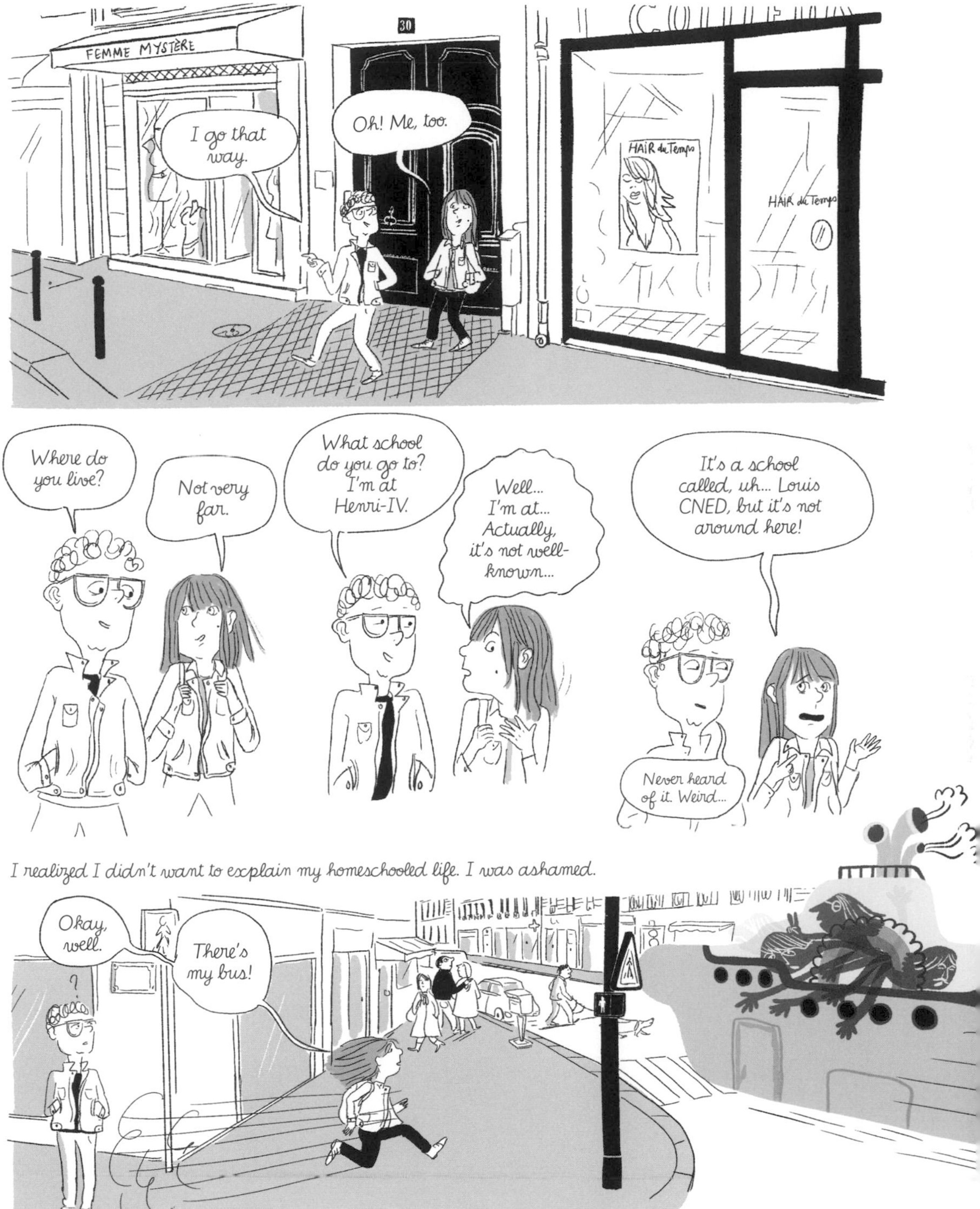
FEMME MYSTÈRE
30
I go that way.
Oh! Me, too.
HAIR du Temps
HAIR du Temps
Where do you live?
Not very far.
What school do you go to? I'm at Henri-IV.
Well... I'm at... Actually, it's not well-known...
It's a school called, uh... Louis CNED, but it's not around here!
Never heard of it. Weird...
I realized I didn't want to explain my homeschooled life. I was ashamed.
Okay, well.
?
There's my bus!

I was spending more and more time drawing, with a fierce concentration that was stronger than ever before.

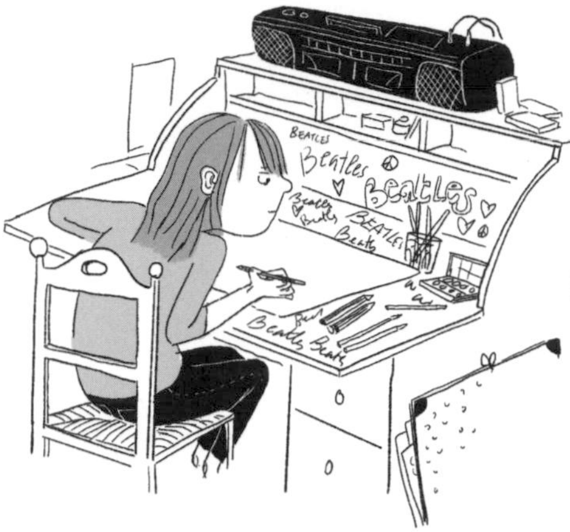
BEATLES
Beatles
Beatles
BEATLES

I liked it more and more.

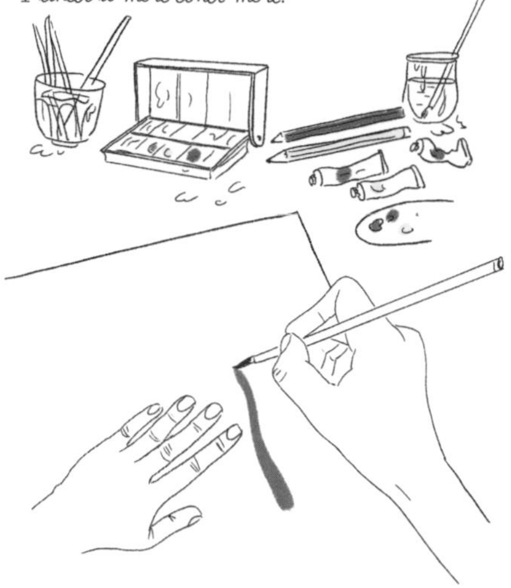

My imaginary world was so real.

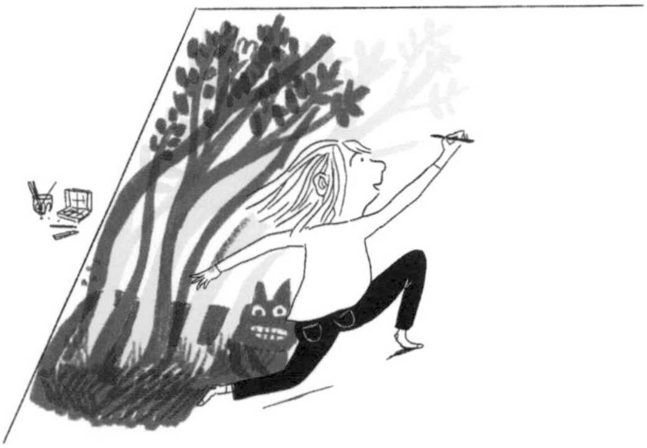

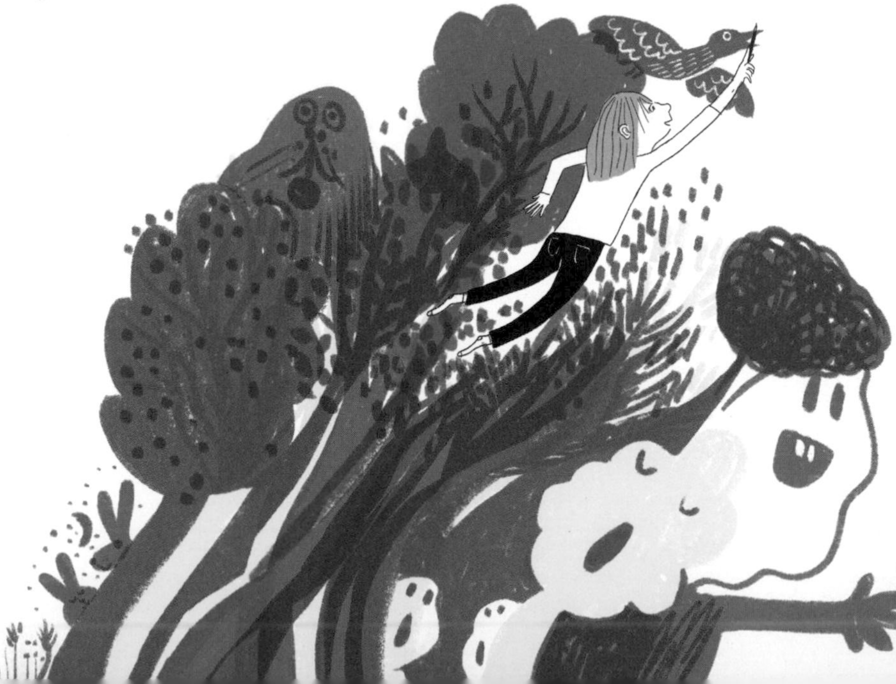

I could do anything I wanted there.
I alone was in charge.

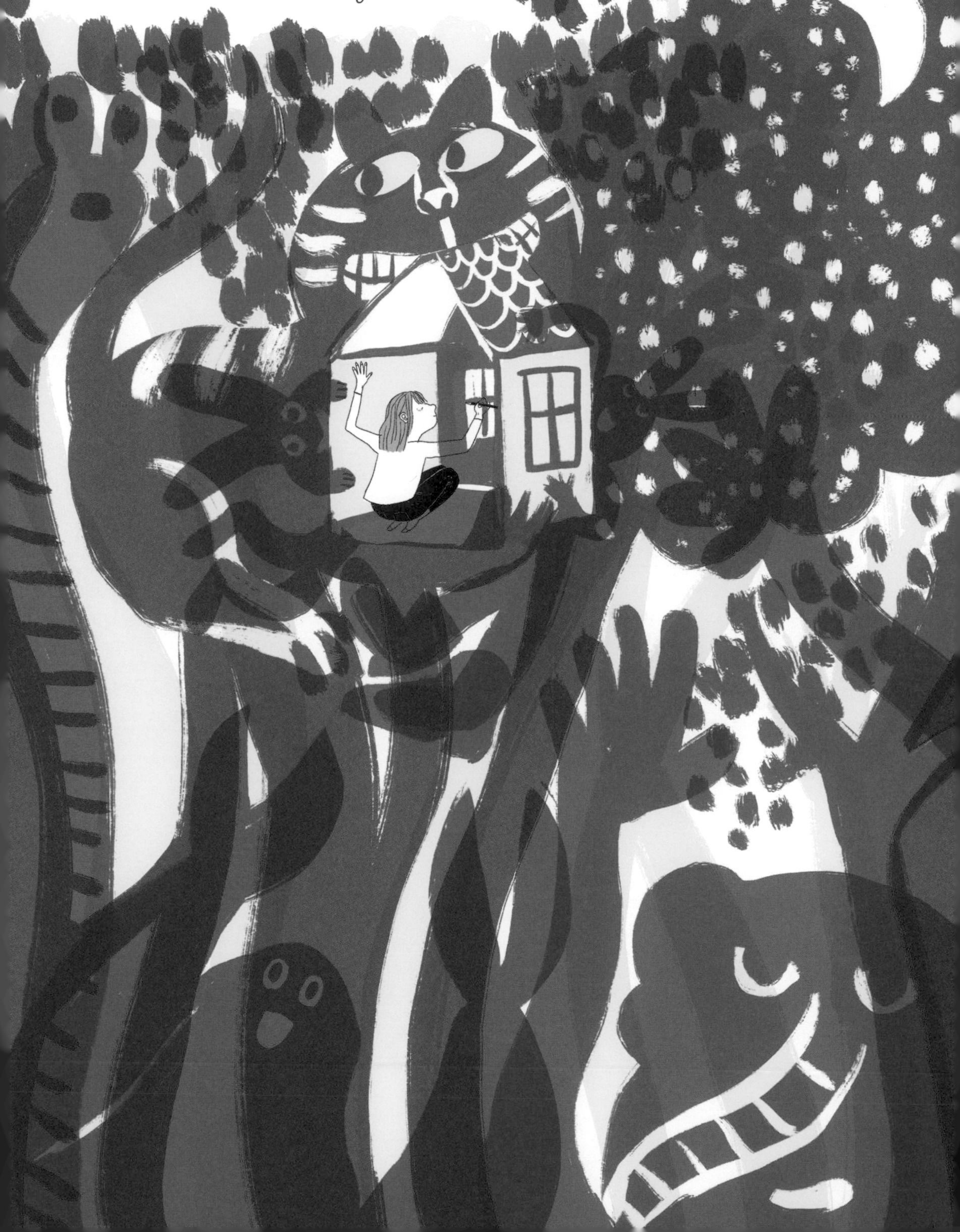

The end of seventh grade was approaching, but I hadn't thought about the following year. If I thought about it, I would have to deal with it. My parents wanted to consult my therapist.

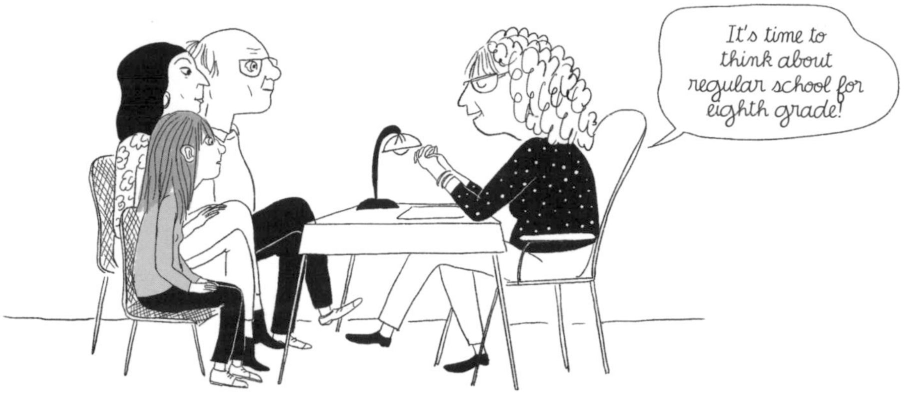
It's time to think about regular school for eighth grade!

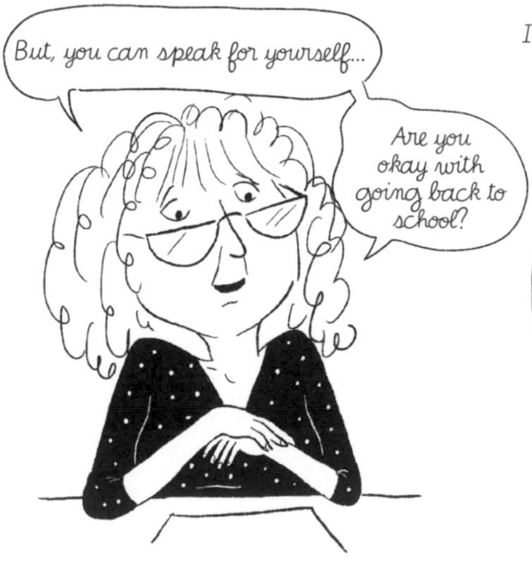
But, you can speak for yourself...
Are you okay with going back to school?

I knew she was right.

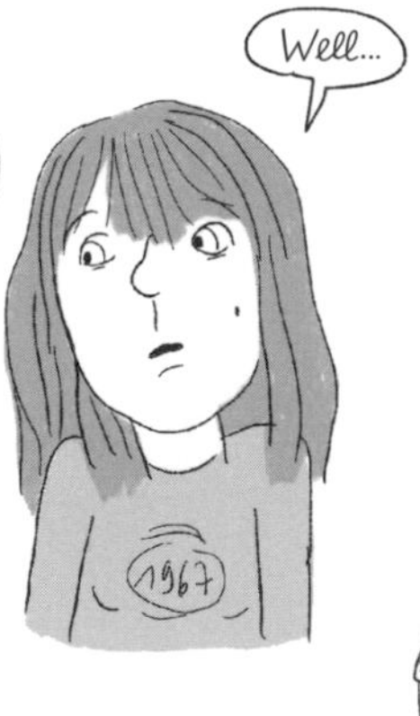
Well...

It was time.

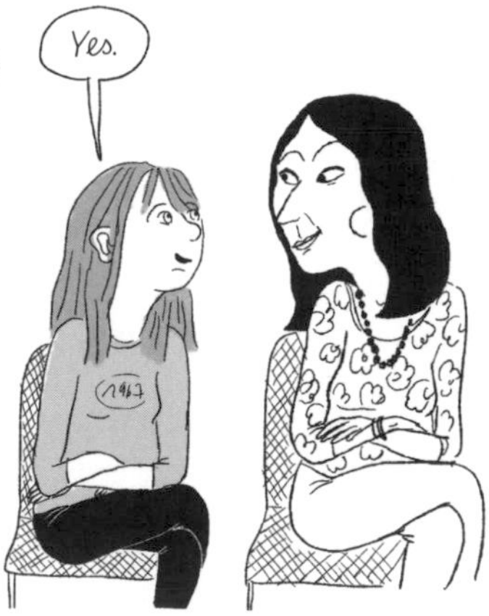
Yes.

First, I took the exam to get back into public school.

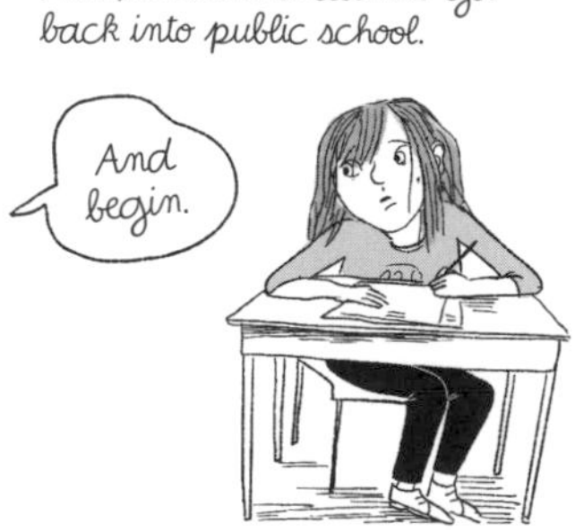
And begin.

But I failed.

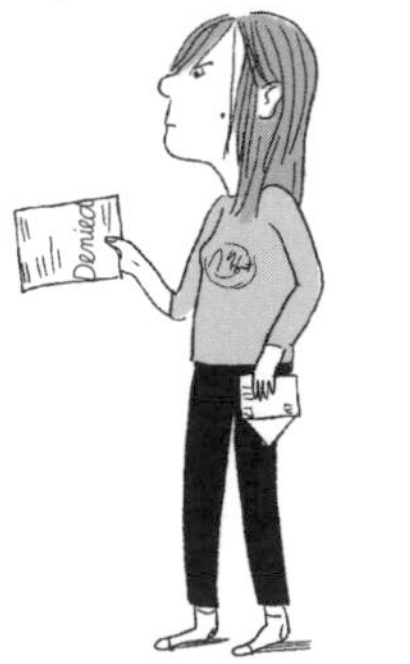
Denied

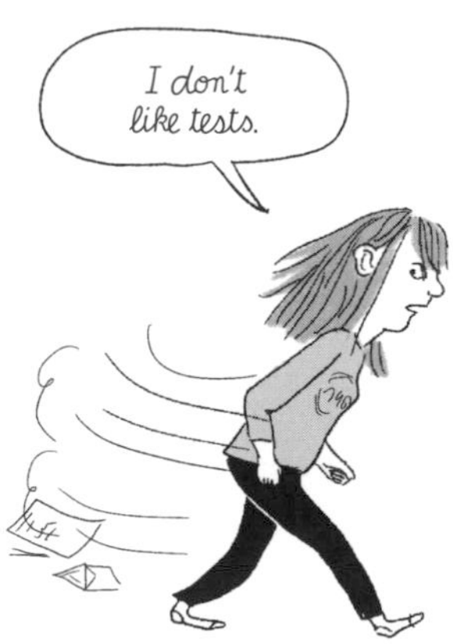
I don't like tests.

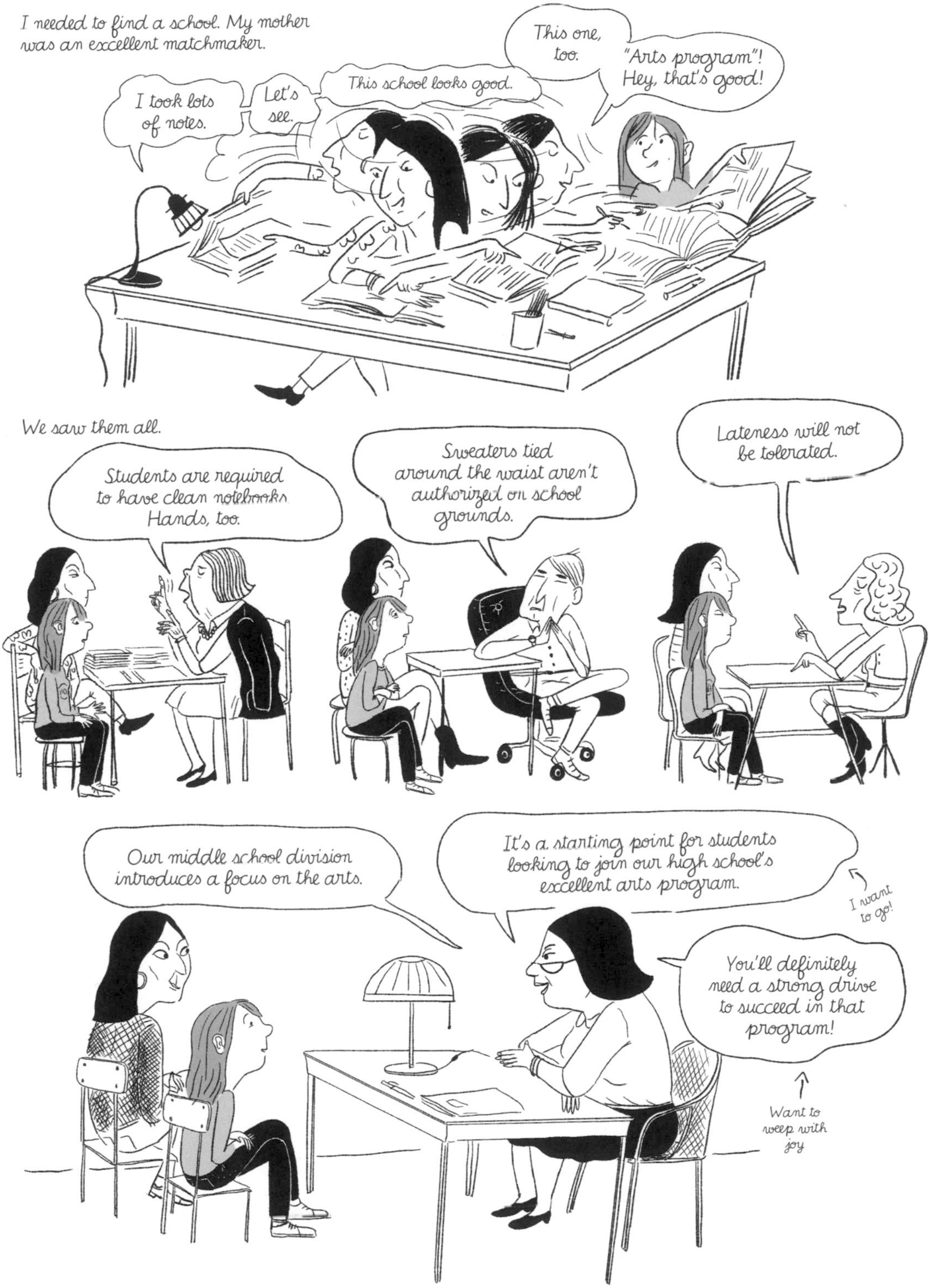
I needed to find a school. My mother was an excellent matchmaker.
I took lots of notes.
Let's see.
This school looks good.
This one, too.
"Arts program"! Hey, that's good!
We saw them all.
Students are required to have clean notebooks. Hands, too.
Sweaters tied around the waist aren't authorized on school grounds.
Lateness will not be tolerated.
Our middle school division introduces a focus on the arts.
It's a starting point for students looking to join our high school's excellent arts program.
I want to go!
You'll definitely need a strong drive to succeed in that program!
Want to weep with joy

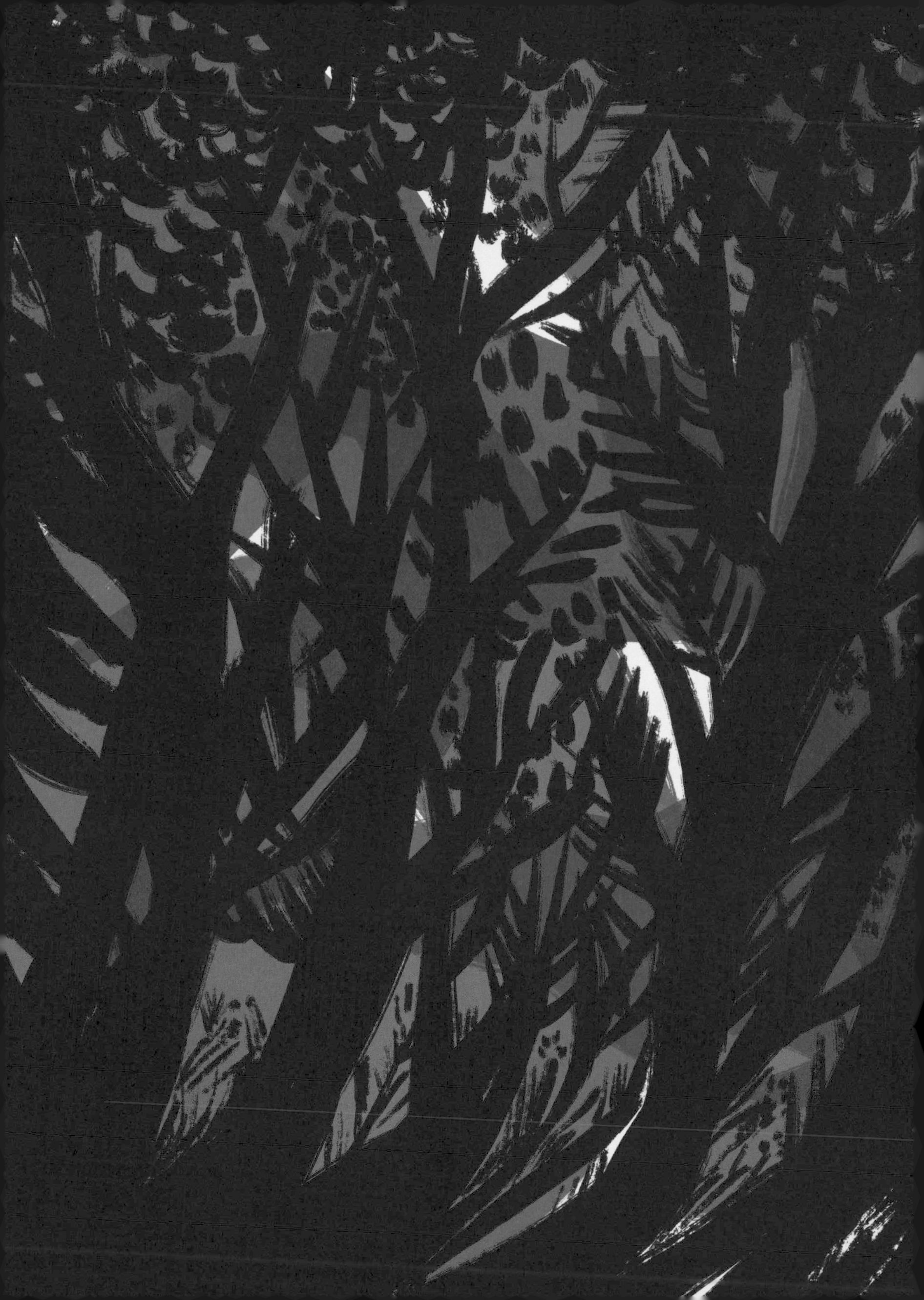

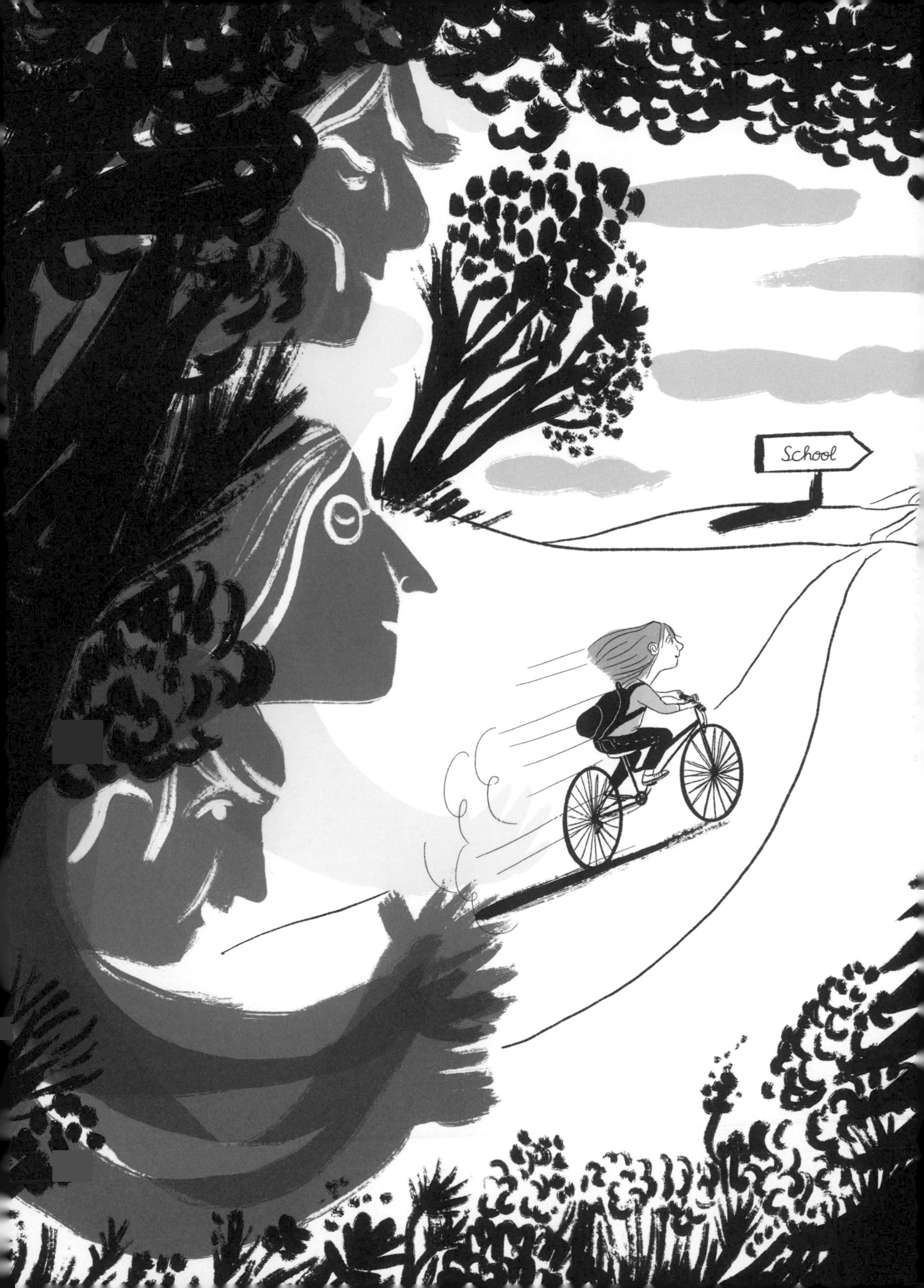
School

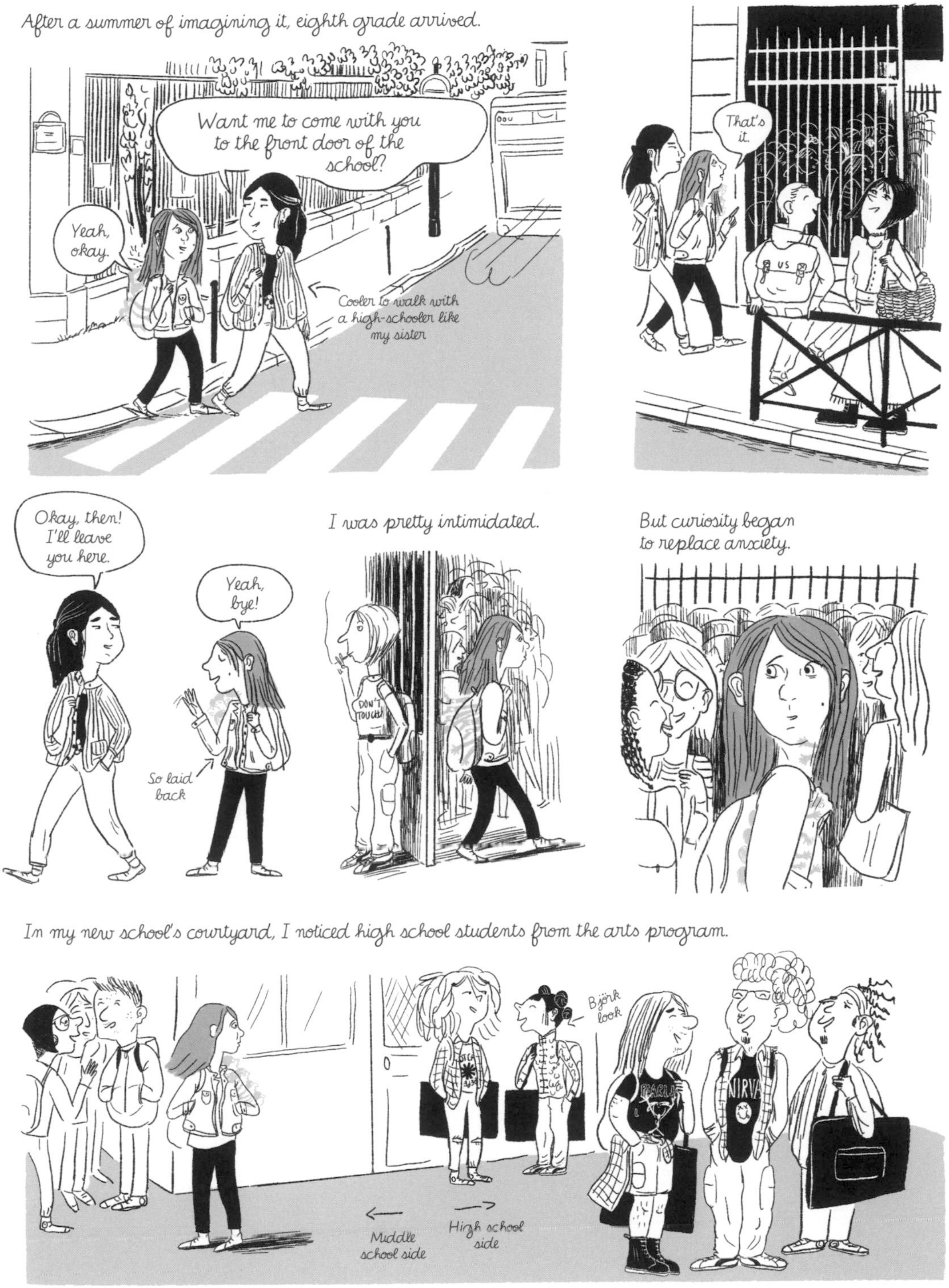
After a summer of imagining it, eighth grade arrived.
Want me to come with you to the front door of the school?
Yeah, okay.
Cooler to walk with a high-schooler like my sister
That's it.
Okay, then! I'll leave you here.
Yeah, bye!
So laid back
I was pretty intimidated.
DON'T TOUCH
But curiosity began to replace anxiety.
In my new school's courtyard, I noticed high school students from the arts program.
Björk look
Middle school side
High school side

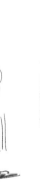

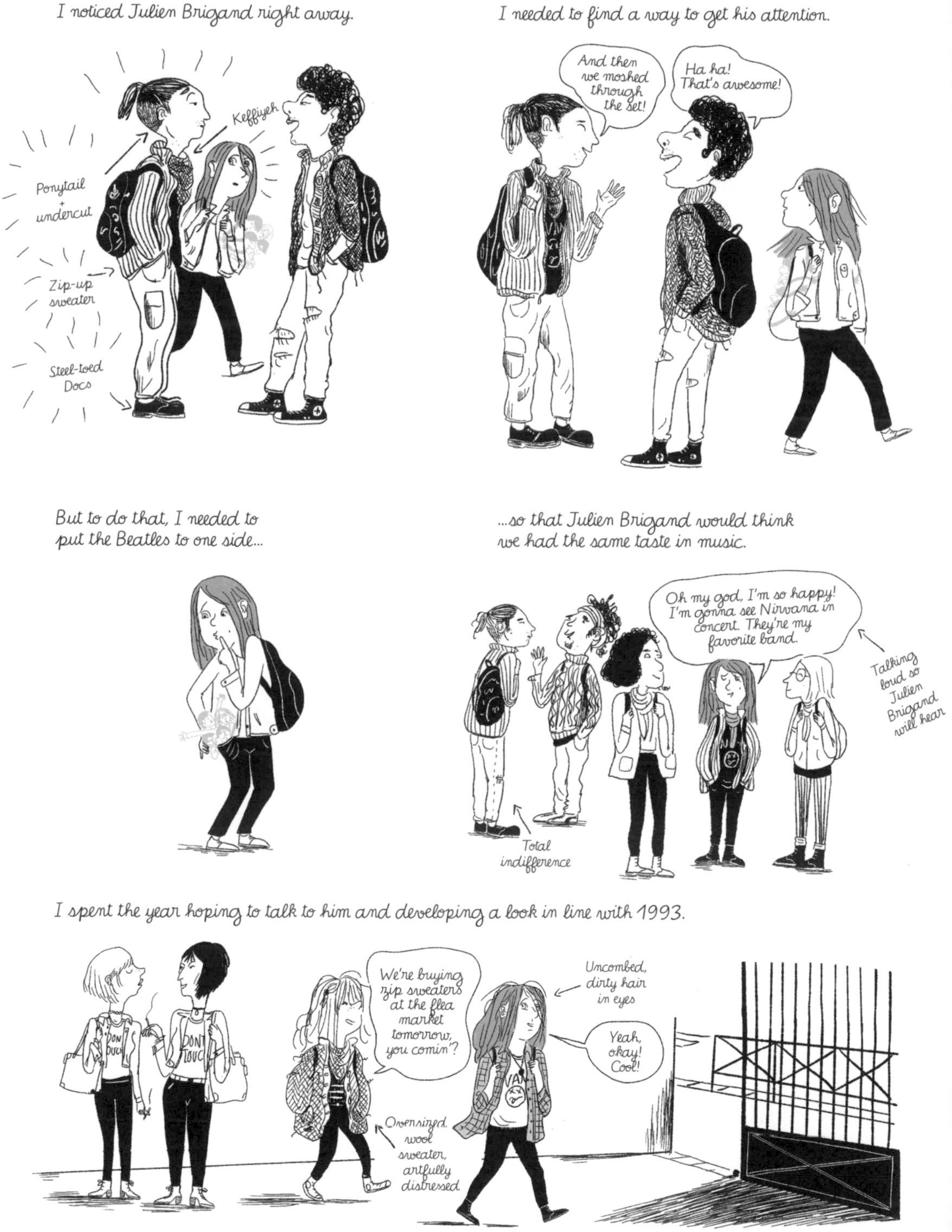

I noticed Julien Brigand right away.
Keffiyeh
Ponytail + undercut
Zip-up sweater
Steel-toed Docs
I needed to find a way to get his attention.
And then we moshed through the set!
Ha ha! That's awesome!
But to do that, I needed to put the Beatles to one side...
...so that Julien Brigand would think we had the same taste in music.
Oh my god, I'm so happy! I'm gonna see Nirvana in concert. They're my favorite band.
Talking loud so Julien Brigand will hear
Total indifference
I spent the year hoping to talk to him and developing a look in line with 1993.
DON'T TOUCH
DON'T TOUCH
We're buying zip sweaters at the flea market tomorrow, you comin'?
Oversized wool sweater, artfully distressed
Uncombed, dirty hair in eyes
Yeah, okay! Cool!

But most of all, something incredible happened.

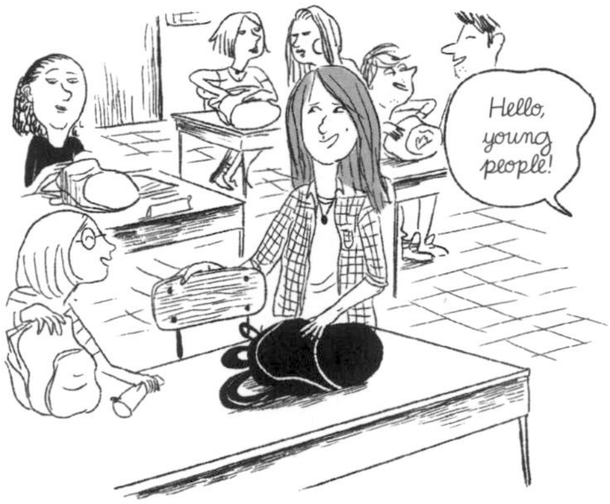
Hello, young people!

I was no longer afraid of being a bad student.

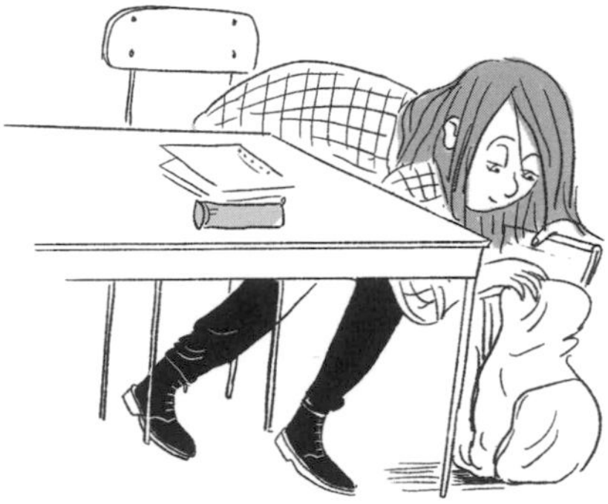

I also didn't care about being the best.

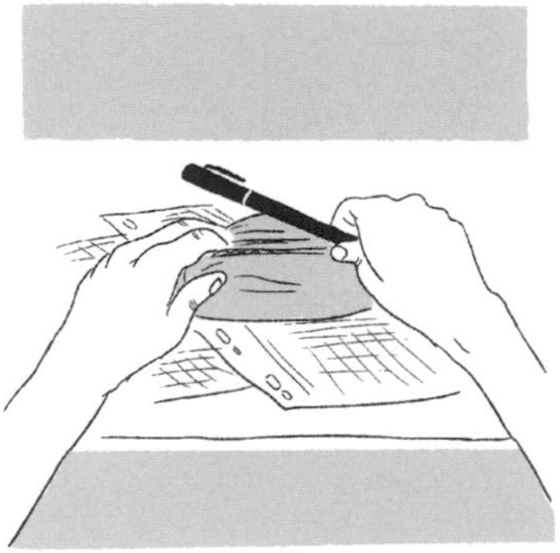

I knew why I was there.

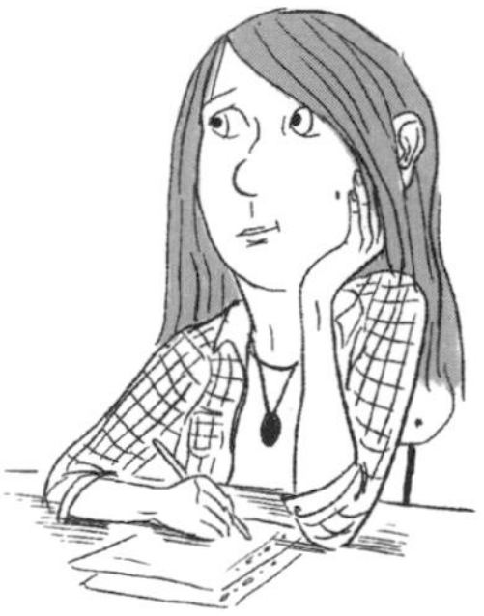

I wanted to grow up... and go live the rest of my life.

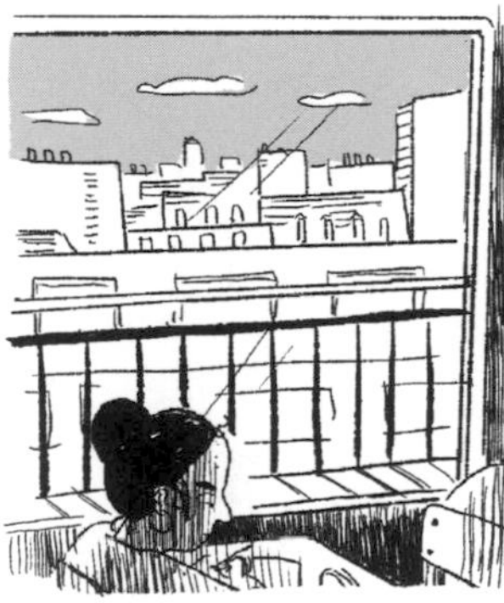

I'd always have the Beatles with me, there in my pocket.

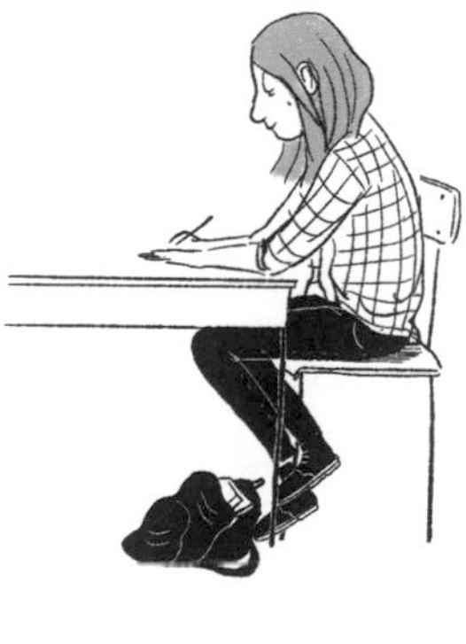

Come what may.

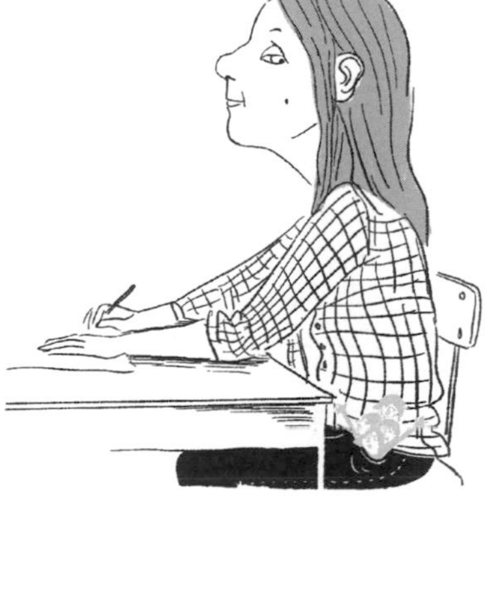

Even if I talked about them less often...

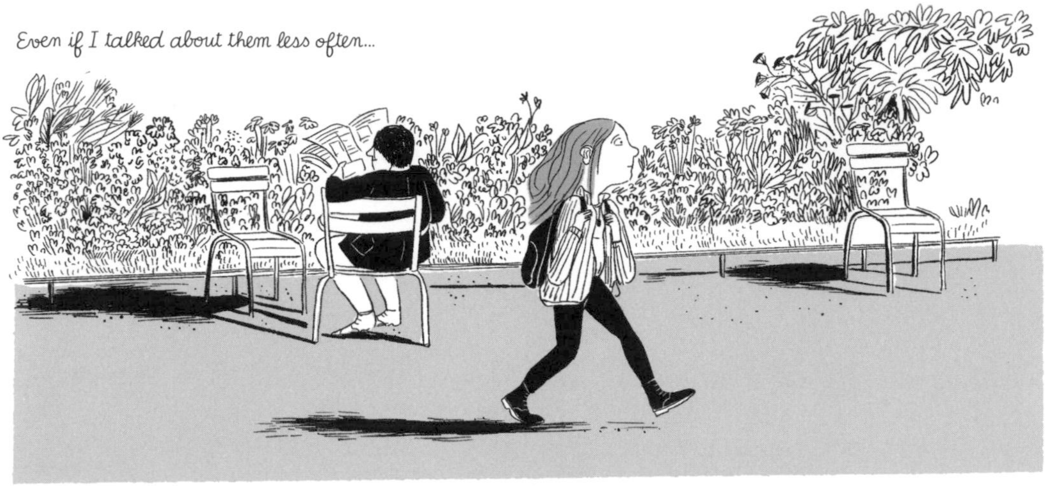

...they never left me.

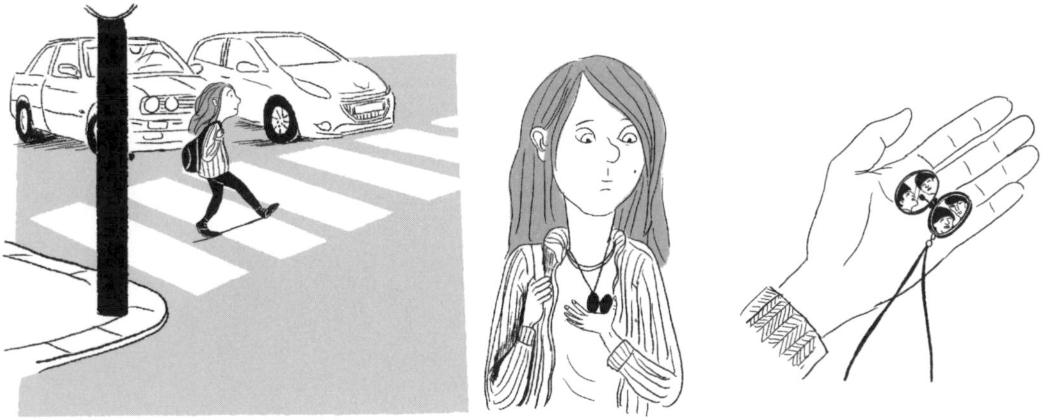

And there were still days...

...when I hurried...

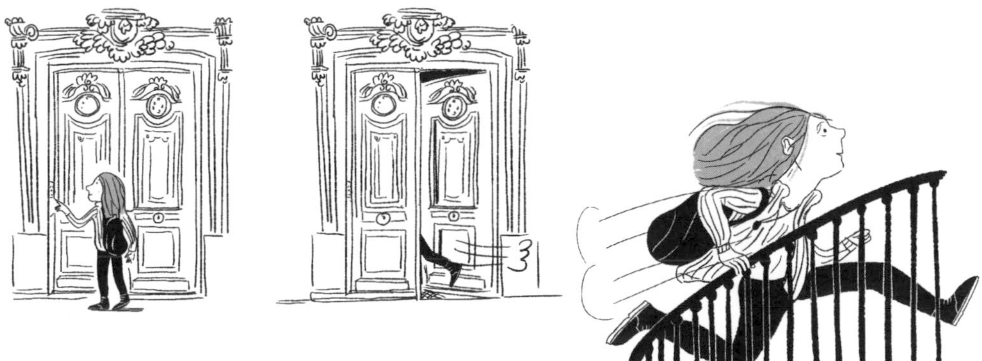

...to get home.

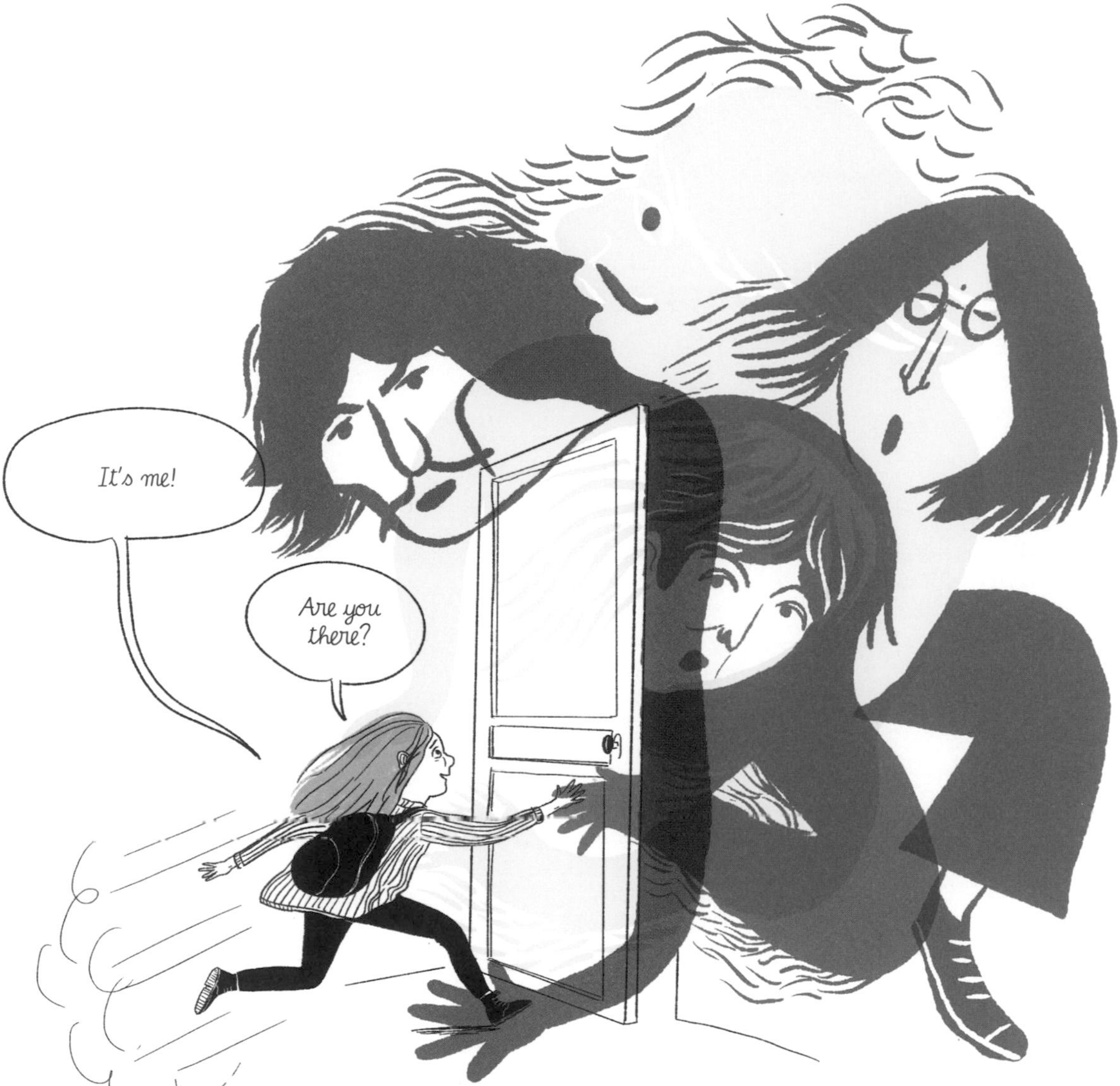
It's me!
Are you there?

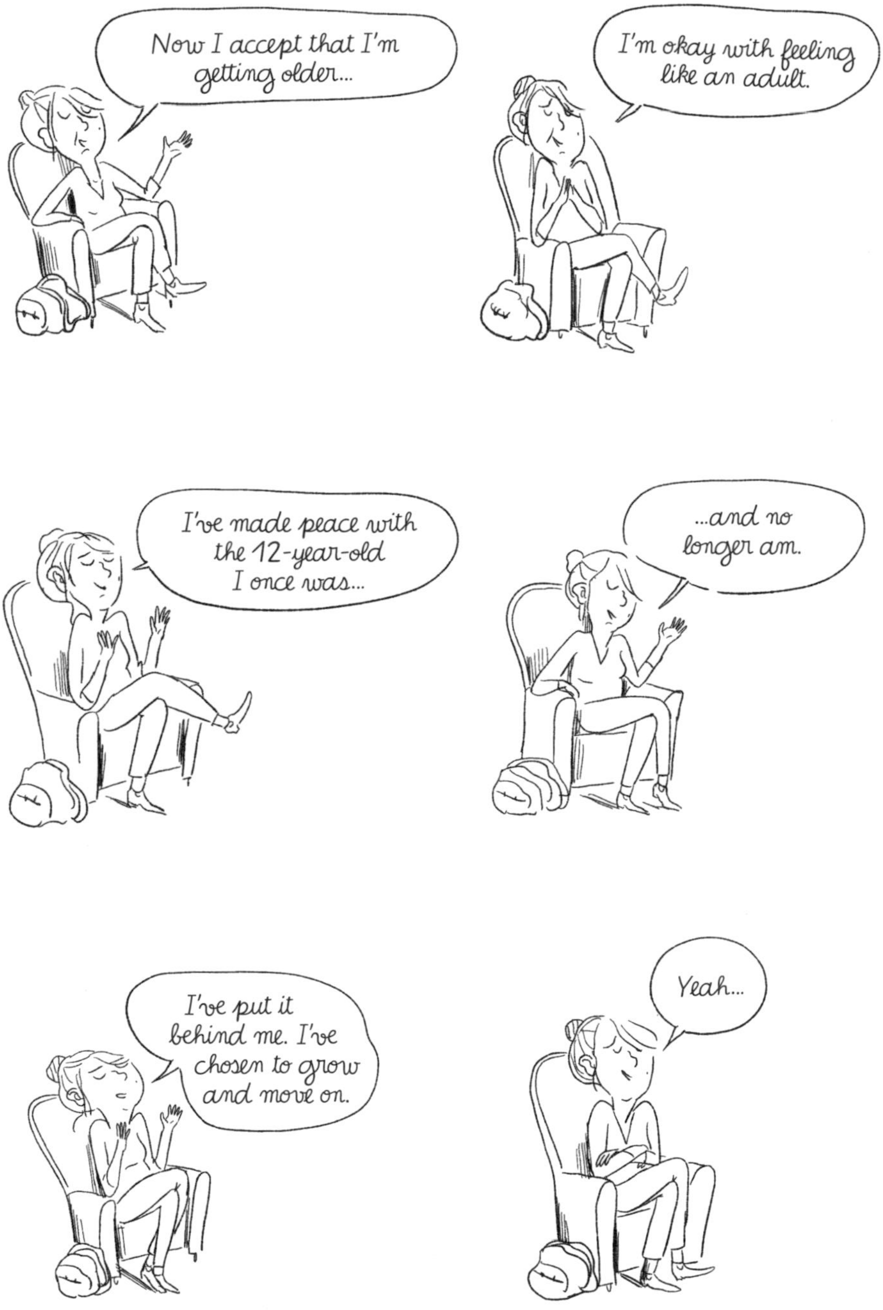
Now I accept that I'm getting older...
I'm okay with feeling like an adult.
I've made peace with the 12-year-old I once was...
...and no longer am.
I've put it behind me. I've chosen to grow and move on.
Yeah...

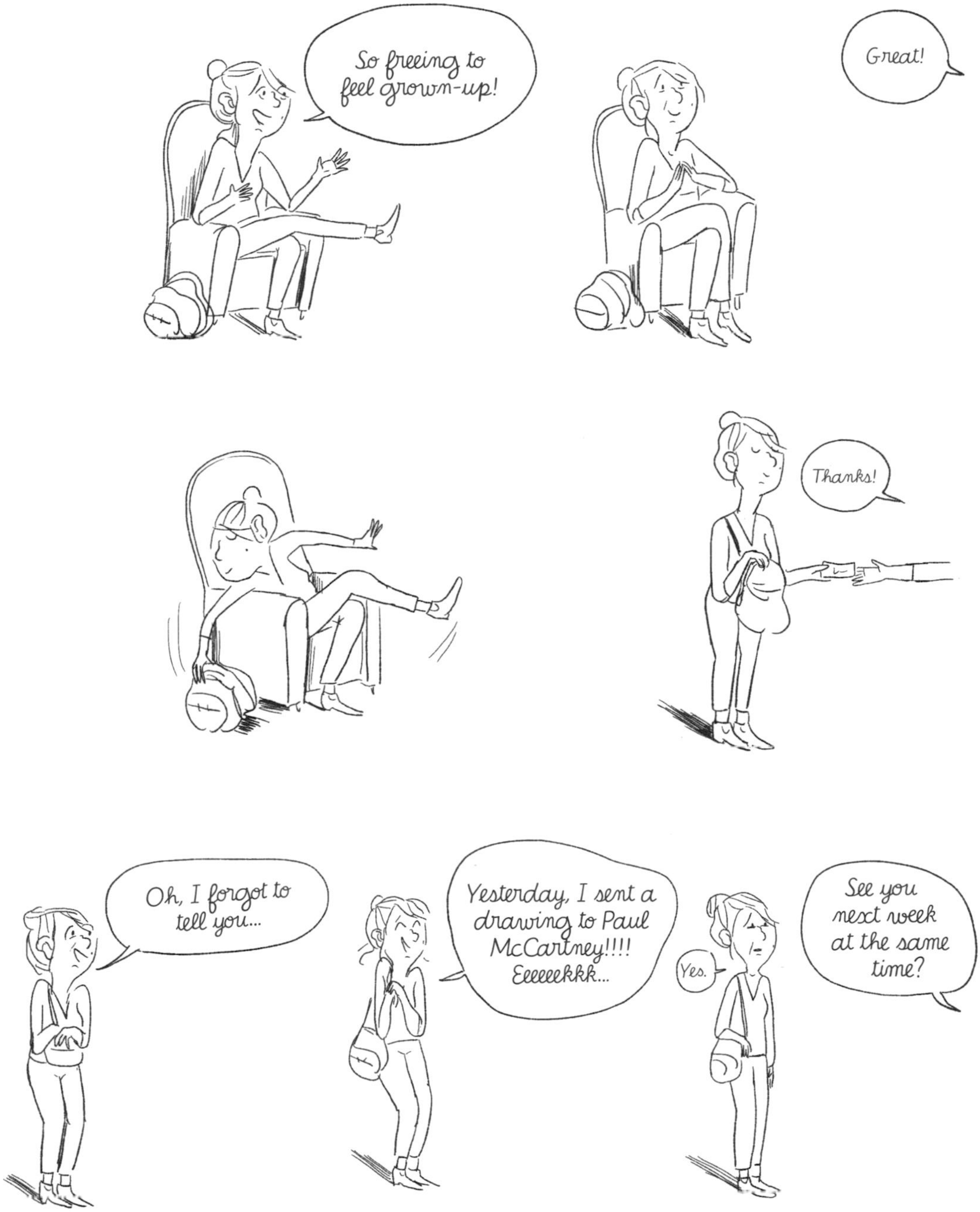

So freeing to feel grown-up!
Great!
Thanks!
Oh, I forgot to tell you...
Yesterday, I sent a drawing to Paul McCartney!!!! Eeeeeekkk...
Yes.
See you next week at the same time?

ACKNOWLEDGEMENTS

Thanks, Tom ♥

Thanks to my parents, my big sister Amélie, and my precious Agathe.

Thanks, magical Elo.

Thanks, Clara and Fanette, my darling pom-pom girls.

Thanks, YenStudio friends, for your advice, your jokes, your Passion Punches, and your super cool playlists.

Thanks to my Atelier 78 Folies friends, where everything started forever.

Thanks, old friends. I still bug with the Beatles, who will always be there.

Thanks, wonder pilates girls! Perineum forever! Friends from 138faubourg forever!

Thanks, Valérie Cussaguet forever!

Thanks, dear cousin Gwen, who I always saw drawing and making comics, which made me dream.

Thanks, TotoBaas, for your accelerated Procreate training and your homemade pencil that I used to make this comic.

Thanks, Marion Montaigne, for your Aligre-Mokonut-title-cover coaching. Special Beatles poke to Anne Simon!

Thanks to my friends from the Café de Matin at Charolais.

Thanks, Mme Lopez.

Thanks to La Bestiole, Olivier, and Delphine for happy rock madness.

Big thanks to Camille, Louise, Mathias, and the entire book office of the French
Institute of London and the South Ken Kids Festival, thanks to whom I was able
to do a residence in Liverpool and London, alone with my neuroses.

Thanks to Gregory from Liverpool for your incredible house.

Thanks, Philippe, Élise, and the whole Dargaud graphic studio team.

Thanks also to Little Richard, Chuck Berry, Elvis, Bob Dylan,
Joe Strummer, Thom Yorke, PJ Harvey, Kurt Cobain, John Cleese,
Lewis Caroll, Edourad Lear, Daniel Pennac, Jean-Marc Barr,
Vic Beretton, Richard Dean Anderson, Jesus, and Santa Claus...

Thanks to Linda McCartney.

And a thousand thanks to Pauline,
my wonderful editor, for believing
in my story from the beginning,
when I didn't know where
I was going!

And finally, thank you to John, Paul,
George, and Ringo. I will never
abandon you.

ABOUT THE AUTHOR

Magali Le Huche was born in Paris in 1979. She spent five years at the school of decorative arts in Strasbourg, three of which she specialized in illustration. She left the school in 2004 and came back to Paris with her first two children's books tucked under her arm: "Les Sirènes de Belpêchao" (2005 Didier) and "Bertille Bonnepoire" (2006, Sarbacane). Ever since then, she's been working regularly as an author and illustrator for the press and children's publishing.

"À la recherche du nouveau père" (2015, Dargaud) is her second graphic novel in collaboration with Gwendoline Raisson. In 2021, Magali created "Nowhere Girl" (Dargaud; Europe Comics in English), a touching and humorous autobiographical tale about a young girl overcoming school phobia by listening to The Beatles. "Nowhere Girl" received the 2021 Pépite Award in the Comics category of the Salon du livre jeunesse de Montreuil and a special mention from the jurors of the 2022 Bologna Ragazzi Awards in the Middle Grade Comics category.

This book is supported by the Institut Français (Royaume-Uni)
as part of the Burgess programme.

INSTITUT
FRANÇAIS
ROYAUME-UNI

Translated in English by Jessie Aufiery for Europe Comics

First published in English in 2022 by Nobrow Ltd.
27 Westgate Street, London, E8 3RL.

Originally published in French as 'Nowhere girl' by Magali Le Huche.

1 3 5 7 9 10 8 6 4 2

Published in the US by Nobrow (US) Inc.
Printed in Latvia on FSC® certified paper.

FSC www.fsc.org MIX Paper from responsible sources FSC® C002795

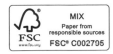

ISBN: 978-1-91312-319-2
www.nobrow.net

IF YOU LIKED NOWHERE GIRL, YOU'LL ALSO LIKE...

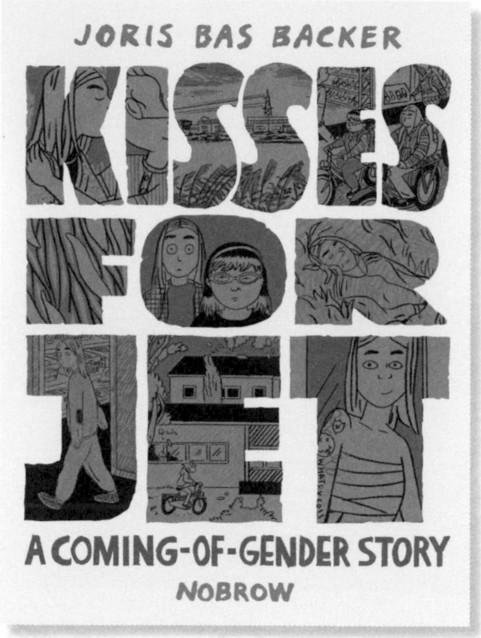
JORIS BAS BACKER
KISSES FOR JET
A COMING-OF-GENDER STORY
NOBROW

"Kisses for Jet is a sensitively-written, beautifully-illustrated depiction of a trans-masculine experience so rarely shown in media. It made me smile, laugh and cry, and packed a real punch when depicting some seriously powerful topics. Visually arresting, genuinely entertaining and a huge step forward for trans representation".

– Jake Hall,
author of *The Art of Drag*

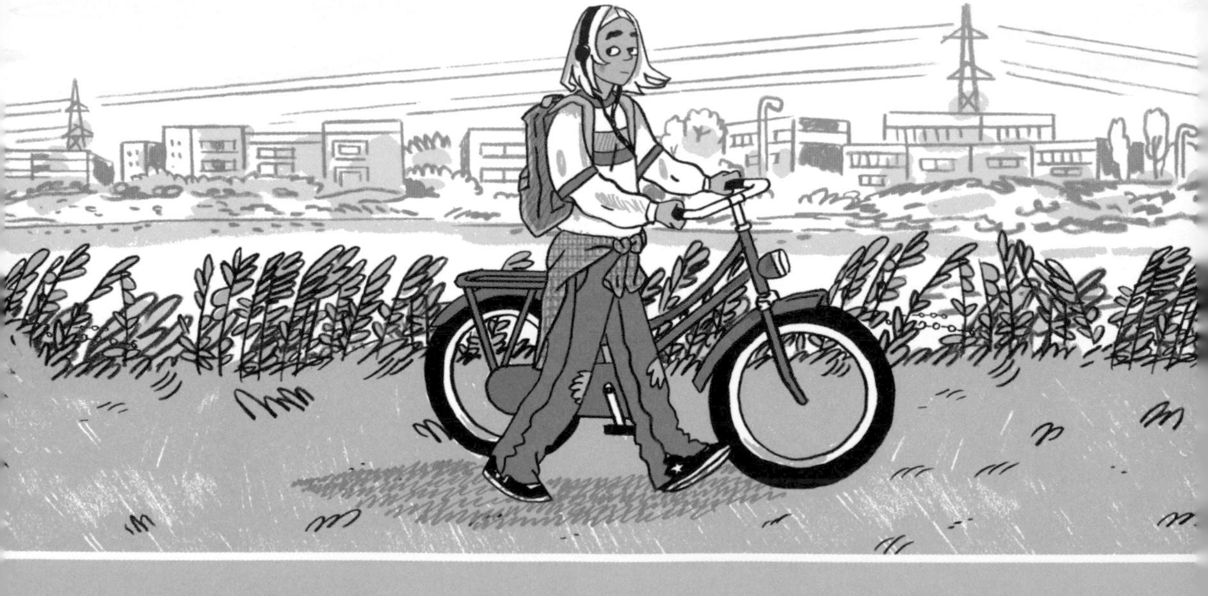

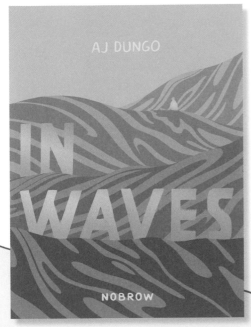

AJ DUNGO

IN WAVES

NOBROW

"I love this book deeply. AJ writes and draws like a surfer, with such fluidity, grace, and breathability, managing to flow with the most profound love and loss, without it dragging us under. He surrenders to the infinite power and mystery of the ocean to heal the void within... this book is a clean line that glides, rolls, and truly moves you. Currently my favorite graphic novel in the universe."

— Craig Thompson,
Eisner award winning author
of the bestselling *Blankets*

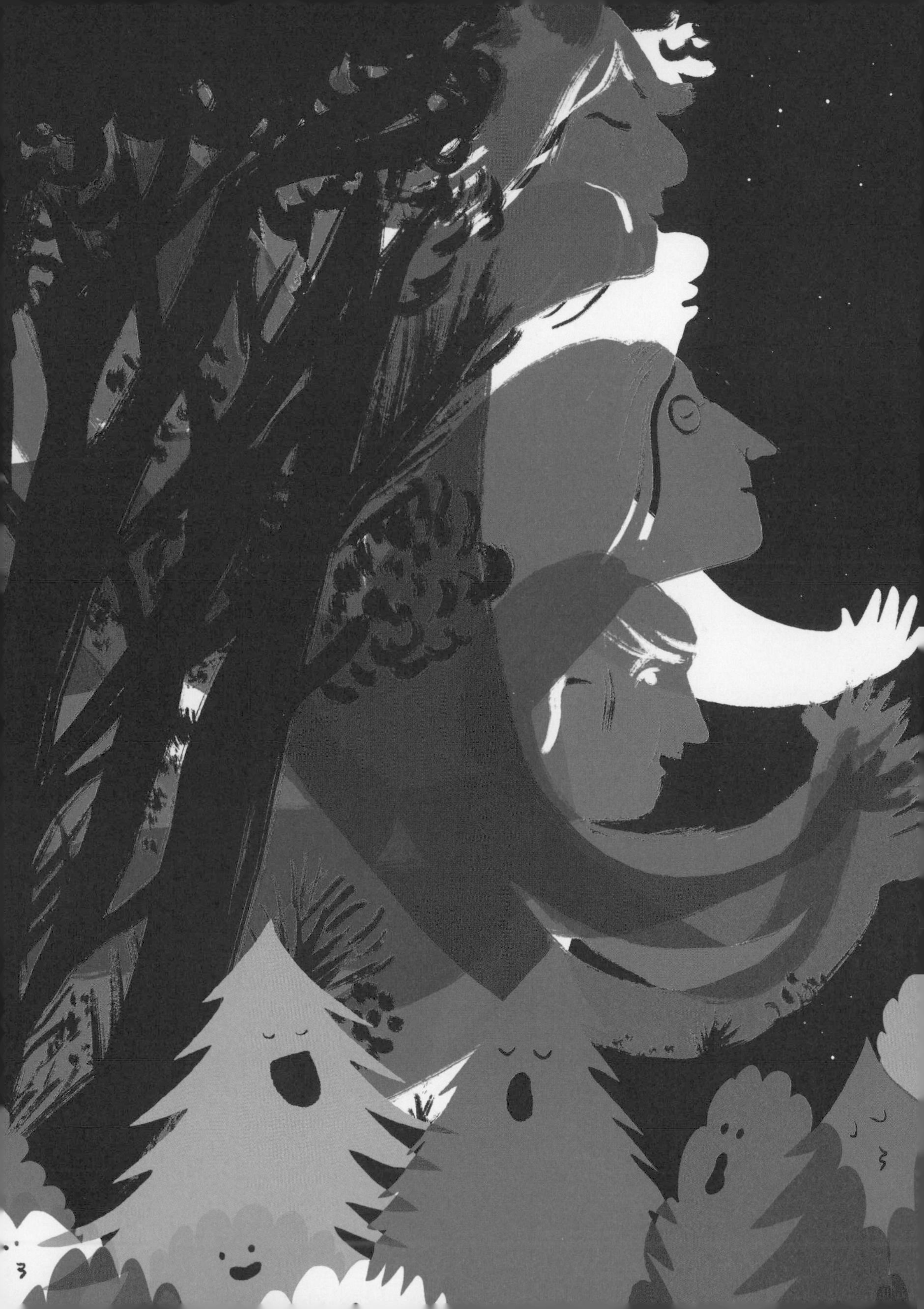

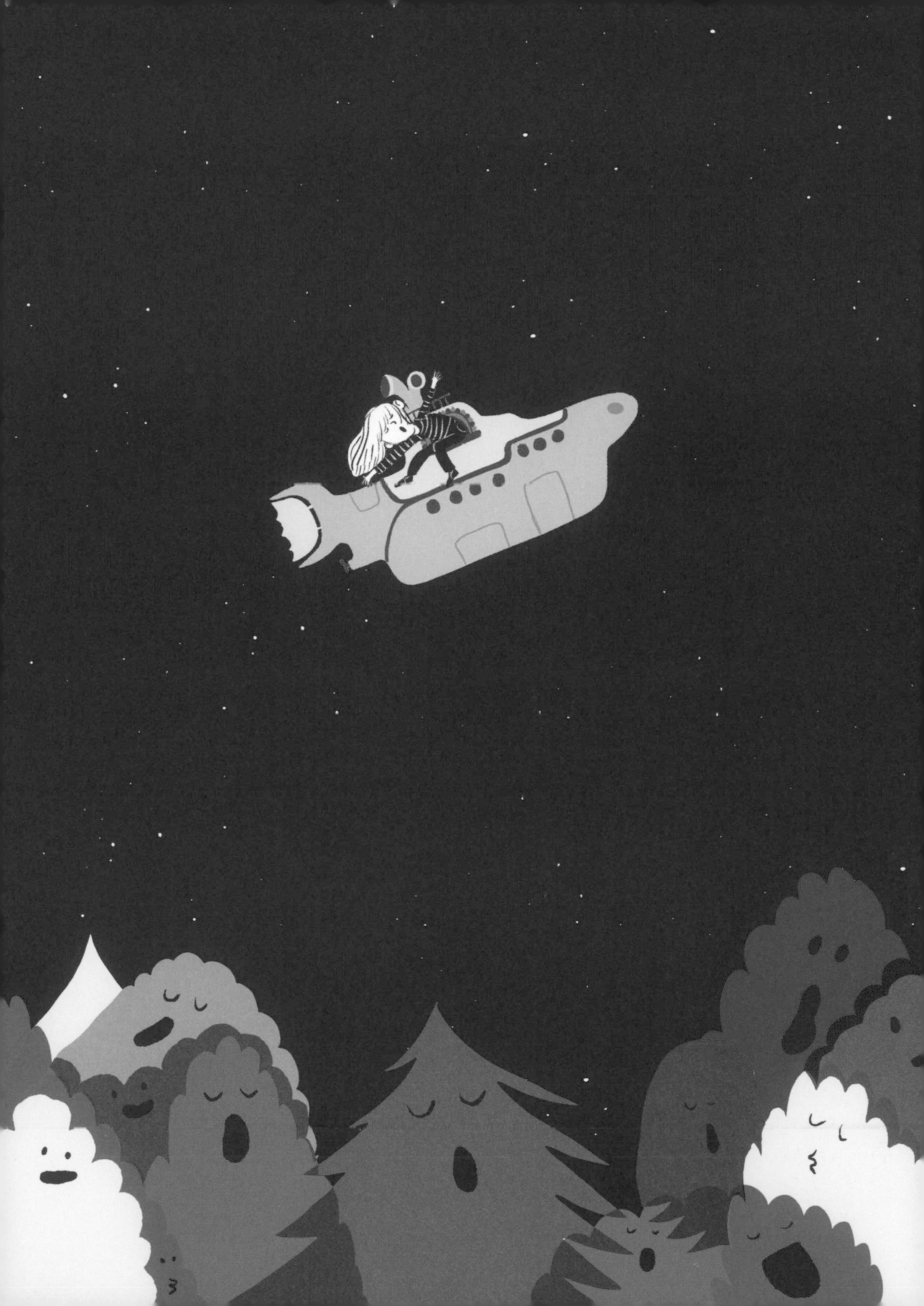